ALLAN KEMP

HALL OF FAME

Norwich City's All Time Greats

DB PUBLISHING

THE AUTHOR

Allan was born in Suffolk in June 1974 and raised in Harleston on the Norfolk/Suffolk border. It was a time when Bobby Robson's Ipswich was becoming one of the nation's leading sides and his footballing loyalties could easily have fallen either way.

A school visit in the spring of 1982 from Norwich Manager, Ken Brown and striker Ross Jack was soon followed by Allan's first game at Carrow Road, a memorable 4–2 win over a Watford side featuring future England international, a young John Barnes. The win-kick started a late and unlikely surge to promotion and Allan was hooked.

Allan has followed Norwich ever since, enjoying that memorable 1992–93 Premier League season while a student in Leeds. He also witnessed, from a seat in the Leeds home end, Norwich's relegation from the premiership two years later.

Like many Norwich fans, Allan has experienced highs such as the UEFA cup adventure, the win in front of the last standing Kop at Liverpool and the Play-off semi-final victory over Wolves. He has also suffered lows that come with supporting your team, with the 1992 FA Cup semi-final defeat and of course the 1–7 home defeat to Colchester coming to mind.

Allan is a qualified accountant whose passion lies in football. He has coached at soccer schools in the USA and played regularly until injury ended his playing days, but also gave him an opportunity to start writing. He currently lives in Bristol with his wife Libby and despite the long distances still gets to see Norwich City play as much as he can.

Hall of Fame – Norwich City's All Time Greats is his first title.

First published in Great Britain in 2012 by The Derby Books Publishing Company Limited, 3 The Parker Centre, Derby, DE21 4SZ.

© Allan Kemp 2012

ISBN 978-1-78091-037-6
Printed and bound by Gomer.

Contents

Introduction

In 2000 Glasgow Rangers became the first British club to set up an official Hall of Fame. Its purpose was to formally recognise the achievements of the footballers that were held in admiration by the Rangers supporters and had made the greatest contribution to the club's success over its long and illustrious history. Since 2000 many other clubs in both England and Scotland have established Halls of Fame, based on a wide variety of differing selection criteria.

In this book I shall look at some interesting statistics about Norwich City's Hall of Fame and its members. I will then provide a short biography of the 128 members elected to Norwich City Football Club's Hall of Fame, through which the history of the club is relived through their experiences and contributions.

In chronological order, I will focus on each 'famer's' time at the club, from their first involvement with Norwich through to their life after Carrow Road. I will particularly focus on their time at Norwich, looking at their role, their achievements, their characteristics and specific memories that made them so popular with Canary supporters around the world and ultimately led to their presence in the Hall of Fame.

Norwich's Hall of Fame

To celebrate the club's centenary during the 2002–03 season Norwich City Football Club initiated a Hall of Fame. More so than other football clubs – and demonstrating Norwich's reputation as a community club – the Norwich Hall of Fame was to include non-playing members of staff including managers, board members and even the long standing physio and groundsman. The club was determined that the Hall of Fame would represent '100 personalities who made the greatest contribution to the club both on and off the pitch'. Of the initial 100, 25 were nominated by the club and 75 were selected by supporters.

Since its conception in 2002, the Hall of Fame membership has grown to reflect the club's history over the last decade.

In 2006 a further 10 Norwich personalities were added to the Hall of Fame following a fans' vote, while on 13 November 2009, at an induction dinner and ceremony, an additional 10 were inducted. These 10 were chosen based on slightly differing criteria from past selections. Five were selected by Trustees of the Norwich City Football Club Historic Trust and focused on the key contributors to the club's foundation in the early 1900s, while the other five were selected by supporters who voted for one individual from each of the last five decades.

The final eight Hall of Famers, bringing the total up to 128, were inducted at a gala dinner held at Carrow Road on 20 March 2012. Three were selected by the historical trust and the remaining five chosen following a supporters' vote.

Norwich City Football Club – The Beginnings

The formation of Norwich City Football Club can be traced to a meeting held on 17 June 1902, in the Criterion Café, White Lion Street, Norwich.

Three of the attendees at this historic meeting, **Joseph Nutchey, John Howes** and **Arthur Turner** are members of the Hall of Fame, in recognition of their roles as founding fathers of the club and as pioneers of football in the city.

While today's Norwich City can trace their origin to that meeting in 1902, they were not the first football club in the city. The leading club at the time were Norwich CEYMS, a club whose roots lay within the church, and whose vice-captain at the turn of the century was Joe Nutchey, a Yorkshireman whose day job was headmaster at a local school. John Howes was also a school teacher who played in goal for a Norwich teachers' side, while Arthur Turner had played for Norwich based team Thorpe Hamlet, in addition to his position of club secretary for another team in the city, Swifans football club.

All three, through their involvement in grass roots football, identified the potential for another club in the city, and despite opposition from members of CEYMS, that day at the Criterion Café saw these ambitions finally fulfilled. Nutchey's first role for the new club was treasurer. Howes and Turner were appointed club secretaries with Howes in charge of administration and Turner, a born organiser, tasked with finding players to fill the squad. This proved to be a difficult challenge. Because of the amateur status of the game, Turner had to be confident of finding employment for players that moved to Norwich. Turner also had to face resistance and hostility from the region's clubs and their fan bases who took issue to the poaching of their best players (something Norwich City supporters could relate to many decades later). In spite of the inherent difficulties, Turner, using his connections, scouted for talent throughout East Anglia and delivered a squad in time for Norwich City's debut season in the Norfolk and Suffolk League.

On 6 September 1902, dressed in blue and white halves and in front of 2,000 people at Newmarket Road, the newly formed Norwich City played their first ever game, drawing 1–1 in a friendly versus Harwich and Parkeston. The first competitive game was to soon follow, a 0–5 defeat, in the FA Cup preliminary round to the region's top side, Lowestoft Town. A week later Norwich opened their League campaign with the club's first win, 4–2 versus Beccles Caxton, at Newmarket Road. A scorer in that victory and an ever-present in Norwich's first three games was forward and Hall of Fame member, **Robert 'Bob' Collinson**.

Born in Yorkshire in 1875, Collinson was one of life's genuine all-rounders. Academically brilliant, he obtained a Bachelor of Science degree at Manchester and had broadened his experiences by travelling to Zurich, Switzerland to continue his studies. However, it was at sport that Collinson truly excelled. He represented Yorkshire at both rugby and cricket, where he played against the legendary W.G. Grace. As for football, Collinson's game started to develop while in Zurich where he represented his college team. He was even selected to represent a Swiss side, albeit in the days before they were a formally recognised international team.

After completing his education, Collinson moved to Norwich in 1900 and soon became a key player for Norwich CEYMS where his association with Nutchey, Howes and Turner began.

Collinson soon established himself as the star player for CEYMS, scoring 30 goals in 25 games. It was therefore a major scoop for Nutchey when he 'sold' Collinson the idea of a new club in the city and persuaded him to join Norwich City as the club's first player. Collinson was the only player at the conception of Norwich City in June 1902 before Turner began his recruitment drive.

Collinson's ability and leadership skills made him an obvious choice to captain Norwich in that first ever game versus Harwich and Parkeston where, naturally, he scored in the opening minutes. Over the course of that first season, 1902–03, in the Norfolk and Suffolk League, Collinson was to achieve a number of club firsts. He was the club's first captain and he scored in Norwich's first ever competitive game. He played (and was captain) in Norwich's first ever derby game versus Ipswich, a 1–0 victory, as well as leading Norwich to victory in the following game, their first, at Portman Road. Despite this early double over Ipswich, the real derby took place on Boxing Day 1902 in the highly anticipated clash against Norwich CEYMS. A crowd of 4,700 (over double the attendance that watched Ipswich) saw Collinson score Norwich's first ever penalty (shortly followed by their second penalty in the same game). Norwich came out on top with a 4–2 victory, much to the frustration of the CEYMS management and supporters who had lost a number of players to their new city rivals and who, at the end of the season, saw their side finish below Norwich on goal difference. Norwich CEYMS would never again be the city's top side.

The following season, 1903–04, Collinson scored in Norwich's first FA Cup victory, a shock 4–1 win over the Norfolk and Suffolk League champions, Lowestoft Town. In the next round Collinson scored the winner against Yarmouth before scoring a hat-trick in the second qualifying round against Harwich and Parkeston. Again Norwich finished the season in third place and again Lowestoft Town won the Championship.

Norwich's third season in the Norfolk and Suffolk League, season 1904–05, proved to be their last. In December 1904 Turner and Howes were answering a Football Association (FA) commission of inquiry, which challenged Norwich's status as an amateur side. This was proving to be a grey area around generous payments to players to cover travelling expenses, payments made to players leaving the club and provision of training, massage and gymnasium facilities in exchange for fees. In short, the commission judged Norwich to be acting as a professional club, a decision which, at the time, shook the club with the Amateur Cup, a prestigious trophy, being the club's top priority. In January 1905, on the FA's recommendation, the board – including Nutchey and Turner – were suspended. Captain Collinson stepped up as acting chairman, probably the only player-chairman in the history of the Football League.

Despite the FA ruling, Norwich were allowed to play out the remaining season and in April 1905, who else but Collinson scored two in a 3–1 victory over Norwich CEYMS to secure their first and last Norfolk and Suffolk League title. This proved to be Collinson's last goal for Norwich. As a believer in the spirit of amateurism he refused to continue with the new professional club that was emerging. Collinson instead focused on cricket and athletics, representing Norfolk in both fields.

In the summer of 1905 and with Collinson's focus elsewhere, Nutchey and Turner were reunited with Howes to lead the newly professional Norwich City. All three used their extensive contacts, providing hospitality and building relationships to ensure that Norwich obtained enough votes to gain election to the Southern League at the expense of Crystal Palace. The Southern League at the time was semi-professional and a viable alternative to the official Football League, which at the time was very Northern/Midlands focused. The Southern League included a number of big name clubs such as Tottenham Hotspur, West Ham and Portsmouth, who went on to have distinguished histories. This new chapter in Norwich's existence signalled the end of regional rivalries with Lowestoft, Beccles and of course CEYMS. Ironically, the most successful side in the region, Lowestoft Town, were also punished by the FA for breaches in their amateur status, but unlike Norwich they decided to amend their procedures and remain an amateur side.

Norwich finished a very respectable seventh in their debut season 1905–06 in the Southern League. At the beginning of the season Nutchey had appointed John Bowman as the first professional manager. Meanwhile Turner, as assistant manager, continued to play an active role in player recruitment. He also was responsible for presenting the team news to Howes' newly formed supporters' club.

It was during this period that Nutchey, Howes and Turner oversaw a number of key events that to this day are still widely associated with Norwich Football Club. Firstly, the famous yellow shirts replaced the old blue and white halves. This was followed with the first reference to Norwich as the Canaries (the previous nickname had been The Citizens), and the world's oldest football song, *On the ball city* was adopted as the club's anthem. It was also during this period, in response to increasing crowds and costs, that Norwich relocated from Newmarket Road to an old chalk quarry in Rosary Road, a unique ground called The Nest.

Turner became manager in March 1909. His promotion from assistant manager came just a month after Norwich had completed an amazing FA Cup giant-killing, winning 3–2 at Anfield, the famous home of First Division Liverpool. The game was watched by 32,000, four to five times the crowds Norwich were used to at the Nest. Turner's first game as manager saw Norwich lose 0–1 to Reading, their first defeat at The Nest. The following season, 1909–10, was Turner's only full season in charge, with Norwich finishing a disappointing sixth from bottom. By March 1910 Turner's long association with Norwich was over, after he was replaced as manager by James Stansfield.

By the time of Turner's departure another founding member, Joe Nutchey, had already ended his association with Norwich. He resigned in the summer of 1907 in support of the then chairman Wilfred Burgess, over a matter of principle regarding the sale of star striker, Davie Ross.

The final member of the founding fathers in the Hall of Fame, John Howes, stayed with Norwich until summer 1947. He had loyally served the club as a director, and for the majority of his 45 years in office as financial secretary.

Nutchey, Turner and Collinson continued to follow the fortunes of Norwich up to their respective deaths. Nutchey was the first to pass away in February 1931 and in recognition of his part in establishing Norwich City, many thousands of supporters attended his funeral. Arthur Turner died in January 1956 aged 87. Finally, the last of the founding fathers, player and captain Collinson, died Boxing Day 1963 aged 88. Bob Collinson made 46 appearances for Norwich, scored 28 goals and achieved many firsts for the club.

Davie Ross

January 1885, Lancashire   Player 1905–07

Davie Ross was Norwich's first star player. He was a terrace idol and Norwich's first player to be known on a national level.

Born in Lancashire to a footballing family, Ross was destined to become a professional footballer. His three brothers all played professionally with the eldest, George, the most successful, winning the FA Cup twice with Bury and scoring in the second of those Finals, a 6–0 thrashing of Derby in 1903.

Six months after his brother's Cup victory, Ross made his debut for Bury – then an established First Division team – against Notts County and his first goal in the top division was soon to follow in the home game versus Aston Villa. Despite this promising start, Ross failed to establish himself in the Bury first team and in May 1904 he signed for Luton Town of the Southern League.

One year on, Ross had scored 12 goals in 32 League games and based on this form he was expected to make a return to the Football League. It was something of a surprise, therefore, when he joined Norwich in May 1905, as they were about to embark on their first season as a professional club in the Southern League.

Ross played in Norwich's first ever Southern League game, a long trip to Plymouth that ended in a 0–2 defeat, and the following first home League game, a 1–1 draw with Southampton at Newmarket Road. As an inside-left, Ross played just behind the main forwards and it was in a friendly on 28 September 1905 that Ross opened his account with Norwich in spectacular style, scoring six goals in an 11–0 rout against French club Athletique Professionel Parisian, Norwich's first ever game against overseas opposition. Two days later and back to the more serious business of the League, Ross scored in the 1–2 loss at Brighton. Two weeks after the Brighton game, Ross scored Norwich's first penalty in the Southern League, again in a 1–2

defeat, this time to Fulham. In total that season, Ross played in all bar one game and ended the season as Norwich's top goalscorer with 21 goals (17 in the League); Norwich exceeded expectations by finishing seventh (in an 18 team League).

The season included many highlights for Ross, a double against QPR in a 4–0 victory, the winner in a 1–0 win versus Swindon in front of the first 10,000+ crowd at Newmarket Road and a hat-trick in the FA Cup first round victory over Tunbridge Wells Rangers. This earned Norwich their first meeting with Manchester United (which Norwich lost 0–3).

Ross' striking partner that season was the experienced Scottish forward Duncan Ronaldson, who scored Norwich's first goal in the Southern League and had been instrumental in Ross' development as a youngster at Bury. However, by the end of 1905–06 season Ross had succeeded his one-time mentor to become the leading goalscorer at Norwich. In addition to his clever footwork and neat interplay he was a master at the volleyed shot, an Edwardian Mark Hughes, and many of his 21 goals were spectacular efforts that wowed the Norwich support.

Ross' reputation continued to grow in the next season, 1906–07. By the time Norwich travelled to the Hawthorns for the FA Cup second round tie versus WBA on 2 February 1907, Ross had already overtaken the previous season's total, scoring 28 (including 19 League goals). His League tally included five doubles with two doubles in consecutive weeks versus Luton and Crystal Palace in October 1906. Norwich's and Ross' reputations were further enhanced with a battling performance in a narrow 0–1 defeat to a WBA team that were founder members of the Football League and twice FA Cup winners.

The WBA FA Cup game proved to be Ross' last for Norwich. A number of the country's bigger clubs had been watching his progress and in February 1907 a bid of £650 was accepted from First Division Manchester City. In addition to the transfer fee, a Southern League record, Manchester City agreed to play a friendly believed to be worth a further £250. Ross' move to Manchester set the trend in Norwich's history as he became the first of many star players to be sold for substantial fees. His move prompted demonstrations by the supporters and split the boardroom, eventually leading to the resignation of chairman Wilfred Burgess and one of the club's founders, Joe Nutchey.

The following season, 1907–08, Ross went on to help Manchester City to a third place finish in Division One. Although he could not break into the England team, he did play in a North v South exhibition game. Norwich without Ross finished the 1907–08 season in 16th place, their lowest Southern League finish (although they did shock the FA Cup holders, beating Sheffield Wednesday 2–0 at Newmarket Road).

Davie Ross made 71 appearances for Norwich scoring 49 goals. He was Norwich's top goalscorer in two consecutive seasons and his goals/appearances ratio of 0.69 is the club's second best.

Joe Hannah

November 1898, Norfolk   Player 1921–35

Norfolk born and a one club man, Joe (official name James) is a true Canary legend.

Hannah was born in Sheringham, north Norfolk, in 1898 and became a prolific striker for his local side and he was destined for a career at a higher level after scoring an outstanding 70 goals in one season for Sheringham.

His soccer education continued when he played with seasoned professionals while serving with the Royal Engineers in World War One. After the war Hannah joined Norwich as a trainee and actually made his debut versus Newport County, on 13 January 1921, five months before signing professional terms in the summer 1921. It was nearly a year after his debut when Hannah made his second appearance, scoring in a 2–4 defeat at Bristol Rovers. Despite his goal, this

proved to be Hannah's only appearance in the 1921–22 season and it was not until the second half of the 1922–23 season that he finally established himself as a first-team regular.

Hannah's debut back in January 1921 was in Norwich's first season in the new Third Division South. By the end of the 1919–20 season, with football in the country booming, the Football League had decided to expand, incorporating the Southern and Northern Leagues into the Football League and so creating a new Third Division. Under the League's pyramid structure, Norwich could now dream of the possibility, one day, of First Division football. Norwich's first game in the Football League was a 1–1 draw at Plymouth (ironically their first Southern League opponents). It was another 13 games though before Norwich experienced their first win in the Football League, beating Reading 1–0 on 6 November 1920.

When Hannah broke into the Norwich first team, who were making their Football League debut, he played as a centre-forward which was not surprising after his goalscoring exploits with Sheringham. However, the Football League was a much higher level than Hannah was accustomed to and he struggled to score, scoring twice in 11 games during his first run in the team, towards the end of the 1922–23 season. The following season, 1923–24, manager Gosnell converted him to full-back, a position he was to make his own for the next 11 seasons, including three as captain.

Despite Norwich consistently finishing in lower mid-table positions throughout the 1920s, Hannah had established himself as the best full-back in the Third Division with his consistent performances and ability to tightly mark the opponent's winger. Such were the high standards set by Hannah that he famously walked the 25 miles back to his home in Sheringham as a self-punishment for a poor performance. Luckily he did not have to make many of these long walks as a poor game by him was rare.

In January 1925 his performances were rewarded when he was selected to represent the South v North at Stamford Bridge. The following month he played for a Rest of England side at Maine Road, Manchester, and the 1925 season culminated in his selection for an England FA select XI on a summer tour of Australia. Hannah played in the three Test games against Australia select XI, including the highlight of the tour, an 8–2 win in July 1925. For his efforts Hannah was awarded with a gold medal as well as having had the experience of representing his country (albeit not for the official England international side).

After the 1925 tour Hannah was brought back down to earth when he played for Norwich in a 1–3 FA Cup first round shock defeat to non-League amateurs Clapton. It was a low point in a season, 1925–26, that ended with Norwich finishing 16th.

The next season, 1926–27, Hannah was promoted to captain. In the following seasons he experienced mixed fortunes including a bottom place finish in 1930–31, his testimonial in April 1932, a 2–2 draw against First Division Derby County and a Championship winners' medal in 1933–34.

It was towards the end of that first Championship winning season that Hannah suffered a serious knee injury in a Division Three South Cup semi-final versus Torquay at Highbury. The injury was so bad that it was to end his career. He did manage one more League game, his first in the Second Division, a 1–0 away win at Plymouth, but that was it for the first team. Hannah did continue to play for the reserves before serving in the Observers Corps in World War Two. After the war he spent one season back with Norwich as assistant trainer before retirement.

Joe Hannah made 427 appearances for Norwich scoring 21 goals. He is fifth in the all-time list of Norwich appearances and third for an outfield player.

Percy Vargo

April 1904, Cornwall   **Player 1927–29**

'Give it to Vargo' was the chant from the terraces for the goalscoring machine, Percy Vargo, arguably the first Norwich player to have their own supporters' song in recognition of their performances.

Cornishman Vargo's early career had been a bit nomadic. He started out with his local club Torquay, in August 1923, before signing for Aston Villa six months later for £200. This was a great opportunity; Aston Villa were founder members of the Football League, six times champions and one of the most famous names in English football. The season Vargo joined Aston Villa, 1923–24, they finished sixth in Division One. However, Vargo had failed to establish himself in the first team, making only 10 appearances in two and a half years. He eventually moved to QPR in June 1926, the summer after they had finished bottom of Division Three South and had to apply for re-election. Vargo's short stay at QPR was again unsuccessful; he scored only four goals in 16 appearances. One of those goals came against Norwich in a performance that caught manager Cecil Potter's eye as QPR completed the League double over Norwich that season. After just one season at QPR, Potter signed Vargo in July 1927.

At Norwich, 23-year-old Vargo finally began to fulfil his potential. He scored four in a pre-season friendly and began the 1927–28 season with a debut goal in the 4–1 win at home to Crystal Palace. He followed this up by scoring in the next six games, taking his total to 10 goals in seven games and by the end of his first season he had finished with 32 goals (29 League and three FA Cup). Interestingly, it could have been 33 but for Vargo's honesty. On 24 March 1928 Norwich were hosting Charlton at The Nest. With the score at 0–0, a Vargo shot missed the goal and rebounded back into play off the large concrete wall that The Nest was famous for. Instinctively Vargo was first to the rebound, tucking the ball into the net. To everybody's surprise the goal was given, until Vargo put the referee straight, the goal was disallowed and the game finished 0–0. Despite costing Norwich a point, Vargo was rewarded for his gamesmanship with a gold sovereign by the chairman, Ernie Morse.

A fine debut season marked many personal achievements for Vargo. He became the first Norwich player to score over 30 goals in one season and the first to score more than 25 League goals. His total of 32 became a Norwich City record for the next 27 years until Ralph Hunt scored 33 in 1955–56. His opening tally of 10 in seven was also a club record and included three doubles (scoring two in a game). He went on to score doubles on another four separate occasions that season including in consecutive games versus Plymouth and Merthyr in October–November 1927. Vargo also became the first Norwich player to score a hat-trick in both the League and FA Cup in the same season. Perhaps with something to prove, his League hat-trick came against his old club QPR at The Nest on 21 April 1928, helping Norwich to a 3–1 victory. Four months earlier he scored three, again at The Nest, as Norwich knocked non-League Poole Town out of the FA Cup in a first round replay. This set up a second round tie away to fellow Third Division opponents Luton, who inflicted Norwich's joint worst ever FA Cup defeat 0–6. In the League too, Norwich disappointed – despite Vargo's goals – finishing a poor 17th, only six points off bottom place.

With Vargo's scoring prowess, Norwich supporters were optimistic about the forthcoming 1928–29 season. In the first home game, Vargo looked to continue where he had left off with a brace in the 5–1 win over Bournemouth. However, the goals failed to flow in an injury interrupted season which restricted Vargo to five League goals in only 12 appearances. There were some highlights in that injury hit season, including a four goal haul in the FA Cup second round 6–0 victory over Newport (a Newport team that actually finished above Norwich that season). In the third round, Vargo and Norwich were given a football lesson by the world famous amateur side Corinthians, who scored five without reply in front of a record attendance of 20,129 at The Nest.

Again, Norwich finished 17th in the League and the 1929–30 season started with Vargo in the treatment room. While he did make a scoring comeback against Newport in late November 1929 he had been out for almost a year and he was given a free transfer back to the South West with Exeter. His last game for Norwich was Boxing Day 1929 against his old club QPR, with Vargo scoring in a 2–3 defeat.

Percy Vargo made 65 appearances for Norwich scoring 47 goals. His goals/appearances ratio of 0.72 is an all-time best for a Norwich player.

Doug Lochhead

December 1904, Scotland

Player 1929–35
Manager 1947–50

In his 20 years at Carrow Road Doug Lochhead served the club loyally in many capacities including player, coach, interim manager, manager and scout.

He first joined Norwich in the summer of 1929, one of new manager Jim Kerr's first signings. A midfielder, he had started his career with St Johnstone in his native Scotland before crossing the border to join Walsall in Division Three South. His transfer to Norwich was overshadowed by the re-signing of his more experienced Walsall teammate Mike O'Brien. O'Brien was seen as Norwich's big summer signing and was immediately made club captain.

On 31 August 1929 Lochhead lined up alongside O'Brien, with both men making a disappointing debut in a 0–4 home defeat to Fulham. In spite of this poor start, Lochhead became a regular in a Norwich side that finished eighth, their highest position since joining the Football League. The highlight of the season came on 15 March 1930 when Coventry were the visitors to The Nest. Just over three months earlier Coventry had knocked Norwich out of the FA Cup in a first round replay, while the corresponding League fixture at Highfield Road had ended in a 1–3 Coventry win. Nobody, therefore, in the crowd of 8,230 was expecting Norwich to record their biggest ever victory (a record that is still held today). Three goals in the opening 14 minutes set the tone and despite Coventry replying, Norwich kept scoring and scoring. Lochhead was one

of the scorers as Norwich hit double figures, winning 10–2 – a fantastic achievement.

After the highs of the Coventry win, Norwich were soon brought back down to earth. The next season, 1930–31, they failed to win in their first eight games including a 0–7 thrashing at Lochhead's old club, Walsall. The season did not get any better and a year after finishing eighth (at the time a club record League finish), Norwich finished joint bottom and had to go through the process of re-election.

While 1930–31 was a low point for Lochhead, the following seasons were more successful, culminating in the Championship winning season in 1933–34; Lochhead earning his medal playing in 31 of the 42 games.

Norwich's success that season also meant that crowds were increasing and the facilities at The Nest were becoming increasingly inadequate.

The Nest had been Norwich's home since 1908. The terraces and grandstands were squeezed into an old chalk quarry where there was a 50ft retaining wall at one end and steep cliffs at the other, giving the ground a cauldron feel that was both unique and intimidating. As Norwich grew as a club and attendances increased, the ground became more and more unsafe both for supporters and players. Reading had already refused to play an FA Cup fixture there while 60 people had suffered minor injuries when a wall collapsed. On 16 February 1935 Lochhead was involved in the FA Cup fifth round tie versus Sheffield Wednesday that attracted a record gate of 25,037. The ground simply could not accommodate such numbers and with increasing threats from the FA of ground closure and suspension from the League, a new ground was built in the summer of 1935 on the banks of the River Wensum. This ground is still Norwich's home today, Carrow Road.

In the opening Division Two fixture of the 1935–36 season, 29,779 saw the first ever match at Carrow Road. On this momentous day, Lochhead was not only captain but also had the honour of scoring the opening goal in a 4–3 win over West Ham, earning his place in history as the first Norwich player to score at Carrow Road. Lochhead only scored five goals in his entire Norwich career but, as we have seen, two came in historic matches: the record win against Coventry and the opening game at Carrow Road.

Lochhead only played another two matches at Carrow Road – both as captain and both ending in defeat – before he was dropped. He later worked as chief scout and assistant manager under Bob Young and then, after the war, first as interim manager during another difficult season of re-election and finally as manager in December 1947. In his two years as manager he stabilised the club, making a number of shrewd signings, including fellow Hall of Famers Johnny Gavin and Billy Lewis. A believer in youth, Lochhead also gave a debut to another Hall of Famer, Roy Hollis. Sadly, before these players were to blossom, Lochhead's health deteriorated. He retired in March 1950, heading for the warmer climate of Turkey as scout for Galatasary.

Doug Lochhead made 222 appearances for Norwich scoring five goals. He was manager for 104 games with a respectable win ratio of 40 per cent.

Bernard Robinson

December 1911, Cambridgeshire   **Player 1931–49**

Despite being born in Cambridgeshire, Bernard Robinson became a Norfolk institution and went on to become one of Norwich's finest servants. He was educated in King's Lynn and represented the Norfolk County side before progressing to Norwich as a trainee in 1931. This started an association with Norwich which was to last 18 years.

Robinson was a wing-half, which today would equate to a more defensive midfield position. His strong performances, particularly for the County team, had created a lot of interest for his signature – including that of the famous Aston Villa – but manager James Kerr persuaded him to sign for his local professional team as he looked to rebuild the club after winning re-election to the Football League at the end of 1930–31 season.

The first of his 380 appearances came in April 1932, the first season after re-election. Despite losing to Exeter 0–3 (a game that saw Hall of Famer Percy Vargo score twice against Norwich), Robinson impressed and was selected for four of the last five fixtures that season. He missed the first game of the 1932–33 season, a home defeat to Watford, but went on to play in every other game that season as the James Kerr revolution began to take shape and Norwich finished third (unfortunately in the pre Play-off days when only the champions were promoted).

Robinson played a key role in the 1933–34 Championship winning season that followed and missed only one game in Norwich's first ever season in Division Two. His consistent performances

and ability to link defence with attack meant that he was often the first name on the team sheet. He had a presence on the pitch and could dominate his opponent. Never injured or suspended, Robinson missed only two games in the next three seasons, including being ever-present in Norwich's first season at Carrow Road, 1935–36. Robinson, in particular, was relieved to be playing in the new stadium; as a wing-half he saw how dangerous the proximity of The Nest's wall to the pitch was for wingers and felt the ground had been unsuitable for playing football.

After playing in the inaugural game at Carrow Road, Robinson's form dipped as Norwich lost their next seven games in a row, a run finally halted in October 1935 with a 1–1 draw away to Fulham. Four games later Robinson finally scored his first goal for the club, coming in his 135th League game, a 3–2 win at Barnsley. His first goal at Carrow Road was to follow only a week later in a classic tussle with Manchester United, ending in a 3–5 defeat to the eventual champions.

As the club's penalty taker, Robinson would have scored far more goals if he played today, rather than in an era where you practically had to be assaulted to get a penalty. For those penalties that he did take, he developed a unique and successful technique, where he would stand with his back to the goal before turning and shooting. Robinson was also one of the pioneers of the long throw, a rare but useful weapon in those days, which Norwich used to their advantage.

Robinson scored two goals in the following season, 1936–37, with one in a crucial 5–1 victory over fallen giants Aston Villa, a win that was to secure Norwich another year in Division Two.

Still a regular in the first team up to the war, Robinson made a further 160 appearances in wartime friendlies before returning to League action for the first post-war season 1946–47. These were difficult times for Norwich, and Robinson's presence as a senior player was important as Cyril Spiers and then Hall of Famer Doug Lochhead steadied the ship.

His knack for scoring important goals continued when, on 31 January 1948, Robinson scored a long distance winner at Portman Road to secure Norwich's first ever League win over their Suffolk rivals, who had finally been elected into the Football League. Fittingly, Robinson's last game for Norwich was again versus Ipswich on 12 March 1949, a 2–0 win in front of Carrow Road's first 35,000+ gate.

Robinson had a belated but much earned testimonial against Luton in April 1949 before retiring to run a pub. He was the oldest surviving player at Norwich's centenary celebrations in 2002 before his death in November 2004.

Bernard Robinson made 380 appearances for Norwich scoring 14 goals. This places him 12th on the all-time appearances list, but if you add in his 160 appearances in unofficial war games his total of 540 would place him third behind Hall of Famer Kevin Keelan and Ron Ashman. His 18 years of consecutive service to Norwich is the most of any player in the club's history.

Stan Ramsey

August 1904, Tyne and Wear   Player 1932–35

Born in the footballing hotbed that is the North East, Ramsey was destined for footballing success when he began his career with his local club, Sunderland, in May 1924. He was joining one of the country's most successful teams at the time – they had won the League Championship four times – and in his time there, Sunderland achieved two third place finishes (enough for Champion's League football today). However, competition for places was tough in a side full of seasoned internationals and Ramsey's opportunities were limited to 23 appearances in three seasons with the club. Despite scoring a top flight hat-trick against Leeds, he was soon sold to Second Division Blackpool in February 1928.

In a sign of things to come later at Norwich, he was instrumental in Blackpool's Division Two title win in his first full season, 1929–30. He then helped Blackpool to First Division survival the following season, 1930–31, the same year that Norwich were propping up the football League. After 105 games for Blackpool, Jim Kerr persuaded him to join his revolution at Norwich and Ramsey signed on 1 July 1932. This was a significant signing as at 27 years old, Ramsey was at his peak, with an experience of top flight football that few of his new teammates at Norwich could rival.

Ramsey made a headline-grabbing debut in the first game of the 1932–33 season when he scored an own-goal in the first minute against Watford at Carrow Road (a feat to be repeated by Hall of Famer Steve Bruce some 50 years later). He recovered from this start to score at the right end the following week at Cardiff (his only goal for Norwich). Ramsey went on to make 32 appearances that season, playing an important part in Norwich's third place finish (their record finish at the time).

After Ramsey's successful first season it was no surprise when new manager and Hall of Famer Tom Parker promoted him to captain. He was a natural leader, leading by example on the pitch with his committed displays. Hard in the tackle, he was rarely beaten by his opponent. He played a pivotal role in leading Norwich to their first professional Championship, the Division Three South title, in the season 1933–34. That season Norwich lost just six games. In fact, since Ramsey's debut in August 1932, Norwich had only lost 13 out of 84 League games. The statistic is even more impressive when you consider that for three of those 13 defeats Ramsey was missing from the first team. With Ramsey in defence, Norwich conceded only 49 goals (an impressive tally in an era of five forwards and high scoring games) including 16 clean sheets; this compared to 67 goals in the season before Ramsey joined and 76 the season before that. Ramsey's impact on the side was therefore tangible as Norwich went on to win the title by seven clear points.

Top by November and with the best away record in the entire Football League (only five defeats), the title was clinched when nearest rivals Coventry visited The Nest on 21 April 1934. The Nest, with its close crowds and steep banks, was an intimidating venue for visiting teams and Norwich had lost at home only once all season (0–2 to Torquay). In front of an expectant and large gate of 16,903, Ramsey helped settle the pre-match nerves with a convincing performance. He marshalled the defence against a free-scoring Coventry (they finished the season with 100 goals, 12 more than champions Norwich), restricting the visitors to a single goal as Norwich triumphed 3–1 to seal both promotion and the Championship title.

Ramsey was the first Norwich player as captain to lift a trophy. He soon lifted a second trophy on 7 May 1934 when Norwich defeated the Second Division champions, Grimsby Town by 7–2, to win the Norfolk and Norwich Hospital Cup, the traditional end of season finale.

Ramsey was part of the first Norwich team to play in the Second Division, although he was no longer captain, as manager Parker looked towards youth in the form of Hall of Famer Tom Halliday. He played just nine games in that 1934–35 season before retiring. After nine months out of the side, in the summer of 1935, he became player-manager at non-League Shrewsbury in the same season that his first club, Sunderland, won the First Division title. He had only one season with Shrewsbury before returning to Norfolk to play for Dereham Town and run a newsagent in Norwich.

Stan Ramsey made 82 appearances for Norwich scoring one goal.

Tom Parker

November 1897, Hampshire **Manager 1933–37 and 1955–57**

Apart from the founding members, Tom Parker is the first Hall of Famer that never played for Norwich, instead leaving his legacy with the club in his two spells as manager.

Parker had an illustrious career before joining Norwich. He signed for his home-town club, Southampton, in 1919 and played in the inaugural Division Three South season which Southampton finished as runners-up. The following season, 1921–22, he won the Third Division South Championship and was a regular in the side that held their own in Division Two. His abilities at full-back were recognised with his one and only England cap, a 3–2 victory against France in 1925.

Destined for bigger things, it was no surprise when Parker signed for Arsenal in March 1926, at the beginning of the great Herbert Chapman's revolution. At Highbury his career flourished. He captained Arsenal to their first FA Cup win in 1930 against the mighty Huddersfield, and the following season, 1930–31, he led Arsenal to their first Division One League Championship. In addition to his FA Cup and Championship medals, Parker went on to appear for Arsenal in two further FA Cup Finals (both as runners-up) and made a record number of consecutive appearances for the Arsenal first team (172), a record which he still holds to this day.

With Arsenal on their way to another Division One title, Parker, now aged 35, made his first move into management when he joined Norwich in March 1933. At the time, Parker was the most successful individual, in terms of medals won and achievements at the game's top level, to be employed by Norwich.

As well as being new to football management, and having to adjust to life outside the First Division, Parker faced the added challenge at Norwich of replacing previous manager Jim Kerr. Kerr had died suddenly in February 1933, the only Norwich manager to die in service. He was much liked and respected by both players and fans and had been steadily rebuilding the club after the re-election season in 1930–31. With five first-team players having been bearers at Kerr's funeral, it was an emotional dressing room that Parker walked into in March 1933.

To Parker's credit, at this difficult time, he not only maintained but built upon the foundations laid by Kerr. So positive was his impact that he guided Norwich to their first Third Division South Championship in his first full season in charge (1933–34) and so became the first manager to lead Norwich into Division Two.

Parker's role in the team's achievement that season should not be understated. He had a good eye for a player, signing Jack Vinall and Tom Halliday (both Hall of Famers) in the summer of 1933, with both playing central roles in Norwich's success. He promoted the inspirational Stan Ramsey to captain and introduced a very modern philosophy that would not look out of place in today's Premiership. His new approach involved the team staying together at the Pier Hotel, Gorleston, before all home games. He introduced pre-match routines and encouraged players to watch their diets. His man-management skills were good, encouraging players to socialise on the golf courses. He also became popular, with players wanting to play for him. Overall he brought a new level of professionalism to Norwich.

After overseeing the move to Carrow Road and keeping Norwich in the Second Division, Parker could not resist the opportunity to return home, and in February 1937 he accepted an offer to become Southampton's new manager. With him he took a young Norwich reserve, Ted Bates, who was to later become an iconic figure at The Dell, serving the club for over 66 years including over 200 games as a player and 850 as manager.

Parker's service with Southampton was interrupted by the war, and in 1943 he resigned to spend a period of time outside of football with Lloyds and the Ministry of Transport. After 12 years he was tempted back into football when Norwich came calling in May 1955. By this time Norwich were back in Division Three South and the Board were hoping for a repeat of the successes achieved under his first tenure in the 1930s. Unfortunately, as is often the case in football, the second coming was not so good, and in sharp contrast to his previous first season, Norwich finished bottom of Division Three in 1956–57. Parker did not see out the full season and was sacked in March 1957 following a run of only two wins in seven weeks.

While Parker's second spell as manager ended in disappointment on the pitch, he did bring back fans' favourite Johnny Gavin and signed Ralph Hunt (both in the Hall of Fame). He was also hampered by financial constraints caused by the debt that Norwich found themselves in.

Tom Parker managed Norwich for 271 games. His overall win ratio was a credible 38 per cent, although if you look at his first spell alone, the ratio is an even better 43 per cent.

Jack Vinall

December 1910, West Midlands   **Player 1933–37**

All supporters, of any club, love a traditional goalscoring number nine. Jack Vinall did this shirt proud for three seasons, as he became one of the most deadly forwards in Norwich's history.

Born within a stone's throw of Villa Park, Vinall never got an opportunity with his renowned local club. Instead he started a career in engineering while playing non-League football in Folkestone. His big break came in October 1931 when he travelled 340 miles to sign for First Division Sunderland for £500. Five days after signing he was thrown into the deep end, making his debut versus Middlesbrough in the fiercely contested Tees/Wear derby.

Although he played well in those early games, Vinall was in a strong and established First Division squad and opportunities were limited. After only 16 appearances and two goals in 18 months, and before the days of the loan system, Vinall decided to drop down two divisions to obtain regular first-team football with Norwich City.

Vinall was one of Tom Parker's first signings, in June 1933, as Parker looked to kick on from a third place finish in Division Three South the previous season. He made his debut in the opening game of the 1933–34 season, a 3–0 win over Clapton Orient. His decision to move was vindicated as he went on to play consecutively in the next 164 games, an ever-present for three seasons, a run finally ending in the away game to Leicester in February 1937.

Vinall's popularity with the Norwich supporters was sealed in his second game when he scored four goals in a 7–2 thrashing of Bristol City. He went on play a central role in his first season as Norwich romped to the Third Division South Championship, the club's best ever finish. Vinall was key to Norwich's success, forming a formidable partnership with Billy Warnes, with each finishing the season joint top goalscorer with 24 goals (21 League goals). Vinall's total included the winner against Newport in front of a record League crowd at The Nest (22,433) and a vital goal in the title clinching win against Coventry. His unofficial total that season was actually 29, as he scored five in the end of season Hospital Cup game versus Grimsby.

In the following season, 1934–35 – Norwich's first in Division Two – Vinall proved that he could play and score at a higher level when he again finished the season as Norwich's top goalscorer with 19 goals (16 League). His highlights that season included a goal in Norwich's first ever win in Division Two when they beat Bury 4–1 in August, a hat-trick at The Nest when Football League founder members Notts County were put to the sword in a 7–2 win, and a goal that resulted in Norwich's first ever win over Manchester United in February 1935. That season, Vinall also proved that he could score against First Division defences when Norwich drew Leeds out of the hat in the FA Cup fourth round. Leeds went into an early two goal lead at The Nest before goals from Vinall and two from Hall of Famer Alf Kirchen (who later went on to star for Arsenal) secured a replay at Elland Road. With home advantage gone, nobody gave Norwich a chance, but Vinall scored again in a shock 2–1 win. Vinall played in the fifth round game against Sheffield Wednesday in front of that record crowd at The Nest of 25,037, but unfortunately could not find the net as Norwich lost 0–1.

The 1935–36 season began well for Vinall, he scored two in the first ever game at Carrow Road and on 8 February 1936 he became the first Norwich player to score a hat-trick at Norwich's new home, helping Norwich comfortably beat Southampton 5–1. This was Vinall's fifth hat-trick in a Norwich shirt, a club record that has since been equalled by Hall of Famer Johnny Gavin but still stands to this day. The season ended with Vinall's best tally in the League, scoring 24, as he became Norwich's top goalscorer for the third successive season.

Despite scoring against Sheffield United on the opening day, the 1936–37 season proved to be more difficult for the free-scoring Vinall. All forwards have a goal drought at some stage in their careers and Vinall finished the 1936–37 season with 12 (10 League), five behind top scorer Frank Manders. Still a decent total, but short of the high standards he had set himself.

Vinall scored in the season's opener in 1937–38 (for the third successive year) but he only played another three games before moving to Luton for £3,000 in October 1937. He had a relatively successful time at Luton including, inevitably, a hat-trick against Norwich. He scored a total of 18 goals in 44 games before his career was interrupted by the war.

Jack Vinall made 181 appearances for Norwich scoring 80 goals, a total that leaves him fifth in Norwich's all-time top goalscorer chart.

Tom Halliday

September 1909, County Durham   Player 1933–39

When manager and Hall of Famer Tom Parker signed Tom Halliday on 30 June 1933, just three days after the signing of Jack Vinall, he had the final piece of his squad in place for what was to be the momentous title winning team of 1933–34.

Tom Halliday was a tough, uncompromising defender, a child of the industrial North East. He was a promising footballer from an early age; he excelled in his school teams and progressed to represent England schoolboys against Wales schoolboys in 1924. Unlike many of his young teammates, Halliday made the transition from schoolboy promise to professional football, first signing for Sunderland in 1927 and then, in 1928, for Darlington.

Halliday spent the next five years learning his trade in the hard environment of the Third Division North. He made 118 appearances for Darlington, with his last season, 1932–33, being particularly challenging as Darlington finished bottom with Halliday part of a defence that had shipped 109 goals. With this record it was perhaps a surprise when Parker signed him in June 1933.

Originally signed as a squad player, Halliday's debut came sooner than expected when he replaced the injured Tom Williamson for the second game of the 1933–34 season. Williamson's boots were big to fill. He had been Norwich captain for the previous two seasons and he had scored in the opening day win against Clapton Orient. Nevertheless, Halliday rose to the task, with Norwich trashing Bristol City 7–2. From this point, Halliday never looked back, missing only one game (Norwich's only home defeat that year) in that title winning season as Williamson drifted out of football.

Much of Norwich's success that season was based on the midfield three of Robinson, Lochhead and Halliday (all Hall of Famers).

Each complemented the others' games, with Halliday the central-defensive rock of the trilogy. So impressive were Halliday's performances in his debut season that Parker made him his captain for Norwich's first season in Division Two.

As captain, Halliday led his team out at some of the most famous grounds in English football, as Norwich made their competitive debut at Manchester United, Newcastle and Bolton. Halliday played in 41 of the 42 League games, leading Norwich to a respectable 14th place finish as they consolidated their position in English football's second tier. Halliday's defensive role that season was highlighted by the fact that Norwich's defence conceded 61 goals, which was better than eight of the teams that finished above them including 63 conceded by third place West Ham.

Halliday was an inspirational captain both on and off the pitch. He was a 'larger than life' character in the dressing room with a love for fast cars and nights out. A true premiership footballer!

He continued to lead Norwich in their debut season, 1935–36, at Carrow Road (although Lochhead was captain in that first game). A personal highlight for Halliday that season came in the FA Cup third round, when First Division Chelsea were restricted to one goal in a 1–1 draw at Carrow Road before Norwich were narrowly beaten in the replay.

The following season, 1936–37, in the FA Cup third round, Norwich went one better when the defence, protected in midfield by Halliday, kept a clean sheet in a 3–0 victory over First Division Liverpool (A Liverpool team featuring Matt Busby in attack). The Norwich captain that day and for that season was Sam Bowen. Despite losing the captaincy, Halliday was still an important player, appearing in 33 games that season.

Halliday briefly regained the captaincy during the 1937–38 season but by then he was beginning to look to the future, passing his FA coaching badges and taking sessions at Norwich High School for Boys. His final game for Norwich was on 27 December 1938, in the impressive surroundings of St James' Park. It was not to end happily for Halliday, with Newcastle winning 0–4. Six weeks later he was granted a transfer to Exeter, where he played briefly until retiring during the war.

Tom Halliday made 203 appearances for Norwich but never managed to score a goal. He was captain in 84 of those 203 games.

Alf Kirchen

April 1913, Norfolk   **Player 1933–35**

Alf Kirchen was one of the most talented players of his generation. He excelled in his short time at Norwich before starring in an Arsenal side that were all-conquering in English football. England caps were to follow; a proud moment for the County of Norfolk was Kirchen becoming the first Norfolk born player to play for his country.

Kirchen began his journey to the England team as a free scoring winger, firstly with King's Lynn Boys and then in the local Leagues, including the Norfolk and Suffolk League and the Eastern League. He was soon offered a trial at Norwich in 1931 aged 18, but an injury intervened and he was left to concentrate on his carpentry apprenticeship.

His ability continued to stand out at amateur level and, undeterred by his missed trial, he finally signed for Norwich in November 1933. He joined a Norwich team enjoying their best ever season since turning professional in 1905, and had to bide his time before making his debut in the penultimate game of the 1933–34 season. The disappointing 0–0 draw against Southend came a week after the title and promotion party had begun, following the 3–1 victory over Coventry, but Kirchen's single late appearance that season meant that he missed out on a Championship medal.

In the traditional end of season finale, the Hospital Cup, Kirchen played and scored two goals. Best remembered for Hall of Famer Jack Vinall's five goals, Norwich won the game 7–2 against Second Division champions Grimsby. Kirchen's overall performance in the Cup game set the tone for Norwich's debut season in Division Two, a season that would turn out to be his last in a Norwich shirt.

Kirchen had to be patient in the 1934–35 season as manager and Hall of Famer Tom Parker kept faith in the side that had got City promoted. After a couple of appearances Kirchen got his first run in the team, starting with a goal in a 1–1 draw at Swansea on 22 December

1934. The Swansea game marked a run of 15 consecutive League and Cup games with a return of 10 goals. The run included four in three games, the highlight being a double away to Fulham and a goal in a thrilling 3–2 home win, Norwich's first against the famous Manchester United.

In the FA Cup fourth round Kirchen proved he could compete at the highest level by scoring twice against First Division Leeds United, as Norwich came back from 0–2 down to earn a replay at Elland Road.

Kirchen's performances were soon attracting interest from First Division sides. He was a winger with pace and trickery who was difficult to knock off the ball. He had a fierce shot and a goalscoring ratio that any striker would be satisfied with. His last Norwich goal came on 23 February 1935 in a 1–1 draw with Blackpool and a week later he was sold to manager Parker's old club Arsenal for £6,000. It was a lot of money in those days and was to prove valuable in helping to fund the move to Carrow Road that summer.

Within 14 months of becoming a professional and still only 21 years old, Kirchen was joining the top team in English Football. Under Herbert Chapman, Arsenal had become invincible, dominating the First Division winning two consecutive titles. Under new manager George Allison they were well on their way to their third title when Kirchen signed.

Kirchen had a dream debut scoring two in a 6–0 win against North London arch rivals Tottenham, instantly winning over the fans. He played another six games but, as in 1933–34 season with Norwich, it was not enough to qualify for a medal. In a squad full of internationals, Kirchen again missed out on a medal, this time in the 1936 FA Cup Final. He finally established himself in the 1936–37 season with 22 goals as Arsenal finished third.

At the end of the 1936–37 season Kirchen got his call up to the England squad for a tour of Scandinavia, winning his first cap on 14 May 1937 and scoring in a convincing 6–0 win over Norway. He played in all three of the tour games in what proved to be his only England caps.

Kirchen finally got his hands on a deserved domestic medal in the 1937–38 season when Arsenal won their fifth title of the decade. Now in his prime, World War Two cut short his career. Serving with the RAF, Kirchen still managed another 113 appearances before an injury sustained by a tackle from future Norwich player and Hall of Famer Bill Lewis, forced him into retirement in 1943.

After the war, Kirchen played bowls to a good standard and represented England at clay pigeon shooting. He returned home to Norfolk, spending some time on the Norwich board during the 1950s before later taking on the job he was ideally suited for; Honorary President of the Norfolk Arsenal Supporters Club.

Alf Kirchen made 18 appearances for Norwich scoring 10 goals.

Bob Young

September 1893, County Durham　　　　　　　　　　　　　　Manager　1937–46

Bob Young served both his club and country with distinction – as both World Wars were to shape his career – as a player and a manager.

As a youngster coming through the ranks at Sunderland, the future looked bright for Young. Sunderland had won the First Division Championship in 1912–13, reinforcing their reputation as one of England's top sides. Two seasons later, in April 1915, Young made his debut in a home draw with Bradford. Sunderland finished the 1914–15 season eighth in Division One. This proved to be the last season of competitive football for four years; with the country in the depths of war the Football League was suspended. Young, like so many of his generation, left his club to fight in the trenches; he received a military medal for his bravery.

Despite being wounded in the war, Young returned to first-team football with Sunderland as the League resumed in 1919.

He played his second game for Sunderland, an away win at Everton, four and a half years after his debut. Although restricted by his wartime injuries he went on to make another 54 appearances for Sunderland, the last, again against Everton, in February 1925.

After a few years in the footballing wilderness, he was appointed – in the summer 1929 by new manager Jim Kerr – as Norwich coach, replacing the popular and long serving Charlie Miles. Young played an important back team role in the successes that Norwich enjoyed, first under Kerr and then Hall of Famer Tom Parker.

With Norwich established in Division Two, Young was rewarded for his efforts when he was appointed Norwich manager in February 1937, replacing the departing Parker. Norwich were facing a relegation battle at the time and

Young's first decision was a shrewd one, appointing Hall of Famer Doug Lochhead as his assistant. Together they steadied the ship, guiding Norwich to 17th and safety.

In his first full season in charge, 1937–38, Young bought in fellow Hall of Famer Billy Furness to lead the attack, as Norwich consolidated their Division Two status with an improved mid-table finish.

Despite further investment in the team, Young was unable to build on this position and Norwich lost their first four games in 1938–39. Another defeat followed on 29 October 1938, this time to Millwall, in front of King George VI. November and December then brought heavy defeats 0–7 and 0–6 to Sheffield Wednesday and Blackburn respectively, leaving Norwich in the relegation zone. By January things had not improved and almost a year after his appointment, Young was released from his duties.

Young's replacement in January 1939 was a surprise choice, ex-FA Cup Final referee James Jewel (probably the only referee to move into football management). The experiment did not work and Norwich was relegated at the end of the 1938–39 season. With the outbreak of World War Two in September 1939, Jewel left the club after only six months in charge and Young returned as manager at this turbulent time.

Young deserves much credit for his role in preserving football in Norwich over the war years. He understood the positive impact that football had on morale, particularly in a region at the geographical forefront of the war, with many regiments based in East Anglia and the region under sustained attack by the Luftwaffe. Under Young's guidance, Norwich played against other professional sides in a regional League as well as numerous friendly matches against Army, Navy and RAF sides. He would try to ensure that Norwich could fulfil their fixtures where possible and would improvise, such as playing seven-a-side games or loaning players to the opposition, rather than postponing a fixture and letting the crowd down.

The end of the war in 1945 brought much relief to the country, but with resources scarce and many players either still in service or retired, it was decided by the League to run an unofficial transitional season based on regional Leagues. Under Young, Norwich finished second in an 11 team League. That season also saw the return of the FA Cup. For the first and only time in the competition's history, games were played over two legs. Norwich lost both legs to Brighton in the third round.

After playing his part in ensuring Norwich's future as a football club, Young retired in 1946, with his former assistant Lochhead taking the reins.

Bob Young gave 17 years' loyal service to Norwich as coach and manager. He was manager for 78 games with a 33 per cent win percentage. However, unofficially he managed another 240 games during World War Two making him one of Norwich's longest serving managers.

Billy Furness

June 1909, County Durham   Player 1937–46

Billy Furness became a Norwich legend during the difficult years of World War Two. His positive attitude and goalscoring ability brought some relief to those involved in the war effort and played a significant part in improving the morale of spectators.

Another Hall of Famer from the North East, Furness was no stranger to hard work. He began his working life in the coal pits and spent his spare time playing football for the Washington Colliery team. In August 1928 he swapped life as a miner for that of a professional footballer when he signed for First Division Leeds United.

An energetic centre-forward with a powerful shot and eye for goal, Furness broke into the Leeds first team during the 1930–31 season, scoring 10 goals in a Leeds side that got relegated to Division Two. The next season, 1931–32, saw Leeds bounce straight back to Division One at the first attempt, with Furness spearheading the attack from the inside-left position.

Back in the First Division, Furness helped Leeds to a respectable eighth place finish and earned himself a call up to the England squad. He won his one and only England cap in a 1933 friendly versus Italy.

With Leeds established in the First Division, Furness became an ever-present in the team. He enjoyed his best goalscoring season in 1934–35 with 16 goals but was an FA Cup loser in a shock defeat to Norwich. This was Leeds' first competitive game against Norwich and the experience must have made an impression on Furness, as he later signed for Norwich in June 1937.

A victim of a squad clearance after a disappointing season by Leeds, Furness was signed by new Norwich manager and Hall of Famer, Bob Young. At 28 years old and with his First Division experience, he was a big signing for the Canaries. Costing £2,700, it was the most Norwich had ever paid for a player and a real statement of intent after a disappointing season. On the opening day of the 1937–38 season an expectant crowd of 23,407 watched Furness make an instant impact on his debut, with two goals in a 4–3 win against Southampton. Overall though, the season proved to be an anti-climax with Norwich finishing 14th (an improvement of only three places), despite a respectable 11 goal finish by Furness.

The following season, 1938–39, proved to be a massive disappointment for both Norwich and Furness. He played in every game that season, but managed only seven goals as Norwich slid towards a return to Division Three South. On 6 May 1939 the season boiled down to a 'winner takes all' clash against Nottingham Forest. A tall order, but if Norwich beat Forest 4–0 they would survive at the expense of the Midlands club. With Furness up front the crowd were hopeful of a miracle but in the end a 1–0 victory was not enough and Norwich, after five seasons in Division Two, were relegated on goal difference.

So, for the first time in his career, in August 1939, Furness started a Third Division South game, scoring in a 1–2 loss against Cardiff. One week later, Norwich made their professional bow at Portman Road, in the first ever East Anglian derby in the Football League. Furness has the distinction of being the first Norwich player to score a Football League goal against Ipswich.

The day after the 1–1 draw at Ipswich, war was declared, the League suspended and Furness' derby goal wiped from official records. With the intervention of war, it would have been understandable if Furness saw this as the time to retire from the game and reflect on a long and

successful career. To his credit, Furness, driven by a sense of duty to the club and its supporters, went on to represent Norwich in 177 wartime games scoring 69 goals. Highlights of that wartime campaign included an 18–0 thrashing of an under-strength Brighton, and lining up alongside international players who were stationed in the area and were allowed to represent Norwich as guest players. Perhaps the most famous to have played alongside Furness was the one and only Bill Shankly.

By the time the Football League resumed in August 1946, Furness was 37 years old. He played and scored in the opening Division Three South match against Cardiff. He was one of only five players to have played in the last match pre-war and the first match post-war. Eleven games later, on Boxing Day 1946, Furness finished playing. He stayed with Norwich as a coach and eventually as a physio, until retiring in August 1970.

Billy Furness made 96 appearances for Norwich scoring 21 goals. Unofficially he played in a further 177 games scoring 69 goals during the war, which would have given him a career total of 273 games and 90 goals, making him Norwich's fourth highest goalscorer.

Ron Ashman

May 1926, Cambridgeshire   **Player 1946–63**
                                                       Manager 1963–66

Ron Ashman is the ultimate Norwich City clubman. He was a one club player with a long list of personal records, honours and achievements, guaranteeing him a place forever in the history of Norwich City Football Club.

During World War Two Ashman served his country first as a 'Bevan Boy', conscripted down the coal pits, and secondly in the RAF. In breaks in service he was under contract with Norwich as a trainee and first played in August 1944 in a friendly against an Anti-Aircraft XI.

He signed as a professional when discharged post-war in January 1946, but had to wait until October 1947 before making his first-team debut versus Aldershot. At the time there were few signs of what was to come as Ashman made only five appearances that season and was yet to win over a sceptical Norwich support, who were disappointed with the club's second successive bottom two finish in Division Three South. During his debut season, despite being remembered today as an outstanding midfielder, Ashman played up front and the following season, 1948–49,

he finished as top scorer with 13 goals (12 League). A low total but impressive considering he had played in only 26 games.

In spite of winning Norwich's top goalscorer award, Ashman soon switched to a more defensive position that he felt better suited his game. However, it was not until the end of the 1949–50 season that Ashman finally established himself in the first team and from that point onwards he never looked back. After playing in the 1–1 draw against Ipswich in March 1950, Ashman played 192 consecutive games, until he missed the 0–0 draw with Brighton in April 1954.

The 1950–51 season was Ashman's first as an ever-present in the team and it coincided with one of Norwich's best seasons for many years. Ashman's presence in the midfield helped Norwich to a second place finish (unfortunately in the days when only the champions went up).

Ashman went on to set a club record, playing every game in the following six seasons; 1950–51, 51–52, 55–56, 59–60 and 60–61. Not surprisingly, this represented a fruitful period for Norwich, with two second, a third and two fourth place finishes.

It was on the last game of that successful 1950–51 season that Ashman first wore the captain's armband, putting in a captain's performance, with two goals in a 3–1 win over Crystal Palace. However, it was not until the 1955–56 season that Ashman made the captaincy his own, holding the armband right up to his last game in 1963. By this time he had become Norwich's longest reigning captain, leading the side on an incredible 472 occasions.

As the club's leader, Ashman captained Norwich in the famous 1959 FA Cup run, promotion to the Second Division in 1959–60, lifted the League Cup in 1962 and a highest ever League position of fourth in the Second Division in 1960–61. An impressive list, but there were also some bad days. Ashman played in and captained Norwich for 35 games in the fateful 1956–57 season which ended with Norwich propping up the Football League and facing the rigours of re-election (fortunately for the last time). That season also saw Ashman captain Norwich in arguably their biggest FA Cup embarrassment, a 2–4 home defeat to non-League Bedford Town.

The 1956–57 season proved to be only a minor blemish on a hugely successful career. Other accolades included being Norwich's record penalty scorer – with a career total of 17 – and scoring in 11 successive seasons (another club first). Ashman also became Norwich's second (after Norman Low), and to this date their last, player-manager. Ashman was the natural choice to steady the ship after the club was rocked by manager George Swindin's departure for Cardiff after only six months in the job.

Ashman's first game as player-manager and captain was on 15 December 1962, a home match against Preston. He held this joint responsibility for another 35 League and Cup games before finally hanging up his boots, after the home draw with Southampton in October 1963. His retirement marked a playing career that had spanned 17 seasons and resulted in 662 appearances. In all competitions this was second only to Kevin Keelan, although the best for an outfield player. He holds the club record for League and FA Cup appearances (590 and 56 respectively). The length of his career is illustrated by the fact that he played alongside Hall of Famer Bernard Robinson, whose career had started in 1932, and Kevin Keelan, whose last game was in 1980.

As a manager, Ashman served the club for a further two and a half years, finally ending his association with Norwich in June 1966, 20 years after signing as a pro. During his time as manager he had stabilised the club, enjoyed another famous FA Cup run and bought in three players that are in the Hall of Fame, including, ironically the man who was to beat his appearances record, Kevin Keelan. He was also the first Norwich manager, after a change in the League's rules, to make a substitution, bringing on Gordon Bolland in place of the injured Terry Anderson.

Ashman went on to manage in Lincolnshire with both Scunthorpe (where he gave a young Kevin Keegan his debut) and Grimsby, before leaving football in May 1981. His Norwich testimonial was, fittingly for a centre-half, a 0–0 versus Ipswich. He has also received an FA long service statuette and has been honoured with an MBE.

Ron Ashman made 662 appearances for Norwich scoring 56 goals. He was manager for 162 games.

Les Eyre

January 1922, Derbyshire   Player 1946–51

Les Eyre was the first of many great post-war strikers that played for Norwich. He represented hope for Norwich at a low point in their history, a club struggling to find its feet, both on and off the pitch, after the disruption of war.

For Eyre, his opportunity in football came during the war. Serving with the RAF he was spotted by Cardiff playing exhibition games in India. On his leave from service he followed Cardiff manager Cyril Spiers to Norwich, signing professional terms on 9 July 1946 in time for the resumption of the Football League programme after the transitional season.

He made his Norwich debut on 26 September 1946, partnering the great Hall of Famer Billy Furness in a 2–3 defeat to Crystal Palace. While not scoring, Eyre impressed and played in all bar one game for the remainder of the 1946–47 season, becoming a beacon of consistency in a struggling season where Norwich used a record 37 different players.

After a slow start in his debut season, with two goals in his first nine games, his defining point came on 30 November 1946. Brighton were the visitors in the FA Cup first round and had a 1–2 lead at half-time. In worsening playing conditions, Norwich overwhelmed their opponents in the second half, running out 7–2 winners with Eyre scoring five. The score was even more remarkable considering Brighton had won 2–3 at Carrow Road in the League clash only a couple of months earlier (incidentally the only League game Eyre had missed since his debut).

The five against Brighton equalled Thomas Hunt's club record for most goals scored by the same player in one match and it helped Eyre finish his first season as the club's top scorer with 18 goals, eight more than the second top goalscorer, Ralph Johnson.

Eyre's fine goalscoring form continued in the following season of 1947–48. He missed only two games and again finished as Norwich's top goalscorer with 16 goals. In doing so he joined an elite group including Hall of Famers Davie Ross, James Jackson and Jack Vinall, who had finished top goalscorers in two consecutive seasons. Eyre's goalscoring achievements are put into perspective when you consider that, in both of these seasons, Norwich had finished second bottom of Division Three South and twice had to apply for re-election. In a side short of confidence and creativity, Eyre had to rely on his pace and a high conversion rate. He also had high levels of stamina and was a nuisance to opposing defenders for the full 90 minutes. This was illustrated by the fact that just under half of his total Norwich goals were scored in the last third of the game.

The final two seasons of the 1940s saw improvements in Norwich's League position as the team evolved. The goalscoring burden on Eyre was lightened by the emergence of Hall of Famer Noel Kinsey as an advanced midfielder; Norwich finished both seasons in mid-table. The team continued to improve in 1950–51 season based around a now potent attacking force. Eyre again ended a season on double figures with 16, and while this was enough to lead the scoring charts in 1947–48, he finished the season third behind Hall of Famers Johnny Gavin and Roy Hollis.

The highlights for Eyre, in the 1950–51 season, again came in the FA Cup. In the first round, he scored Norwich's 100th goal in the competition in a 2–0 home win over Watford and after scraping through the second round against non-League Rhyl, Norwich landed a plum third round tie at home to Liverpool. First Division Liverpool had been beaten finalists the previous year and were expected to proceed with comfort. However, in the true traditions of the FA Cup, Norwich won 3–1 with Eyre scoring in front of 34,693 at Carrow Road. This proved to be Eyre's last goal in the Cup and his 11th FA Cup goal for Norwich in total, leaving him joint second in the list of Norwich's all-time FA Cup goalscorers. His last game in the Cup came in the fifth round in front of 65,125 at Sunderland, but Norwich could not repeat their heroics losing 1–3.

In the summer of 1951, a joint club record of £9,500 was paid to Hull for centre-forward, Alf Ackerman. This was a significant fee for a Third Division club and Ackerman was always likely to start. Ackerman scored on his debut and with the presence of Gavin, Kinsey and Hollis, Eyre found his opportunities limited. He played just five games before moving to Bournemouth in November 1951. He went on to score 10 in 38 games for Bournemouth before ending his career in the non-League.

Les Eyre made 201 appearances for Norwich scoring 69 goals. He is the ninth highest goalscorer in the club's history.

Denis Morgan

September 1925, Wales   **Player 1946–56**

Denis Morgan was a stylish full-back who, but for injuries, would certainly have played the game at the highest level.

Welsh born, Morgan was one of the first of a growing link between South Wales and Norfolk. A relationship that had begun with the appointment of new Norwich manager, Cyril Spiers.

Before joining Norwich, Spiers was the manager of Cardiff City. Dictated by high debt levels and the interruption of the League during the war, he set about developing the youth set-up at Cardiff (a strategy that Norwich would later benefit from). One product of the Cardiff academy was Denis Morgan who joined Cardiff as a 17-year-old in August 1942.

As a youngster at Cardiff, Morgan must have made quite an impression, as he was one of Spiers' first former players to be signed in October 1946. The following week Morgan made his Norwich appearance in a 2–3 home defeat to Brighton, his debut coming only a fortnight after that of his former Cardiff youth teammate and fellow Hall of Famer, Leslie Eyres. Morgan was soon joined by George Morgan and Hall of Famers Norman Low, Noel Kinsey and Don Pickwick, as Spiers added a Welsh backbone to his new-look Norwich side.

Spiers returned to manage Cardiff in December 1947, the same season that Morgan was beginning to establish himself in the Norwich first team. He was a defender who was comfortable on the ball, happy bringing the ball out from the back and rarely losing possession. He was a classy defender with lots of pace that enabled him to recover from forays forward as well as providing cover for his teammates across the Norwich backline. In the 1949–50 season, Morgan played in 28 games (25 League), establishing a partnership with Hall of Fame member Bill Lewis (the two went on to play together in 149 games for Norwich).

Just as his career was about to take off he suffered a knee injury that was to restrict him for the rest of his career. He only featured in the first five

games of the successful 1950–51 season, including a defeat to eventual champions Nottingham Forest. Norwich finished second in Division Three South that season but could only wonder what might have been if Morgan had been fit.

Despite the serious nature of the knee injury and the subsequent loss of pace, Morgan returned to first-team action on 25 August 1951, after almost a year out. This game versus Leyton Orient marked the start of three seasons where Morgan enjoyed his best run of games. He played 32 League games in 1951–52, helping Norwich finish third in Division Three South. These included a derby double over Ipswich, both 2–0 in two consecutive days over Christmas.

Morgan's most influential season was in 1953–54 where he made 48 appearances. Missing only three games, he played his part in another good season ending in a seventh place finish (a finish only tarnished by Ipswich winning the Championship). He also ended a run of 179 games without a goal, scoring in a 4–1 win over Watford. After ending this record he only had to wait another week before scoring again, this time at The Den, Millwall. Morgan's 48 appearances included six in the FA Cup, the highlight of which was a shock 2–1 victory against Arsenal in front of 55,767 at Highbury.

A further 39 appearances were made in season 1954–55 before the knee injury struck again, in an away game at Watford. It was a cruel blow as he was on the verge of being capped by Wales. Previous injuries had prevented a call up earlier in a career that had deserved international recognition.

Again Morgan picked himself up, as he set out on the long road to recovery, building up his fitness in the reserves. He played a total of 111 reserve team games during his Norwich career as he battled back to the first team from injury. After his latest setback, Morgan returned to action in October 1955 and had one further career highlight, testing himself against a First Division Sunderland forward line, in front of 46,380 in the FA Cup third round. Three weeks after his experience at Roker Park, Morgan played his last game for Norwich, a disappointing 1–4 home defeat to Southampton, on a cold January afternoon in 1956.

Unable to continue at professional level, Morgan returned to South Wales and non-League Merthyr Tydfil. He remained in Wales until he sadly had to have his left leg amputated, a condition which eventually lead to his untimely death at the young age of 54.

Denis Morgan made 250 appearances for Norwich scoring three goals.

Norman Low

March 1914, Scotland

Player 1946–50
Manager 1950–55

Norman Low was born into a footballing family and destined to follow in his father's footsteps as a fearless centre-half and inspiring captain.

Wilfrid Low, a tough Scotsman, had already been an FA Cup winner with Newcastle by the time his son Norman was born in 1914. Wilfrid went on to make over 300 appearances with Newcastle and won five Scottish caps.

As a youngster Norman learnt much about the art of defending from his father. By his late teens he had developed the required physique to back up this knowledge and become a top-class defender. At 19 he got his first career break, signing for First Division Liverpool, but after struggling to hold down a first-team place he dropped down the Leagues signing for Newport County in 1936.

Low soon captained Newport to success winning the Third Division South in 1938–39 for the first time in the club's history. However, like many of his generation, Low's career was disrupted by war just when he was reaching his peak playing years.

After playing for many clubs as a guest player, Low emerged from the war back with Newport. He soon signed for Norwich, in October 1946, after Newport had turned down a higher offer from Welsh rivals Cardiff.

When he signed for Norwich, Low was following a well beaten path from South Wales to Norfolk, but unlike many who had made or were to make this move he was a seasoned professional rather than promising youngster. As a result he was made club captain in only his

10th game and he remained captain until his last game in May 1950. In total, he captained Norwich in 154 of his 163 games.

During his captaincy Norwich were struggling on the pitch at the wrong end of Division Three South, but throughout these difficult days he never wavered from the task and always gave 100 per cent. He was strong in the air and tough on the ground as he dominated the opposition forwards.

Norwich's problems at the time were not helped by managerial disruptions; Cyril Spiers returned to Cardiff and then Hall of Famer Doug Lochhead's health deteriorated. When Lochhead retired, in March 1950, Low was the natural choice to replace him in the hot-seat. On 4 March 1950 Low became Norwich's first player-manager when he captained the side to a 1–1 home draw against rivals Ipswich. He went on to make another 11 appearances before retiring from playing to become the 19th permanent Norwich manager.

Although he played for Norwich with distinction it is Low's successful reign as manager that he is most well known for. In his first full season he guided Norwich to second in Division Three South. This was followed by third, fourth, seventh and 12th place finishes during his five seasons in charge – a sharp contrast to his playing days with those two bottom two finishes.

Low, as manager, can take much credit for this turnaround in Norwich's fortunes. One of his first actions as manager was to switch Ashman from centre-forward to a more defensive wing-half position. This proved to be a masterstroke in shaping both Ashman's and Norwich's future. Low also developed the Gavin/Hollis partnership and despite his defensive background he encouraged an attacking philosophy that produced many high scoring games. Low was not afraid to spend money to strengthen the team. During his tenure he twice broke the club transfer record; he bought Alf Ackerman in 1950 for £9,500 and then paid £15,000 in July 1953 for Hall of Famer Bobby Brennan. However, Low did not have an open chequebook; therefore he also had to focus on youth. One of the highlights of his time as manager was the emergence of Hall of Famer Maurice Norman, who was given his first-team debut by Low, aged just 21.

In total six Hall of Famers made their debuts under Low, including his replacement in central defence, Reg Foulkes.

Despite his success in turning Norwich's fortunes around promotion had still proved elusive and the board, perhaps surprisingly, decided to end his contract in April 1955. He is one of only seven people to have both played and managed Norwich.

After Norwich, Low had a short spell managing Barry Town before returning to the League with Workington. He later had a spell at Port Vale where he won the first Championship in the newly formed Division Four.

Norman Low made 163 appearances for Norwich but did not manage to score a competitive goal. He managed Norwich for 258 games of which he won 129. A win per cent ratio of 50 per cent is the third best of all Norwich managers.

Ken Nethercott

July 1925, Bristol   **Player 1947–60**

Norwich City has always had a tradition of producing great goalkeepers. Seven 'keepers are recognised in the Hall of Fame, between them racking up 2,524 appearances for Norwich. The first of this illustrious group is Ken Nethercott.

Ken Nethercott first appeared at Carrow Road in February 1938 as a 13-year-old with Bristol Colts. Nine years later, after time served with the army in Italy, he was back at Carrow Road making his professional home debut for Norwich in a 0–1 loss to Aldershot. His first-team debut had taken place the previous week away at Northampton, which in turn had come only a week after he was formally demobbed from the army.

Nethercott was signed by Norwich manager Cyril Spiers in an attempt to solve a problem position for the team. In the 1946–47 season, before Nethercott's signature, Norwich had conceded 100 League goals and had used five goalkeepers in search of a solution. Derek Davies began the 1947–48 season but after conceding five against Ipswich was replaced by youngster Don Edwards, who promptly let in five at home to Bristol Rovers. Nethercott himself had a shaky start, conceding six in his third game at Bristol City, but Spiers kept faith as Nethercott went on to establish himself as Norwich's number one.

Keeping the jersey following a change in management, Nethercott played in all bar one of the games in the 1948–49 season. That season Norwich finished 10th in Division Three South, thanks mainly to a marked improvement in defence. With Nethercott playing behind captain and Hall of Famer Norman Low, Norwich, despite their mid-table finish, conceded only 49 goals that season, one better than second place Reading.

Norwich continued to improve after defender Low became manager. In 1950–51 Nethercott enjoyed his best season for Norwich as they finished second. He missed only one game and kept 17 clean sheets, including one against champions Nottingham

Forest. He was also credited with an increase in goals scored, as he had excellent distribution and was the starting point for many attacks.

After missing the game against Gillingham on 17 March 1951, Nethercott went on to appear in 136 consecutive games before injury forced him to miss the trip to Selhurst Park on Christmas Day 1953. During this long run he was ever-present in the Norwich team in 1951–52 and 1952–53 seasons – a time when Norwich re-enforced their position as one of the Third Division South top sides. His consistent performances during that time were awarded with an England B cap in March 1953, in a 2–2 draw against the old enemy Scotland at Edinburgh. The England B cap gave Nethercott some national recognition and he could have progressed his career away from Norwich, but he remained loyal to Norwich and his old teammate, Low.

In 1955 Hall of Famer Tom Parker returned to Norwich replacing Low, and Nethercott found himself no longer the undisputed number one. His long suffering deputy Ken Oxford finally had a run in the team, restricting Nethercott to seven appearances in season 1955–56. The next season, 1956–57, was one of the club's worst. Nethercott played in only 14 games but his last was a 1–7 thrashing at Torquay. It was another 32 games before Nethercott had a chance to make amends for the Torquay game, returning to the team and keeping a clean sheet in the 1–0 win over Plymouth.

After his return to the first team in November 1957, Nethercott enjoyed a run of games under new manager Hall of Famer Archie Macaulay, climaxing in his and one of the club's greatest moments, the 1959 FA Cup run. The 1959 FA Cup run deservedly features heavily among many Hall of Famers. Nethercott's defining moment of that run came in the quarter-final against Second Division promotion chasers Sheffield United. With the game poised at 1–1 Nethercott, typifying the bravery he had become known for, dived at the feet of striker Bill Hamilton emerging from the collision with a dislocated shoulder. In those days there were no substitutes. Therefore, no doubt in agony, Nethercott remained in goal for the remaining 30 minutes and somehow managed to keep the Sheffield United attack at bay to earn an incredible replay.

In 12 seasons and 416 games, the Sheffield United Cup game was Nethercott's most famous. It was also his last. He was replaced by Hall of Fame's Sandy Kennon and later retired from the game after a brief spell at Wisbech. Nethercott remained in Norwich working for 25 years at the city's Rowntree chocolate factory.

Ken Nethercott made 416 appearances for Norwich, leaving him eighth in the all-time listing for club appearances.

Noel Kinsey

December 1925, Wales   **Player 1947–53**

Noel Kinsey was yet another product from the Cardiff youth system who found his way to Norwich in the late 1940s. Later, while at Norwich, he would return to Wales to represent his country, and in doing so he has the distinction of becoming the first Norwich player to be capped at international level by one of the home countries.

When Kinsey signed for Norwich on 2 June 1947 he became the fourth Hall of Famer signed from the South Wales region by Cyril Spiers. Spiers recognised that Kinsey would help solve the lack of creativity in the low scoring Norwich side of 1946–47.

Making his debut in the third game of the 1947–48 season, Kinsey helped the team to a 1–0 victory over Watford. After a difficult first season, new manager and Hall of Famer Doug Lochhead decided to play Kinsey in an attacking midfield role more suited to his strengths, where he could find space and supply the forward line with through balls beyond the opposition defence.

Not only was Kinsey a supplier; he could also score. He ended the 1948–49 season with 12 goals, only one behind top scorer and Hall of Famer Ron Ashman. His tally of 12 was impressive as he averaged a goal every two games, including an away day hat-trick in the 6–1 mauling of Bristol City.

Kinsey started the following season, 1949–50, on fire; he scored eight in the first seven games, including an opening day double back in South Wales against Newport County. Kinsey went on to score doubles in another three games that season, which he finished as top goalscorer with 17 goals. A personal highlight for Kinsey that season came on 7 January 1950, when he scored the opener in the FA Cup third round at Portsmouth's Fratton Park. Portsmouth had emerged from the war as one of England's leading sides, winning the Championship in 1948–49 and again in 1949–50. On their way to this second title they had a formidable record at Fratton Park, conceding only 15 goals. Against these statistics Kinsey's strike, in front of 42,059, was even more impressive. Portsmouth equalised in the second half and won the replay 0–2 at Carrow Road but Kinsey had had his day in the national limelight.

The 1950–51 season saw the Norwich team finally come of age with an impressive second place finish; Kinsey was again instrumental in the team's success. He finished the season with 14 goals, including scoring in both games versus champions Nottingham Forest and a crucial late FA Cup second round winner that spared Norwich's blushes against non-League Rhyl, setting up a glamour third-round tie at home to Liverpool. As well as contributing with goals, Kinsey also played a key role providing many assists to Johnny Gavin, Les Eyre and Roy Hollis (all Hall of Famer, who all finished ahead of him in the goalscoring chart that season.

Kinsey's fine form that season was recognised in March 1951 when he was selected by the Welsh FA panel (in the days before an international manager) for the squad to play Northern Ireland. Kinsey started the game that ended in a 2–1 Welsh win and in doing so he became the first Norwich player to appear for his country since Mike O'Brien represented Eire back in 1930. Kinsey went on to win a further three caps while with Norwich during a golden era for Welsh football with established internationals Ivor Allchurch, Cliff Jones and John Charles all playing at their peaks.

Kinsey continued his impressive form into the next season 1951–52. He scored on the Christmas Day derby at Portman Road and finished the season with 12 goals. This was the fourth season in a row that he had achieved double figures, not bad for a deep lying forward.

The 1952–53 season was to be his last for Norwich. He scored on his last game for the club in a 4–0 home win against Colchester. In June 1953 he signed for Second Division Birmingham City. He enjoyed a successful career with Birmingham, winning the Second Division Championship in 1954–55, playing in the First Division, and scoring in the 1956 FA Cup Final – a Final won by Manchester City that became part of FA Cup folklore after goalkeeper Bert Trautman carried on playing after breaking his neck. While at Birmingham he also added another three Welsh caps, the highlight being a 2–1 win over an England side lead by the great Billy Wright.

In 1958 he joined Hall of Famer Norman Low, his old captain at Norwich, at Port Vale where he was part of the side that won the first ever Fourth Division Championship. He eventually ended his career with Norwich's old foes Lowestoft Town, leading them to three titles as player-manager.

Noel Kinsey made 243 appearances for Norwich scoring 65 goals. He is 13th in the all-time goals listing.

Don Pickwick

February 1925, Wales   **Player 1947–56**

Don Pickwick was born just two months after Hall of Famer Noel Kinsey and was from the same area of South Wales. Both were amateurs at Cardiff City and both signed professional terms for Norwich within two months of each other. Both players also made their Norwich debuts in the same game, a 1–0 home win over Watford on 30 August 1947, Norwich's first win of the season after losing the opening two fixtures. It is therefore only natural to draw comparisons between the two.

   While it would appear that Pickwick's career closely followed that of Kinsey, he actually signed for Norwich as a young trainee in February 1946. As a youngster he was a promising rugby union player and represented Wales' schoolboy; however, during the war he focused on football, with more opportunities to play football than rugby in the services. As fate would have it, he was based in Norfolk with his regiment, the Royal Welsh Fusiliers, and was spotted and signed by Norwich manager and Hall of Famer Doug Lochhead a year before Cyril Spiers' Welsh revolution took off.

   Pickwick learnt his trade in the Norwich reserves and had played over 50 reserve games before Kinsey was signed. Pickwick was a right-sided midfielder, who was tenacious in the tackle and played with an attitude and enthusiasm that warmed him to the City faithful. Of all the

signings from Wales, Pickwick was arguably the most promising and had the most expectations for his career ahead.

   After breaking into the Norwich first team in August 1947, he failed to hold down a position and made only nine appearances in the 1947–48 season. The season ended in disappointment with Pickwick fracturing his ankle and Norwich finishing second bottom in Division Three South. This meant that for the second season running Norwich had to seek re-election. In the days before the Football League was linked to the non-League pyramid, teams finishing in the bottom two of Division Three South and North had to apply to be

allowed to continue in the League. It was a nervous time, with the club's future relying on the votes of fellow League clubs and with plenty of new clubs looking to enter the League. Fortunately Norwich secured enough votes, at the expense of challengers and East Anglian rivals Colchester.

After recovering from injury in the summer of 1948, a fresh Pickwick went on to establish himself in the Norwich starting XI during the 1948–49 season. His run in the side no doubt contributed to an improved finish of 10th and the comforts of mid-table security. Pickwick's importance to the team was highlighted by the fact that Norwich lost three and let in 11 goals in the four games that he missed. That season, Pickwick played in both victories over Ipswich as well as the home win over eventual champions Swansea.

He continued to play a key role for Norwich over the next two seasons, missing only five games in two years. In the 1950–51 season Norwich finished second in Division Three South; one factor behind this achievement was the settled midfield three – all Hall of Famers – of Foulkes, Ashman and Pickwick. They knew each others' games inside out and together played in 41 of the 46 League games.

One game that season that was particularly memorable for Pickwick. On 3 February 1951 Pickwick took his place in the starting line-up in the home match versus Colchester just hours after his marriage to fiancée Lottie. Although unsure what the new wife thought of his decision to play, his appearance in the 1–1 draw illustrated Pickwick's dedication and loyalty to his teammates and Norwich City. Two days before the big day he scored his first goal of the season in a 3–1 win over Leyton Orient, while his honeymoon the week after the wedding was spent at Roker Park, Sunderland, for Norwich's biggest game of the season, a 1–3 loss in the FA Cup fifth round.

Pickwick continued to be a mainstream in the Norwich team, until disaster struck in September 1952. In one of Norwich's greatest games, an 8–1 away win at Shrewsbury, Pickwick suffered a broken leg. Such was the extent of his injury that, while he did recover to play another 60 games over the next three seasons, he was never the same player.

He eventually retired in May 1956, three months after his last game, a 1–4 defeat at home to Southampton. A match that, coincidentally, was also the final game for Hall of Famer Denis Morgan.

He went on to play for and manage non-League Spalding, who later hosted Norwich in a benefit match for Pickwick in recognition of a career cut short by injury. After leaving Spalding Pickwick retired from football to begin a new life down under in Australia.

Don Pickwick made 244 appearances for Norwich scoring 11 goals.

Roy Hollis

December 1925, Norfolk   Player 1948–52

Roy Hollis scored goals throughout his career with a goalscoring ratio up there with the best in the country.

Hollis' potential as a forward was evident, from an early age, as a youngster with Yarmouth. As a local lad, he was on Norwich's radar during his school days and was promptly signed, initially as an amateur in May 1947, after serving with the RAF during the war.

With 54 goals in 88 reserve games it was inevitable that Hollis would break into the first team. Hollis was emerging during a period of financial instability for Norwich, brought about by loss of revenue after the wartime suspension of League football, and there was little money available to strengthen a team struggling on the pitch. In addition, Norwich managers Spiers and then Hall of Famer Lochhead envisaged youth development as central to the club's future. With all these factors in place it was only a matter of time before Hollis would make his first team debut.

When he made his much anticipated first start on 21 April 1948, it proved to be one that would live long in the memory of the 30,052 watching spectators. Within 30 minutes Hollis had completed his hat-trick as Norwich went on to beat QPR 5–2. His debut was even more impressive when you consider that Hollis had scored his three against the eventual Division Three South champions with the League's second best defence; Norwich meanwhile were struggling at the foot of the table. He went on to play in the next two games as the season drew to an end, scoring another goal to take his season tally to 4 in 3 games.

Hollis' breakthrough in the Norwich team came at a boom time in football with attendances in all leagues at all-time highs. Hollis' third game at home to Notts County (featuring the great Tommy Lawton) was watched by 37,863 – a Carrow Road League record.

Hollis had set the tone on his debut and in the following four seasons he never let these standards slip. As a classic centre-forward he was fast, direct and had an ability to score all types of goals. He scored seven in 12 games in the following season, 1948–49, including a double in his first game versus Northampton, as he looked to establish himself in the first team.

Despite his predatory instincts in front of goal, it wasn't until the 1950–51 season that he enjoyed a consistent run in the team, under new manager and Hall of Famer Norman Low. Low was rewarded with 16 League goals in 33 games, a total including two hat-tricks that contributed to Hollis finishing second highest goalscorer that season.

Season 1951–52 was even better for Hollis, climaxing in a remarkable five goals in one game on 29 December 1951. Hollis' victims that day were Walsall who slumped to an 8–0 defeat at Carrow Road. His five that day equalled Thomas Hunt's record set in March 1930 (League only, Hall of Famer Les Eyre scored five in an FA Cup game) and is still to this day unbeaten. That season Hollis' goalscoring was a regular occurrence; he finished the season Norwich's top scorer with 22 goals including 20 scored in just 27 League games. Were it not for injury, based on his scoring ratio, he could easily have finished the campaign on 35 goals.

It was no surprise that Hollis' scoring exploits were attracting the attention of some of the country's biggest clubs. In December 1952 Hollis signed for Tottenham, for an undisclosed fee, becoming the first of many players to have been associated with both clubs. He scored two on

his debut but never settled in the top flight, eventually returning to Division Three South with Southend United.

His much anticipated return to Carrow Road came on Christmas Day 1954. Inspired by the familiar surroundings, Hollis scored a hat-trick to earn Southend a 3–3 draw. In doing so Hollis became the only player to have scored hat-tricks at Carrow Road both for and against Norwich. Ironically one of his Norwich hat-tricks was against Southend four years earlier.

Hollis ended his professional career as Southend's greatest ever goalscorer, topping the charts with 135 goals in 260 games. No doubt he could have achieved the same honour at Norwich, but instead he finished 15th in the Norwich listing with 59 goals. However, his appearances to goals ratio of 0.55 (i.e. he averaged 0.55 goals for every game he played) is the third best among Norwich's top 30 strikers, bettered only by Davie Ross and Percy Fargo, both of whom played in days of more attacking formations and higher scoring games.

Roy Hollis made 107 appearances for Norwich scoring 59 goals.

Johnny Gavin

April 1928, Ireland   **Player 1948–54 and 1955–58**

With 122 in the League and 10 in the FA Cup, Johnny Gavin scored a total of 132 goals for Norwich City making him Norwich's all-time top goalscorer.

Gavin is one of only two Norwich players to have topped the century and he is 36 clear of third place, Iwan Roberts.

It is debatable whether Gavin's total will ever be broken. Modern football is very different from that of Gavin's era. The Bosman ruling and the increased spending power of the major clubs means players are less likely to remain with the same club for long. At Norwich the current challenger and Hall of Famer, Grant Holt, has 70 goals; even at his highly impressive goals ratio, it would take another three to four seasons before Gavin's record would even be threatened.

As a young Irishman, Gavin was more into hurling than football. Hurling was a tough sport and it set the tone for Gavin's future career in football, allowing him to take a physical challenge and develop a steely determination and will to win. After focusing on football with local side Limerick his performances began to attract attention from English club scouts. West Ham were favourites for his signature but Norwich had a trump card in their new signing Kevin Holman. Holman was also from Limerick and friends with Gavin. Gavin signed in August 1948 for £1,500

(an amount that worked out at £11.36 per goal) on the basis that his friend would help him settle.

Gavin did take a while to adjust to the long move to Norfolk. He took a season to break into the first team and, when he did, he scored only 1 goal in his first 19 games, which is surprising when you consider his overall goal record. By the start of the 1950–51 season the pressure was on, especially with other forwards emerging. Gavin responded with 18 goals to finish the season's top goalscorer.

The following season, 1951–52, he beat this by 2 (20 goals) but was this time pipped to top place by the quick scoring, fellow Hall of Famer, Roy Hollis. In addition to Gavin and Hollis, Hall of Famers Ashman and Kinsey also reached double figures as Norwich became an attacking force in Division Three South. Gavin scored a hat-trick of hat-tricks that season, becoming the first Norwich player to do so, all coming in high scoring victories: Bristol City 5–2, Torquay 7–0 and Gillingham 5–0. By the end of his career Gavin had scored a total of five hat-tricks for Norwich, a record he shares with Hall of Famer Jack Vinall.

By this time Gavin was an international player, winning his first cap for the Republic of Ireland in a World Cup Qualifier against Finland in September 1949. Gavin opened the scoring with a goal direct from a corner in a 3–0 win for the Irish. In doing so he became Norwich's first player to play in a competitive international and also the first Norwich player to score in a World Cup game. Gavin went on to win another four caps while at Norwich, scoring one more goal.

Back in Division Three South, Gavin continued scoring with another 20 in 1952–53, becoming the first player since Hall of Famer Davie Ross to score 20 in two consecutive seasons. He failed to extend the record to 20 in three seasons, scoring 14 in 1953–54. Gavin's scoring statistics are even more impressive when you consider that he spent most of his career on the right wing rather than as an out and out striker. He had quick feet and would either attack the back post or drift in deep looking for one-twos to release him beyond the defence. His style of play and goals record alerted First Division Tottenham and he soon followed the path of former teammate Hollis, signing for Spurs in October 1954 for £9,000.

Unlike Hollis, Gavin had a consistent run in the Tottenham side scoring 16 in 34 games. He added to his international caps, playing European giants West Germany and Holland. Tottenham wanted to keep him but were desperate to sign Norwich's hugely talented young defender Maurice Norman, another Hall of Famer. The deal would only happen if it involved Gavin as part of the transfer package. Therefore, in November 1955, he returned for his second spell at Carrow Road.

Gavin continued where he had left off at Norwich. He scored four in his fifth match back, in a 7–2 win over Southend, and ended the 1955–56 season with 15 goals in only 26 games. The following season, 1956–57, he achieved his centenary of goals in the 3–0 win over Plymouth on 15 September 1956.

The 1957–58 season was Gavin's last at Norwich and fittingly he finished it as the club's top scorer with 22 goals, seven seasons after he had first achieved this total. In the summer of 1958, with relatively new manager and Hall of Famer Archie Macaulay looking to build his own team and Norwich in financial difficulties, Gavin moved to Watford before eventually settling in Cambridge where he retired to run a local pub.

Johnny Gavin made 338 appearances for Norwich scoring 132 goals, still to this day a club record.

Bill Lewis

November 1921, London

Player 1949–56

Bill Lewis was a big money signing who delivered during his time at Norwich, playing a major part in turning Norwich from Division Three South also-rans to genuine title contenders.

Lewis, a full-back, began his career at his local club West Ham. Despite playing 129 games for the Hammers he never experienced competitive League football, having signed as a trainee just before the war.

His 129 wartime appearances included an exciting 5–3 defeat to Norwich in the newly formed regional League and a two-leg victory over Norwich (3–5 on aggregate) in the Football League War Cup in February 1941. A teammate of Lewis' during this period was future Norwich manager and Hall of Famer Archie Macaulay.

Before the resumption of the Football League after the War, Lewis signed for First Division Blackpool and in the first post-war season, 1946–47, he helped them to a fifth place finish. In the Blackpool team of that era were the legendary England internationals Stanley Matthews and Stan Mortensen. Lewis' education as a defender was no doubt helped by facing players of this calibre day in, day out, in training.

While never a regular, Lewis still went on to make 42 appearances for Blackpool over three seasons in the First Division as well as featuring in the 1948 FA Cup Final. Such experience would not come cheaply; Doug Lochhead had to break the Norwich transfer record to sign Lewis for £9,500 in November 1949.

At that price it was no surprise that Lewis went straight into the first team, making his debut and keeping a clean sheet in defence alongside Hall of Famers Denis Morgan and Norman Low, in a 0–0 versus Watford. After a solid debut Lewis went on to play every game that season, including the FA Cup draw at First Division Portsmouth where his experience proved invaluable.

After making his debut in November 1949 Lewis missed only 12 games in four seasons, becoming a reliable and permanent fixture in the Norwich defence. He soon became a fans' favourite for his committed approach, with a fearsome tackle that would shake the opposition winger. He was a Stuart Pearce of his day.

The 1950–51 season proved to be a highlight for the Norwich defence. In finishing second Norwich conceded only 45 goals, a club record in the third tier that still stands today. Paul Lambert's outstanding Division Three champions of 2009–10 conceded two more (47). Another record achieved that season was a sequence of 23 games without defeat, stretching from 26 August 1950 to 11 January 1951 (a surprise 1–3 reversal at Leyton Orient). This run went some way towards a final points total of 64 which was also a club record with two points for a win.

Much of Norwich's success that season was down to the stability of the starting XI. The 11 players that started the home game to Swindon on 16 September 1950 went to start the following 21 League and Cup games, until Len Dutton replaced Les Eyre for the FA Cup fourth round tie at Newport on 27 January 1951. Lewis of course was one of the 11 along with eight other Hall of Famers.

Another successful season followed in 1951–52. Lewis missed only two games (both ended in losses for Norwich) as Norwich won 18 of their 23 home games, which was a record until finally bettered in 2003–04.

In 1952–53 Lewis enjoyed his first ever-present season, playing in all 46 League and three FA Cup games. While the season is better known for the explosion of attacking talent, Lewis and the Norwich defence still enjoyed a good season, conceding only 55 goals as Norwich finished fourth. By the end of the season Lewis had made 174 appearances for Norwich, but despite possessing a powerful shot he was still awaiting his first goal for the club. He finally broke his duck on 11 September 1954, in spectacular style, when he scored from a free-kick on the halfway line to earn a 1–1 draw with Northampton. Sadly only 9,560 were there to witness his fine strike.

Unfortunately Lewis failed to add to his token goal as injuries began to restrict his number of appearances. In his last season, 1955–56, he played only nine games before retiring at the end of the season. By this time he had made a total of 256 appearances, with Norwich getting good value for their record signing, working out at £37 per game. His dedication came at a price – he had to have a hip replacement – but he remained at Carrow Road as a coach and reserve team trainer.

Bill Lewis made 256 appearances for Norwich scoring one goal.

Reg Foulkes

February 1923, Shropshire   **Player 1950–56**

Reg Foulkes was the Norwich City captain during the club's successful period in the early 1950s. He was a rock of a man and an inspired leader, demanding 100 per cent every game from every player.

Foulkes was born to be a leader. He was a promising footballer from an early age and rose through various school teams to become the first schoolboy from Shropshire to represent England Under-15's; in 1937 he played in games versus Scotland and Wales.

After 'guesting' for Birmingham during the War, he signed for West Midlands rivals Walsall in August 1945. His first two games for Walsall were both against Norwich in the Football League Division Three South-North Region in the 1945–46 transitional season. Both games ended in 2–1 victories for Norwich, but five months later, in the Division Three South-North Cup, Foulkes and Walsall got their revenge beating Norwich 2–4 at Fellows Park.

Norwich and Walsall renewed their rivalry the following season as Division Three South restarted in 1946–47. In the first two post-war seasons back in the Football League, Walsall enjoyed the upper hand over Norwich with a 0–2 win at Carrow Road, and fifth and third place League finishes as Norwich faced re-election both times. They also knocked Norwich out of the 1947 FA Cup in the second round. Foulkes played an important role during this time and was at the heart of a Walsall defence that conceded only 40 goals in 1947–48. He was also the Walsall captain for most of his 160 appearances, including two consecutive seasons as an ever-present in the team. In 2005 he was selected by Walsall fans in their legends XI squad, where he was recognised as Walsall's greatest ever half-back.

As Norwich looked to recover from their post war slumber, Hall of Famer Norman Low was appointed manager in March 1950. One of Low's first priorities as manager was to replace himself. He had been captain and central-defender for the last four seasons and his promotion to team manager had left a massive void in the Norwich defence. Foulkes was an ideal candidate; as a player he had a similar style, attributes and attitude to Low. Like Low, Foulkes was a strong, fearless and commanding defender as well as an experienced captain.

On 17 May 1950 Low made Foulkes his first Norwich signing, 21 years after Hall of Famer Doug Lochhead (Low's predecessor in the Norwich hot-seat and fellow Hall of Famer) had made the same move from Walsall to Norwich in 1929.

After a summer adjusting to his new surroundings, Foulkes led out the Norwich side on his debut, the first game of the 1950–51 season. He captained Norwich to a 2–0 win over Port Vale and went on to captain in every game that season except the last two. In his first season, a season of many highlights, he led the side to a second place finish in Division Three South. Foulkes was playing alongside Hall of Famers Denis Morgan and Bill Lewis as part of a tight and organised defensive unit that conceded only 45 goals. In the FA Cup that year Foulkes saved his best performance for the visit of First Division Liverpool, where he managed to keep the iconic Billy Liddell quiet as Norwich went on to complete a 3–1 giant killing.

During the 1950–51 season Foulkes also made an impression at the other end, scoring six goals, with all six coming in a spell of 19 games in the second half of the season. By far his most memorable goal of the season came at Portman Road in April 1951 where he scored a late winner with a trademark header from a corner. That goal, combined with a resolute defensive display, gave Norwich a 1–0 win in Suffolk.

Foulkes went on to captain Norwich in 42 games, leading Norwich to another top four finish (third) in 1951–52. It was only an injury during the following 1952–53 season that forced him to miss seven games and lose the armband to Ron Ashman. On his return to the first team, Ashman retained the captaincy. While Foulkes was no doubt disappointed, this did not affect his performances or his commitment to the team.

Playing regularly for another three seasons for Norwich, Foulkes even regained the captaincy in the 1954–55 season, until injury struck in February 1955. His last season with Norwich was 1955–56 which ended with Norwich finishing seventh. In his six seasons at the club, Norwich had finished second, third, fourth, seventh, twelfth and seventh. Foulkes' importance to the team was illustrated when, in the first season after he left the club (1956–57), Norwich finished bottom of Division Three South.

Foulkes left Norwich in May 1956 to start the next logical step in his career as a manager. His first appointment was as player-manager at non-League Wisbech Town, but things did not work out for him and he never did make the step up to management. He did return to Norwich to work with the reserves and even had a spell with Norwich's old foes Norwich CEYMS before he quit football for good to take up accountancy back in his home town of Shrewsbury.

Reg Foulkes made 238 appearances (153 as captain) for Norwich scoring eight goals.

Roy McCrohan

September 1930, Berkshire   **Player 1951–62**

A rarity in today's modern game, and unusual even in the bygone days of the 1950s, Roy McCrohan is one of a select band of players to play for one club for over a decade. In fact he gave Norwich City 11 years of loyal service in a career spanning the 1950s and early 1960s.

Our first Hall of Famer born in the 1930s, McCrohan's career was not interrupted by the War. He played for his home team, Reading Juniors, rising rapidly through the ranks to sign professional terms with Reading in January 1949. By this time he was already on Norwich manager and Hall of Famer Norman Low's radar, and after only 4 appearances for Reading he completed his move to Norwich in the summer of 1951.

Part of the transfer deal saw Les Owens move in the other direction. Owens was an experienced footballer who had played First Division football, so his part in the transfer highlighted the potential Low saw in McCrohan. It proved to be a shrewd bit of business on Norwich's part; Owens went on to make only eight appearances for Reading compared to McCrohan's 426 for Norwich.

As a youngster joining a Norwich side that had finished the previous season second in the Third Division South, McCrohan had to be patient before getting a run in the team. He made his

debut on 12 September 1951 and scored the winner in his second game some five months later versus Bristol Rovers. Originally a forward he scored 7 in 16 in 1952–53, but faced stiff competition from Hall of Famer Johnny Gavin, Alf Ackerman and Tom Johnston. Finally thanks to his ability to adapt his game and the foresight of manager Low, McCrohan switched to a defensive midfield position for the home win over Walsall in January 1954 and from this point never looked back. He played the remaining 19 games, even captaining the team in a thrilling 4–4 draw at his old club Reading.

From season 1954–55 onwards McCrohan was one of the first names on the team sheet. He was a versatile player

who went on to play in every position (bar goalkeeper) for Norwich. He had a great engine to supplement his ability and became the perfect foil for the more attack-minded Hall of Famers Bryan Thurlow and Matt Crowe, adding bite and determination in the Norwich midfield. McCrohan was a player who may not have grabbed the headlines but was appreciated for his contribution by both the team and the manager.

McCrohan completed 45 games in 1954–55, more than any other Norwich player. He went on to play over 40 games a season for the next six seasons including two where he played every game. The first of those ever-present seasons was 1955–56, which included a rare McCrohan goal in front of 46,380 at Roker Park, Sunderland, in a FA Cup third round defeat. McCrohan's second season as an ever-present was in 1959–60 where, as an experienced player, he was an important part of a Norwich side featuring many Hall of Famers that won promotion to Division Two.

Prior to that promotion, McCrohan also played in every game of the famous 1959 FA Cup run. He was a vital cog in that spirited side, holding his own against more illustrious opponents. His best moment in the Cup run came in the semi-final against Luton Town where he claimed an assist for the Norwich equaliser, winning a header before squaring the ball across the area for Hall of Famer Bobby Brennan to finish.

After promotion to the Second Division in 1959–60, at the age of 31, McCrohan played 47 games in his first season at that level of the game. He scored his first goal in the second tier on 10 September 1960 as Norwich exacted some revenge on their semi-final foes Luton in a 2–0 win at Kenilworth Road.

The 1961–62 season was to be McCrohan's last as he missed 11 games towards the end of the season, his longest period outside the first team for many years. His last Norwich game was a momentous one; the final match of the 1961–62 season which ended with a League Cup winner's medal for McCrohan after a 1–0 second leg League Cup Final victory over Rochdale.

In the summer of 1962 McCrohan moved to Colchester. As when joining Norwich, some 11 years earlier, his transfer involved a player exchange. Mike Foster came to Norwich who, in contrast to McCrohan, did not make a single first team appearance. McCrohan played 62 games for Colchester before he moved into coaching after taking his FA coaching badges. He also spent time pursuing his other hobby with his wife, dancing; a sure candidate for *Strictly Come Dancing* if he was a player today.

After coaching at a number of clubs, including Ipswich Town, McCrohan eventually settled in Florida where he worked at a number of local soccer schools and became a respected coach in the USA. He brought some local teams over to Norwich for exhibition games and returned to Carrow Road himself in 2009 to take part in the 50 year celebrations of the 1959 Cup run.

Roy McCrohan made 426 appearances for Norwich scoring 23 goals. His 426 appearances put him sixth in the Norwich all-time list.

Tom Johnston

August 1927, Scotland   **Player 1952–54**

Tom Johnston played for nine professional clubs during his 13 year career. He scored goals for fun at every club, and nowhere more so than during his relatively brief but successful spell at Norwich.

Scotsman Johnston was lucky to be playing football at all after a mining accident left him with a badly injured arm. His arm was saved but he had to spend his entire career wearing a protective cast that became his trademark.

His first professional club was Kilmarnock but after a short time there he decided to move south to test himself in the English League, first with Darlington and then Oldham.

Johnston was spotted at Oldham by Norwich manager and Hall of Famer Norman Low; he cost Norwich just £500 and proved to be a true bargain. He had already demonstrated his striking abilities with 31 goals in just 57 games for his previous three clubs. He was a powerful, tough centre-forward and particularly lethal in the air. He would intimidate his marker and was just the type of player Norwich were looking for at that time to complement Hall of Famer Johnny Gavin and Alf Ackerman.

Johnston made his debut in the opening match of the 1952–53 season, scoring one in a comprehensive 5–0 win over Aldershot. He soon became a fans' favourite, scoring the only goal in a home win over Ipswich, in only his fourth game. Two weeks after the derby delight, Johnstone struck four goals in the 8–1 mauling of Shrewsbury. This result was (and still is) Norwich's record away win and, with his four goals, Johnston became one of only two Norwich players (the other is Hall of Famer Efan Ekoku) to hit four goals in one game away from Carrow Road.

Back at Carrow Road, Johnstone continued his incredible start to his Norwich career, scoring in the next two League games and taking his tally to 10 goals in his first 10 Norwich games. One of these goals, in the 3–0 win against Walsall on 20 September 1952, secured Norwich's 12th successive home win. It was a run stretching back to 15 March the previous season and became a new club record. Who knows what Johnston may have achieved that season but for an injury that restricted his appearances in the second half of the season. Nevertheless, he still finished his debut season with 15 goals.

The 1952–53 season was a particularly memorable one for the Norwich strike force, which Johnston was at the heart of. In finishing fourth in Division Three South, Norwich scored 99 goals – a club record for goals scored in a single season. This compares with 60 in 1971–72, 84 in 1985–86, 79 in 2003–04 and 89 in 2009–10, all seasons where Norwich finished champions. The Norwich home support in 1952–53 certainly got their money's worth with 56 of the 99 goals scored at home, another club record. Therefore, in his first season for Norwich, Johnston had played his part in creating club history.

While Norwich struggled to maintain their promotion push, the following season (1953–54) was another triumph for Johnston. He finished as top goalscorer with 16 goals with his greatest moment in a Norwich shirt coming in the FA Cup fourth round versus Arsenal. Arsenal were an established First Division club with a rich Cup heritage and had beaten Norwich 0–5 in the FA Cup only two years previously; they were expected to comfortably repeat this performance when the teams met at Highbury on 30 January 1954. However, in front of 55,767 – and despite a missed penalty and going a goal down – Norwich hit back through two Johnston goals to secure a famous win, their first competitive win over Arsenal.

The goals at Highbury proved to be the pinnacle of Johnston's Norwich career. Hampered by injuries, he played only seven games in 1954–55 before he moved to Newport County in October 1954. He only played two full seasons for Norwich but his goals ratio of 0.49 is comparable with that of any top Norwich striker.

Johnston continued to score goals in his career, particularly at Leyton Orient where in two spells he scored 123 goals, making him their all-time highest goalscorer. One of his most crucial goals for Orient came at Carrow Road in the penultimate game of the 1960–61 season, when he scored an unlikely winner to ensure Orient survived relegation from Division Two.

After leaving Orient, Johnston played briefly for Gillingham before eventually emigrating to Australia.

Tom Johnston made 67 appearances for Norwich scoring 33 goals.

Maurice Norman

May 1934, Norfolk

Player 1952–55

Maurice Norman was and still is the greatest player to have come out of Norfolk. He was born a few miles south of Norwich and went on to win four major titles and 23 England caps during a 10 year playing career at Tottenham at the very highest level of English football.

Although he only played 35 senior games for Norwich before his move to Spurs, he is rightly recognised in the Norwich City Hall of Fame by club and supporters, reflecting their pride in the achievements of one of their own.

From a very early age it was clear that there was a special talent playing for Norfolk schools. Norman was signed as a 17-year-old trainee by local club Norwich in 1951. At the time of his signing he worked as a farm labourer, a tough living which built up his stamina and muscles to supplement his natural footballing talent.

After impressing in the youth team he signed as a professional in September 1952. Norman continued his apprenticeship in the reserves but it was only a matter of time before this emerging talent would break into the first team. His opportunity came aged just 21 when he made his Division Three South debut on 5 February 1955 away at Watford. He came into the Norwich defence and played in the next 35 games, spanning seasons 1954–55 and 1955–56. Although his time in the first team coincided with a relatively uneventful spell of mid-table mediocrity for Norwich, Norman's performances stood out. He had a great understanding of the game, had excellent positional sense and was a superb reader of the game. He was comfortable on the ball for a defender and was becoming an increasingly important player for Norwich.

Norman's performances were attracting attention from bigger clubs and it was Tottenham who won his signature on 3 November 1955. While it was disappointing to lose a player of Norman's calibre, his transfer did have some significant benefits for Norwich. Firstly, Hall of Famer Johnny Gavin returned to Norfolk as part of the deal where he would eventually become the club's all-time leading goalscorer. Secondly, in addition to Johnny Gavin, Norwich received an £18,000 transfer fee. A large fee for a Division Three South club, the income was particularly important in ensuring Norwich's future as they were still suffering from debts incurred during the War, as well as earlier costs associated with the building of Carrow Road.

Norman, or 'Monty' as he was known, made his Spurs and First Division debut in a November 1955 draw with Cardiff. He played at right-back, replacing the future England World Cup winning manager and star of the 1950–51 Tottenham Championship side, Alf Ramsey. After a spell out injured he returned to the side as centre-back, where he was to remain for the rest of his Tottenham career.

Under manager Bill Nicholson, Tottenham became one of England's greatest teams with Norman's career coinciding with the best period in their history. Norman was a pivotal figure in this legendary Spurs side; Nicholson built the defence around him. He enjoyed a runner-up and third place finish in the late 1950s but could not prevent his Spurs side from slipping to a shock FA Cup fifth round defeat on his one and only return to Carrow Road in February 1959.

For Norman the defeat to Norwich was only a minor blemish, as he and Tottenham went on to become the first team in the 20th century to win the much fabled League and Cup double in 1960–61. Norman played his part in history, missing only one game of the record breaking double season.

Playing alongside Spurs legends such as Dave Mackay, Danny Blanchflower and Jimmy Greaves, Norman added to his honours with another FA Cup winner's medal in 1962, Tottenham's second successive FA Cup win. The following season he experienced success in Europe, with Tottenham winning the recently established European Cup-winners' Cup and in doing so becoming the first English side to win a European competition.

With such success on the pitch, international caps were inevitable. Norman made his England debut lining up alongside the one and only Bobby Moore, in a 4–0 win over Peru in the build up to the 1962 World Cup. Norman went on to play in all four England games in the World Cup including the defeat to eventual winners Brazil.

Norman won 23 England caps in total, but during an international exhibition game in November 1965 against a Hungarian select XI he broke his leg and subsequently ended his career. On retirement Norman had made 411 appearances for Tottenham scoring 19 goals, many of these having come up from defence to attack set pieces, a move pioneered by Norman that is commonplace in today's game.

As well as being a Norwich City Hall of Famer he is also a member of the Tottenham Hotspur Hall of Fame, who described him as 'a cornerstone of our all-conquering side of the early 1960s'. Throughout his time as one of the country's top players he never forgot his Norfolk roots, returning each summer to work on the farm of his youth.

Maurice Norman made 35 appearances for Norwich with no goals.

Bobby Brennan

March 1925, Northern Ireland   **Player 1953–56 and 1957–61**

Bobby Brennan was one of eight Hall of Famers that played every game of the legendary 1959 FA Cup run. He was the creative spark in a team that consistently beat higher League opposition by playing good football.

One of his opponents that year in the fifth round of the Cup was twice Footballer of the Year Danny Blanchflower. Brennan knew Blanchflower well as the two had played together 16 years earlier as youngsters for the same local side in Northern Ireland.

While Blanchflower's career took him to Tottenham and stardom, Brennan got his break in English football with Second Division Luton Town. After 22 goals in 69 games Brennan earned a big money move to First Division Birmingham City, who paid £20,000 for his services in summer 1949. He was a bright light in an ultimately disappointing season that ended with Birmingham's relegation. Brennan remained in the top flight, moving to Fulham for £19,500. Three years and 79 games later he became Norwich's record signing, when Hall of Famer Norman Low paid £15,000 for him in July 1953. This took Brennan's career transfer fees total to £54,500 (at a time when the British transfer record was £34,500).

For his money Low was signing a player with international and First Division experience, close control and a bag of tricks to unlock any defence. Brennan was immediately named captain and scored the winner in his debut in the opening game of the 1953–54 season. He held the armband for the next 19 games before Ron Ashman resumed the responsibility. Respectful of the manager's decision, Brennan put in a Man of the Match performance in the next game, scoring in a 1–1 draw at Ipswich. Later that season he further endeared himself to supporters when he took over from the injured goalkeeper Ken Nethercott and restricted Bournemouth to just two goals in a 0–2 loss. Brennan finished his first season with 15 goals, second only to Hall of Famer Tom Johnston, who could no doubt thank Brennan for many assists for his 16 goals.

In the next season, 1954–55, Brennan went one better, finishing the season as joint top scorer and the only Norwich player to hit double figures in the League. At the end of that season Norwich decided to replace manager Low with ex-boss and Hall of Famer Tom Parker. Players are always at risk when a new manager is appointed; in spite of another decent season it appeared that Brennan had played his last game for Norwich when he was shipped out to non-League Yarmouth in summer 1956 aged just 31 years old.

The decision to release Brennan proved to be Parker's undoing and, after a disastrous season, he himself was replaced by Hall of Famer Archie Macaulay. Macaulay had played with Brennan at Fulham and knew what he could bring to the team. Therefore one of his first moves as manager was to return him from his exile in Yarmouth.

Brennan's second spell at Norwich climaxed in the 1959 FA Cup journey. However, things could have turned out very differently in Norwich's history at the start of the Cup run, as they left the pitch 0–1 down at half-time to non-League Ilford in the first round. Facing an embarrassing exit Brennan stepped up to the mark, providing an assist and scoring two goals to see Norwich safely through to the second round.

Now an out and out winger, Brennan contributed another three crucial assists during the Cup run. The pick of the bunch came in the highly charged quarter-final at Bramall Lane when Brennan

provided a moment of inspiration, beating three men before crossing for Hall of Famer Errol Crossan's equaliser which earned Norwich a replay back at Carrow Road.

Brennan also contributed to the Cup run by scoring goals. Four days after his magic at Sheffield he scored the opener in the replay in front of 38,000 at Carrow Road. He followed this up with a goal in Norwich's biggest game of the season and arguably in their history to date. On 14 March 1959 Norwich faced Brennan's former club Luton Town in the FA Cup semi-final in front of 63,500 at White Hart Lane. On the back foot for much of the game and 0–1 down, Brennan's moment of glory came in the 65th minute when his first time shot found the corner of the net. Brennan had equalised and in doing so became the only Norwich player to have scored in an FA Cup semi-final. Sadly, Norwich succumbed in the replay but Brennan had had his day in the limelight.

His semi-final goal came on Brennan's 34th birthday. While he still made 20 appearances in the following season (1959–60) he had become a squad player, eventually seeing out his time at Norwich in the reserves before retiring in the summer of 1961 to become a coach at King's Lynn.

Bobby Brennan made 250 appearances for Norwich scoring 52 goals.

Bryan Thurlow

June 1936, Norfolk   **Player 1954–64**

Bryan Thurlow was a local man playing for Norwich in the 1959 FA Cup campaign. Born in Norfolk he could relate first hand to the impact that the FA Cup adventure was having on the local people, how it captured their imagination and lifted their spirits.

Thurlow was also the youngest player in the 59er's team. He had signed for Norwich in the summer of 1954 after he was spotted playing at the grass roots level, with local sides Loddon and Bungay.

A quiet, unassuming lad, he worked hard developing his game in the Norwich youth and reserve teams before his opportunity came in the 1955 New Year's Eve fixture against Brentford. Norwich won the game 1–0 with a clean sheet, providing much satisfaction for the young defender.

Over the next couple of seasons, Thurlow continued his footballing education. He only had a brief run in the first team, playing the final 12 games of the ill-fated 1956–57 season as manager and Hall of Famer Tom Parker looked to find a solution to a leaky Norwich defence. During this spell Thurlow scored his only senior goal in the 1–1 draw at fellow strugglers Swindon on 23 March 1957.

At the end of 1956–57 season Norwich manager Parker was replaced by Hall of Famer Archie Macaulay and, after a season back in the reserves, Thurlow finally had a consistent run of games in the first team during the 1958–59 season (Norwich's first in the new national Division Three). These games included Norwich's first ever League fixtures against Bury, Stockport and Rochdale.

By this time Thurlow was beginning to make an impression on Macaulay. He had managed to fill the large boots of injured captain and Hall of Famer Ron Ashman, an intimidating prospect for any player let alone a 23-year-old with relatively little first team experience. He was proving to be a reliable full-back and was appreciated by the team and

supporters for his wholehearted approach and willingness to put his body on the line. Such was Thurlow's growing importance to the team that on Ashman's return Macaulay switched Hall of Famer Roy McCrohan into midfield, to enable Thurlow to continue at full-back.

Thurlow's emergence as a first team regular came at the very start of the 59 Cup run. He went on to play in all 11 Cup ties, which was an FA Cup record for the most games played by one club in the competition. There were many highlights as the team grew in stature from round to round. Thurlow's best individual performance came in the fifth round tie against a Tottenham side, including Norwich Hall of Famer Maurice Norman, who were rapidly becoming one of the best teams in the land and who only two seasons later would complete the double.

Thurlow's opponent in both games was Welsh wonder Cliff Jones, the jewel in the crown of that great Spurs side and arguably the best left-winger in the world. Thurlow more than stood up to the challenge, manfully marking Jones out of the game and restricting the Spurs supply line. The fact that Thurlow managed to keep Jones quiet both in front of 67,633 at White Hart Lane and again four days later in the replay shows that his performance was no fluke. He even earned praise from Jones himself as the modest Thurlow was thrust into the limelight.

The 1959 FA Cup run really kick-started Thurlow's career. Despite breaking his leg in April 1959 he was fit for the first game of the 1959–60 season. Thurlow was an ever-present that season which culminated with promotion and a return to the Second Division after a 21 year absence. Thurlow was an ever-present the following season as well, as Norwich took the Second Division by storm, finishing fourth, the club's highest ever League position. Thurlow went on to make 118 consecutive appearances for Norwich, a run finally ended in a 0–5 loss at Walsall on 18 November 1961.

Injury and a loss of form resulted in Thurlow playing fewer games in the seasons 1962–63 and 1963–64. At the end of the 1963–64 season Thurlow had made only 14 appearances and he was allowed to leave to resuscitate his career at high flying Third Division side Bristol City. Sadly, a ruptured Achilles tendon suffered in pre-season training meant that he never made a first team appearance at Bristol City, and his career ended prematurely at the young age of 29.

Thurlow returned to his East Anglian roots, playing over 200 games for non-League Lowestoft Town, including 152 consecutive games.

Bryan Thurlow made 224 appearances for Norwich scoring one solitary goal.

Ralph Hunt

August 1933, Hampshire   **Player 1955–58**

The signing of Ralph Hunt evoked memories of Roy Hollis, three years after Hollis had left Norwich. Hunt, like Hollis, was an exceptional goalscorer who made a lasting impression on Norwich supporters during a relatively short spell with the club.

Whereas Hollis had emerged through the Norwich youth set up, Hunt had learnt his trade first at non-League Gloucester and then at his home town club Portsmouth. At the time he signed for Portsmouth, in summer 1950, they were champions of England after winning their second successive League title. Breaking into an established side was always going to be a tall order, and in February 1954 Hunt made a career move along the South Coast to Bournemouth where he found regular football in Division Three South.

Hunt played a season and a half for Bournemouth; his 33 games included an away win at Carrow Road. By the end of the 1954–55 season Norwich were in need of a forward. After the departure of Hall of Famer Johnny Gavin, goals were in short supply; Bobby Brennan's 11 were enough to make him top goalscorer (the lowest top goalscorer tally since 1938–39). New Norwich manager and Hall of Famer Tom Parker addressed this problem by bringing in Hunt from Bournemouth, a club that was to later become connected with many Norwich Hall of Famers.

After a good pre-season Hunt started the first game of 1955–56, but could not match Hollis' debut as he failed to find the net. Hunt did score in the next game, his home debut, in a 3–1 win over Shrewsbury. Hunt's next goal came in a 2–1 away win at Brentford on 3 September 1955. A fairly routine Third Division South fixture became part of Norwich history as the first Norwich game to be broadcast on radio, meaning Hunt's goal was brought live into the living rooms of Norwich supporters around the country.

Hunt continued to score regularly throughout that season. He scored one hat-trick and six doubles. His last double of the season was on 21 April 1956 in a 5–2 win versus Southampton. On scoring his second goal in that game Hunt hit the 30 goal mark. He finished the season with 33 goals of which 31 were in the League, 18 more than the second top goalscorer, the returning Johnny Gavin.

Hunt became only the second Norwich player after Hall of Famer Percy Vargo way back in 1927–28 to score more than 30 in a season. He was the first (and to this day only) Norwich player to have scored more than 30 League goals in a single League campaign.

Despite having a natural goalscorer in the team, the following season (1956–57) has to go down as the worst in Norwich's history. The lowlights of the season were a bottom place finish with only 31 points (5 below second bottom Swindon), a goal difference of minus 33, and an unwanted club record of 26 consecutive games without a win, stretching from 22 September 1956 to 2 March 1957. The run included a period of 7 consecutive defeats, the last of which was a 1–7 at Torquay.

It was remarkable that even in this appalling season Hunt still managed to score 21 goals (20 in the League), putting him top of the charts for the second consecutive season. His ability to score so many in a struggling side showed how lethal Hunt was in front of goal – a natural finisher with a goal to chance ratio as good as anybody's in the game.

Ironically, while the 1957–58 season was much better for Norwich, Hunt's total of 18 goals was three fewer than the previous year and his lowest for Norwich. However, he did miss the final five games which, at his scoring ratio, could have made a difference. Hunt's goals had done enough to ensure that Norwich finished eighth in the League and so avoided becoming founding members of the new Division Four (a Division which Norwich have still never played in).

At the conclusion of the 1957–58 season Hunt was keen to test himself at a higher level and in August 1958 he moved to Second Division Derby County. On leaving Norwich he had scored a total of 72 goals and is sixth highest scorer in the club's history. More impressively, his goals to games ratio of 0.54 is the fourth best of Norwich's top strikers, marginally lower than Roy Hollis' ratio.

Hunt continued to score goals away from Carrow Road although he never settled at one club for long. Tragically his life was cut short by a car accident in December 1964 while at Chesterfield, his ninth professional club.

Ralph Hunt made 132 appearances for Norwich scoring 72 goals.

Terry Bly

October 1935, Norfolk   **Player 1956–60**

'Bly Bly babes' was the headline in the local Norfolk sports paper, *The Pink Un*, that greeted its readers on 11 January 1959.

The headline was written in reference to Bly's goals that had defeated the mighty Manchester United in the FA Cup third round – a Manchester United managed by Matt Busby, the manager famed for building squads based on youth that had become affectionately known nationally as Busby Babes.

As top goalscorer during the 1959 Cup run and a local lad, Bly had become the media darling of the local and national papers, a focal point for the intense coverage that Norwich's unlikely Cup run attracted.

It is difficult to imagine now but Bly could easily have missed out on the 1959 Cup run and the fame that it bought, for he was originally rejected by Norwich as a school kid before getting a second chance aged 22 after impressing locally with Bury St Edmunds. He signed in August 1956 and made his debut in the first game of that season, a 1–0 victory over Crystal Palace. At the time he was playing as a full-back but his opportunities were limited in his first season.

A serious knee injury further disrupted the start to Bly's career as he sat out the entire 1957–58 season. He had missed a total of 75 League and Cup games before finally making a first team comeback in a 3–3 home draw with Notts County, the League fixture coming just five days after Norwich had begun the 1959 FA Cup adventure against non-League Ilford.

By the time of his return Bly had reinvented himself as a centre-forward and over the coming weeks proved himself to be a very successful one. He had the forward's knack of being in the right place at the right time, a goal poacher with a thunderous shot on him.

Bly was still settling into his new role when Busby's Manchester United arrived at a snowy Carrow Road for the FA Cup third round tie on 10 January 1959. In those days

players were not rested for Cup games and it was a strong side that City faced including Foulkes, Charlton and Viollet – the same eleven that had just won eight First Division games in a row and went on to finish runners-up at the end of the season. The rest is history; Norwich outplayed their illustrious opponents with Bly scoring twice (only the woodwork prevented a hat-trick). His second, an angled drive from the left, was so good even United 'keeper Harry Gregg was left applauding the effort. Bly's thunderbolt was witnessed by a Carrow Road crowd of 38,000.

The Manchester United game proved to be his defining moment, with Cup fever hitting Norwich. Bly went on to play in the following eight Cup games right through to the semi-final versus Luton.

Bly scored a double including a cracking late winner in the fourth round 3–2 win over Second Division Cardiff to earn Norwich a trip to another giant of the game, Tottenham Hotspur. Even a Spurs defence including Norwich Hall of Famer Maurice Norman could not prevent Bly scoring the winner in the replay at Carrow Road, as he broke the offside trap to apply a cool finish to Hall of Famer Ron Ashman's through ball.

The next higher division victims of Bly were Sheffield United in the quarter-final. After a 1–1 draw at Bramall Lane a capacity Carrow Road crowd enjoyed a Bly double, the second of which in the 71st minute proved to be the winner and the goal that sent Norwich through to their first ever FA Cup semi-final.

While Bly is rightly remembered for his goals in the 1959 Cup run, he was also doing the business back in the real world of Division Three football. Just a week after his wonder goal at Cardiff he scored a home hat-trick in the 5–1 win over QPR. By the end of the 1958–59 season he had scored an incredible 22 League goals in just 23 games. Add to this his seven FA Cup goals and he finished the season's top goalscorer with 29 goals.

1958–59 was truly Bly's season as injuries returned, restricting his appearances, the following season (1959–60) although he still managed to contribute seven goals in Norwich's promotion campaign.

In the summer of 1960, perhaps with Bly's injury record in the back of manager and Hall of Famer Archie Macaulay's mind, Bly was sold to Peterborough. In their first season as a Football League club, Peterborough cruised to the Fourth Division Championship scoring a League record of 134 goals. Bly himself scored 52 goals – another League record and only the second player since World War Two to score over 50 in a single season.

Bly eventually ended his Peterborough career at almost a goal per game (81 in 88 games) and hit a similar ratio at his next club Coventry (25 in 32). He retired from League football in 1964 (aged just 29) after suffering further injuries, before settling in Grantham where he became player-manager for the next 15 years.

Terry Bly made 67 appearances for Norwich scoring 38 goals.

Geoffrey Watling

April 1913, Norfolk   **Chairman 1957–73**

Geoffrey Watling is the longest serving Norwich City chairman, having held office for 16 years between 1957 and 1973. In that period he oversaw Norwich's rise from the very bottom of English football right up to their first season among the elite of Division One.

Watling was born in Queens Road in the very heart of Norwich. A son of an entrepreneur, he was soon to inherit the family business, C. Watling Limited. His father Charles Watling was actually involved in managing the voluntary liquidation process that Norwich Football Club was forced to undertake in 1919 after suffering crippling debts incurred following World War One. He then invested £5,000 capital to ensure that a newly formed Norwich City emerged from liquidation to compete in the 1919–20 Southern League season.

Just under 40 years later it appeared that history may repeat itself when, late in 1956, Norwich again faced the threat of extinction brought on by a financial crisis. A number of factors converged to cause this scenario. Firstly, the final instalment of the loan that was taken out to build Carrow Road way back in 1935 was due for payment, and the board had taken out a further loan of £8,000 to install floodlights at Carrow Road. A terrible season on the pitch had seen Norwich exit the FA Cup in the first round and so miss out on a money spinning tie, while a run in Division Three South of 26 games without a win had seen attendances fall below the 10,000 mark (this

was in the days when gate receipts accounted for most of a club's revenue). Finally, the Board had become bloated with too many members for the club's requirements which created another drain on cash flow. The situation came to a head when players' wages were threatened; drastic action was required.

A new Board was formed, with Watling appointed chairman in February 1957. Under his stewardship, money was raised, investment secured and Norwich's future saved. As well as the financial matters, Watling had the double challenge of obtaining re-election to the Football League and finding a new Norwich manager to take the team forward. Despite Norwich's League position, the club's potential was evident

based on the high number of applications to replace Hall of Famer Tom Parker. Watling showed foresight, and an ability to spot the characteristics that make a good football manager, when he appointed Hall of Famer Archie Macaulay as the new Norwich manager in April 1957. As this was the first League management job for Macaulay, it represented a gamble by Watling. However, as Macaulay went on to achieve a period of success and stability, Watling's decision was vindicated.

During the early years of his tenure, Watling also worked hard on improving Norwich's image and the club soon gained a reputation for hospitality, fair play and sportsmanship. He was congratulated, at the 1961 Football League annual meeting, by Division Two chairmen who were looking forward to hosting newly promoted Norwich.

Like all people at the top Watling was not afraid to make ruthless and unpopular decisions as he looked to take the club forwards. He had to take on team affairs during a turbulent period following Macaulay's departure, while in June 1966 he fired fans' favourite, loyal club servant Hall of Famer Ron Ashman from the manager's position. Also in 1966 he became unpopular with the fans when ticket prices were raised for the FA Cup fifth round tie against Blackburn Rovers. It was a high risk move, but ultimately resulted in record gate receipts and much needed money into the manager's transfer pot.

Throughout most of Watling's time as chairman Norwich had been establishing themselves in the Second Division, but Watling was ambitious to make the next step up. After extensive research Watling was pleased to announce the appointment of Hall of Famer Ron Saunders in August 1969, despite resistance from his current club Oxford United. Saunders was a young but promising manager and Watling was prepared to back his man, making him Norwich's highest paid manager. Again, as with Macaulay, Watling's judgement proved sound. Thanks to Saunders he soon achieved his ambition of seeing Norwich in Division One.

After finally fulfilling his dream, Watling decided to step down as chairman in 1973. He continued to remain close to the club throughout his retirement before briefly returning to the forefront in 1996 when, during the darkest days of Hall of Famer Robert Chase's reign, he purchased 34 per cent of Chase's shareholding. This gave him a controlling stake which he then sold on to Hall of Famers Delia Smith and Michael Wynn-Jones.

As a means of gratitude to Watling for what he had done for Norwich City, the new main stand that was built following a fire in 1984 was renamed the Geoffrey Watling stand. A smart and modern stand housing the changing rooms, club shop and Board room, it was fitting tribute to Watling. After his death, in November 2004, he was further honoured when the pathway behind the River End stand was renamed Geoffrey Watling Way.

Geoffrey Watling was Norwich chairman for 16 years and six Norwich managers worked under him, including three in the Hall of Fame.

Matt Crowe

July 1932, Scotland   **Player 1957–62**

Matt Crowe recovered twice from a broken leg to become one of the most consistent performers in a Norwich side that was enjoying a golden period in the late 1950s and early 1960s.

Crowe first suffered a broken leg as a young 17-year-old at Bradford Park Avenue, then a Football League side. Crowe had come down to England from his native Scotland but his injury was to set him back and it was four years after signing when he finally made his debut. Crowe's debut was also his last game for Bradford Park Avenue as he returned to Scotland with Partick Thistle in the Scottish First Division.

After suffering another broken leg, this time with Partick, it looked as if Crowe's career could come to a premature end. However, with determination and a strong will, he got himself back to fitness and earned another crack at the English League, signing for Norwich in May 1957.

New manager and Hall of Famer Archie Macaulay made Crowe his first signing, as he looked to add some Scottish steel into a Norwich side that had just finished bottom of Division Three South. Crowe made his Norwich debut the following season (1957–58) and scored in a 2–1 win away to Reading. He went on to miss only three games after his debut, scoring four goals including a consolation goal in a freak 1–7 defeat at Brentford.

Crowe had been signed (and initially played) for Norwich as an inside-forward, an attacking position just behind the main striker. However, as with many players, Macaulay saw his potential in a different position and converted him to wing-half – a more defensive minded midfield position. Crowe blossomed in a Norwich team that had learnt to become fluid in formation, alternating between 2–3–5 and 4–4–2.

He became a key player during the 1959 season playing a total of 56 games. Included in the 56 were the

record 11 FA Cup games that Norwich enjoyed on their journey to the semi-final. Crowe played in every game of that Cup run, but it was during one of the early rounds that he had his best game. After drawing the FA Cup second round tie 1–1 with fellow Division Three side Swindon Town, both sides knew that the prize of Manchester United at home lay waiting in the third round. The replay at Carrow Road was a tight affair but Crowe put in a Man of the Match performance that even included a short spell in goal while 'keeper and Hall of Famer Ken Nethercott received treatment for an injury. So good was Crowe's performance that he was singled out for praise by the watching Manchester manager Matt Busby, who identified him as the main threat to his team.

Like all the Norwich players, Crowe rose to the challenges faced in the Cup run against higher level opposition. He worked hard with fellow Hall of Famer Roy McCrohan, protecting the Norwich defence during many periods of sustained pressure.

Crowe continued where he had left off the following season, 1959–60, playing again in all games bar one in the League as Norwich finished second in Division Three and won promotion. He scored four goals that season, all coming in Norwich wins. Crowe also managed to score in the FA Cup against Reading but there was to be no repeat of the previous year; this time Norwich exited at the third round.

In Norwich's first season back in the Second Division (1960–61) Crowe played in every game, meaning he had missed just five games in the last 189 games since his debut in October 1957. The 1960–61 season included the first year of the newly formed League Cup competition, a competition in which Norwich would go on to enjoy many successes in future years. Crowe was in the first Norwich side to play in the League Cup, and became the first ever Norwich player to score in the competition when he scored the opener in a convincing 6–2 win over Oldham in October 1960.

The next season saw manager Macaulay's exit from Norwich and, for the first time in his career, Crowe was no longer guaranteed a first-team place. He did play in 25 games that season including his last for Norwich, a 1–2 loss to Brighton on 20 April 1962.

In July 1962 Crowe was sold to Brentford for £25,000 (50 times the amount Norwich paid for him) and in his first season with Brentford he won a Fourth Division Championship medal. After 73 games for Brentford, Crowe emigrated to South Africa where he managed Port Elizabeth to their first League title before he retired from football to enjoy his new life in South Africa.

Matt Crowe made 214 appearances for Norwich scoring 18 goals, including Norwich's first in the League Cup.

Archie Macaulay

July 1915, Scotland   **Manager 1957–61**

Archie Macaulay's time as Norwich manager was yet another example of the old adage that Scots make good football managers. He also helped dispel the myth that good players often struggle to become good managers.

Macaulay began his career at one of Britain's biggest clubs, Glasgow Rangers, where winning trophies was the norm. From Rangers he moved south and settled in London playing for West Ham, Arsenal (where he won a League Championship medal) and Fulham. He was a Scottish international with seven caps to his name.

After a successful playing career, Macaulay's ambition was to move into management. He was prepared to learn the ropes lower down the League pyramid, taking the manager's job at non-League Guildford Town. His time at Guildford gave him a good grounding and by the time Norwich chairman and Hall of Famer Geoffrey Watling had identified his potential he was ready to make the step up to Division Three South.

Macaulay became Norwich's fifth post-war manager when he joined on 1 April 1957. As well as the famous Cup campaign, he also managed to improve Norwich's League position in each of his four seasons in charge. When he joined Norwich the club was at rock bottom of Division Three South, a difficult time for any new manager, with low morale in the dressing room and few funds available for strengthening the squad.

What money he did have, Macaulay spent well. In his time at Norwich he signed eight players who are in the Hall of Fame, including six of the starting XI for the majority of the 1959 FA Cup games. He also made a masterstroke in bringing Bobby Brennan back from the cold.

As well as buying good players, Macaulay was skilled in blending them into a team with the core of the squad that he had inherited. In his first full season in charge, 1957–58, he guided Norwich to a respectable eighth in Division Three South, 16 places and 22 points more than the previous season. The upward trend continued in 1958–59 with a fourth place finish and, of course, the Cup run that captivated the Norfolk public.

The 1959 FA Cup competition gave Macaulay the chance to pit his wits against the game's biggest managers: Manchester United's Matt Busby and Tottenham's Bill Nicholson. The fact that Norwich not only defeated both Manchester United and Tottenham but beat them by playing attractive football is a credit to Macaulay and his team.

The Cup run was followed by more success in 1959–60 with a second place finish and promotion to Division Two. In his final season in charge, 1960–61, he led Norwich to a surprising fourth place finish in their first season at that level since 1938–39. In just four years Norwich had risen by 42 League places under Macaulay.

Much of Norwich's continual improvement over this period can be attributed to Macaulay. He put an emphasis on player fitness, working hard on this aspect in training. Under Macaulay Norwich became one of the fittest teams in the Football League, an important factor during the draining 11 games of the 59 Cup run. While most managers acknowledged the importance of fitness, Macaulay was one of the first to consider the role of psychology in football. He got to understand his players, realising that players responded differently to varying management styles This attention to his players went some way to developing a bond between Macaulay and his team, who were prepared to 'run through walls' for him.

Macaulay fostered a team spirit and character that Norwich became renowned for, especially in 1959. The players worked hard for each other and enjoyed each other's company on and off the pitch. The players were also well briefed on the opposition, who were analysed and discussed in depth during weekly team meetings.

Another of Macaulay's strengths was his tactical awareness; he was responsible for switching the positions of key men in his team. Hall of Famers Roy McCrohan, Terry Bly, Jimmy Hill and Terry Allcock all benefitted from Macaulay's foresight, flourishing in their new roles within the team. As a consequence the team were adaptable, often playing a 4–4–2 formation which was relatively groundbreaking at the time.

With Norwich's success combined with Macaulay's ambition, it was only a matter of time before he decided to take the next step in his career: managing in the First Division. In October 1961, much to the Board's disappointment, he left to become WBA's new manager. WBA were one of the grand old names in English football but Macaulay never truly settled, completing just one full season (a mid-table finish) before leaving the Hawthorns under a cloud and eventually drifting out of football.

Archie Macaulay managed Norwich for 224 games with a win percentage of 46.9 – one of the best of any Norwich manager.

Barry Butler

July 1934, Teeside   Player 1957–66

The Barry Butler Memorial Trophy is awarded each year to the Norwich City Player of the Season, as voted for by the fans. Butler's name being adopted for the award is a fitting honour to one of Norwich's most inspirational players, who tragically died aged just 32. Since its conception, in 1967, 37 players have won the award with eight players winning it on more than one occasion.

Butler began his career with First Division Sheffield Wednesday, making his debut aged just 19 versus Burnley. Wednesday were relegated that season but won the Second Division Championship the next season. Butler also featured in the Sheffield Wednesday side that got to the 1954 FA Cup semi-finals – an experience that would prove invaluable five years later with Norwich.

With first team appearances limited at Sheffield Wednesday, Butler became Norwich manager and Hall of Famer Archie Macaulay's major summer signing, as Macaulay began to rebuild the Norwich squad after the 1956–57 season. Butler made his debut in the centre of the Norwich

defence in the first game of the 1957–58 season, an exciting 3–2 victory against Crystal Palace. From that point on he became one of the first names on the team-sheet. Butler missed only three games that season and following his return to the team, on 21 September 1957, he went on to play in a record breaking (for Norwich) 208 consecutive League and Cup games. The record was finally ended when he sat out the League Cup second round tie at Lincoln on 4 October 1961, a game he only missed because he had been called up to play an England FA XI representative match. In the League, Butler's record is even more impressive; he played in 219 games in a row until missing the home fixture against Huddersfield on 12 September 1962.

Butler's Norwich City record included four consecutive seasons as an ever-present. During this time he and Norwich enjoyed an

FA Cup semi-final, promotion to Division Two, their highest every League position (fourth in Division Two) and a League Cup-winners' medal. Butler's contribution to this successful period was huge. He had become the defensive rock, strong both on the ground and in the air. He was a terrific organiser, a natural leader and one of the fittest players in the squad. He became the Norwich vice-captain in his first season, first captaining the side to a 5–2 win over Newport on 16 April 1958. He was an able replacement when captain and Hall of Famer Ron Ashman was unable to play and it was no surprise that Ashman, when he became manager in 1962, made Butler his captain.

Butler's defensive prowess was perhaps no more evident than during the 1959 FA Cup run. In 270 minutes of football against two top First Division teams (Manchester United and Tottenham Hotspur) Norwich conceded one solitary goal, the result of a lucky deflection off Butler himself to bring a late equaliser for Spurs.

It was in the quarter-final at Bramall Lane against Sheffield United that Butler enjoyed his greatest game of the Cup run. After goalkeeper Nethercott's injury had rendered him effectively a spectator for the last 25 minutes, Butler inspired a Norwich defence that resisted everything Sheffield United could throw at them in their quest for a winner and so earning a replay that would see Norwich reach the semi-finals for the first time.

After being a permanent fixture in the Norwich side in the late 1950s and early 60s a broken leg restricted him to just 11 games in 1962–63. However, he returned to captain Norwich in the following seasons, 1963–64 and 1964–65, in a Second Division that included some big name teams such as Leeds, Sunderland, Manchester City and Newcastle.

A senior member of the squad by this time, Butler was taking an active role in coaching the new generation of Norwich players. He played his last game for Norwich on 9 October 1965 – a 0–1 defeat at Birmingham – and was due to be appointed as coach for the start of the 1966–67 season. Sadly, fate intervened, and on 9 April 1966 he died of injuries resulting from a traffic accident.

Butler's death left a massive void, shaking all at the club as well as the Norwich supporters. He was a highly respected person and would surely have gone on to become a successful coach and eventually a successful manager. It was understandable that Norwich ended the 1965–66 season with six defeats in nine games following his death, as the club struggled to come to terms with their loss.

A memorial match was played on 5 May 1966 against Ipswich Town and his name was to live on through the Player of the Season awards.

Barry Butler made 349 Norwich appearances scoring three goals.

Terry Allcock

December 1935, Yorkshire   Player 1958–69

Terry Allcock's long and illustrious career with Norwich is littered with personal achievements and club records that reflect a time when Norwich as a club were on the up. They had established themselves as a Second Division team with a reputation as a good Cup side.

Allcock was destined to become a footballer from an early age. He was the youngest ever to play for Leeds schoolboys and went on to captain Yorkshire boys as well as representing England at youth level. He had plenty of options when turning professional, choosing Bolton Wanderers in 1952. Bolton had a rich footballing heritage with a team of household names, none more so than the 'Lion of Vienna' Nat Lofthouse. With England international Lofthouse blocking Allcock's path to the first team he was eventually forced to search elsewhere for regular football. Allcock signed for Norwich in March 1958, just two months prior to Lofthouse scoring both goals and winning the FA Cup for Bolton.

Opportunities for Allcock at Bolton may have been limited because of Lofthouse but he did learn the art of goalscoring through training with the great man, and Norwich were to reap the benefits. 1958–59 was Allcock's first full season; he was deployed by manager Archie Macaulay as an attacking midfielder utilising his footballing brain, work ethic and ability to time his runs into the box. Allcock scored on the opening day of the season in a 3–0 win over Newport. He finished the season with 20 goals, second only to Hall of Famer Terry Bly. Only one goal came in the 59 FA Cup but that was in the cauldron of White Hart Lane where Allcock opened the scoring to stun the 67,633 crowd. By the end of his Norwich career Allcock would finish with 12 FA Cup goals, more than any Norwich player past or present.

The promotion year of 1959–60 saw Allcock finish joint top goalscorer with 16 goals and was to start a run of four consecutive seasons finishing top scorer. He was the first player to achieve this, and his record was held until the early 90s when it was equalled by Hall of Famer Robert Fleck.

In the second of his top goalscoring seasons, 1960–61, Allcock again finished with 16 goals despite missing 17 games after a leg fracture. This was an impressive total considering he was not an out and out striker. He had developed the ability to anticipate any rebounds or deflections within the box and was able to react quicker than the defenders.

By the end of 1961–62 season Allcock had broken the 20 goal barrier, finishing with 21 in all competitions. He opened the season with a hat-trick in the 3–1

win over Bury, but a much more famous hat-trick was to follow on 13 January 1962 when Allcock joined an elite club of players that had scored hat-tricks away at Anfield, home of the mighty Liverpool. To put it into perspective, only Peter Ndlovu has managed this feat since, when he scored three for Coventry in March 1995. Unfortunately for Allcock his Anfield hat-trick was not enough to avoid defeat, with Norwich going down 4–5 to the eventual champions.

The 1962–63 season proved to be the best yet for Allcock. He amassed an incredible 37 League and Cup goals, still to this day the most goals scored by a Norwich player in a single season. Six of these goals were scored in the FA Cup as Norwich embarked on another famous FA Cup run. Two giants of the English game were victims of Allcock's goals; he scored four in the fourth round 5–0 thrashing of Newcastle, followed by a double in the next round to beat First Division Manchester City 2–1 at Maine Road. Allcock also scored five in the League Cup, with his treble against Carlisle completing a new club record: a double of hat-tricks in both the FA and League Cups in the same season.

Another broken leg in the game against Plymouth in November 1963 ended Allcock's goalscoring run. By the time he had recovered from the injury, fellow Hall of Famer Ron Davies was banging the goals in and Allcock returned to first-team duties as a central-defender. Allcock was to spend the next five seasons flourishing in his new position, so much so that he won the first Barry Butler Player of the Season award in 1966–67, an award that was particularly meangingful for Allcock as a teammate and good friend of the late Butler.

More than 10 years after his debut, Allcock played his last game for Norwich against Blackburn in the last game of the 1968–69 season. By the time he retired he had scored 127 goals for Norwich and was second behind Hall of Famer Johnny Gavin in the all-time list. He would surely have been comfortably first if not for his switch to defence.

Allcock went on to coach and manage the youth team before a short spell as assistant manager at Manchester City. He soon returned to Norfolk where he worked at Carrow Road as a match day host for corporate clients.

Terry Allcock made 389 appearances for Norwich, the 10th highest, and scored 127 goals.

Jimmy Hill

October 1935, Northern Ireland   **Player 1958–63**

Not to be confused with his more famous namesake who played for Fulham and managed Coventry before becoming a TV presenter and pundit, Jimmy Hill was one of Norwich's stars of the late 1950s and early 1960s.

Born in Northern Ireland, Hill represented his country at various levels while playing for Linfield. His opportunity to move to England came in a big way when he was signed by First Division Newcastle United. His transfer involved Newcastle legend, three times FA Cup winner and record League goalscorer Jackie Milburn moving in the other direction. Not surprisingly this placed a burden on the young Hill, who struggled to live up to the expectations of a passionate support. Despite the team struggling in the 1957–58 season, Hill made just 11 appearances before making the move to Carrow Road in July 1958.

In spite of his lack of games at Newcastle, Hill, as with a number of Norwich players, still had First Division experience and a bit of quality which would prove invaluable in the big games that Norwich were to play in the coming two seasons.

After signing Hill, the first thing that Norwich manager and Hall of Famer Archie Macaulay did was to move him from the right wing to centre-forward. It was a tactical move which paid instant dividends, with Hill scoring 13 goals in his first season, 1958–59, contributing to the 89 goals scored by the team who finished in fourth place in the newly formed Division Three.

As a member of the '59ers' Hill played in all 11 FA Cup games. Hill may have scored only two goals in that Cup run but both were important. The first brought Norwich back into the game in the first round against non-League Ilford. The second was an equaliser against Swindon in the second round. Up to that point Norwich had been under pressure and playing poorly. Hill's equaliser came against the run of play, instilling confidence in the team, and proved to be the turning point in Norwich's FA Cup – after Hill's goal they never looked back.

The 1959 FA Cup run had helped raise Hill's profile and on 22 April 1959 he won his first Northern Ireland cap, helping his country to a 4–1 victory over Wales. During his career at Norwich Hill won a further 3 caps, including one against West Germany.

In the 1959–60 promotion season Hill finished joint top goalscorer with Hall of Famer Terry Allcock, both hitting 16 goals. Hill hit three doubles as he played an important part in Norwich's promotion. A quiet, timid character, 'Tiger' Hill as he was ironically nicknamed was often more comfortable playing in front of his home crowd, although he did score in six away games that season in which Norwich lost just once. One of Hill's away goals came at The Dell, Southampton, earning Norwich a draw against the eventual 1959–60 Division Three champions.

Hill made the step up to Division Two with ease, finishing the 1960–61 season with 10 goals despite missing 11 games through injury. Hill's success at this higher level was no surprise as he was an immensely talented player who made up for his lack of aggression with a great touch and a high skill level. That season Hill also showed he could perform in tense physical games, scoring in the derby at Portman Road against the Division Two champions and East Anglian rivals Ipswich Town. Later in the season he scored the winner at home to the Division's most glamorous side, Liverpool.

In Norwich's second season back in Division Two, 1961–62, Hill struggled for goals in the League; however, he did manage four in the League Cup. The League Cup was still in its infancy and not yet a priority for the country's leading clubs. In its second year as a competition Norwich won the trophy, beating Rochdale in the Final over two legs. After a comfortable first leg 3–1 win at Rochdale, his goal in the return leg at Carrow Road sealed the trophy for Norwich and a winner's medal for Hill.

Season 62–63 saw Hill hit double figures for the fifth consecutive season when he finished with 16 goals, including his first hat-trick in a 4–2 win over Sunderland in October 1962. At the end of the season First Division champions Everton came in with a £25,000 bid; an opportunity that neither Norwich or Hill could turn down.

Signed as a replacement for Norwich's 1959 FA Cup semi-final nemesis Billy Bingham, Hill never quite made it at Everton, playing only seven games. He moved back down the Leagues to Port Vale before returning to Northern Ireland to begin a career in management that was to last right up to 1991.

Jimmy Hill made 195 appearances for Norwich scoring 66 goals, leaving him joint 10th in the all-time goalscorer listing.

Errol Crossan

October 1930, Canada   Player 1958–61

Errol Crossan is our first Hall of Famer born outside of the British Isles and Republic of Ireland. 'Cowboy' as he became nicknamed was from Canada, a land associated with ice hockey, and a long, long way from Carrow Road and Division Three South football.

It is unlikely that Crossan would have ever got into football in Montreal but as luck would have it his parents relocated to the Isle of Man when young Crossan was eight. He played for various local sides before his shot at the big time came in 1954 when he signed for Manchester City.

After failing to break into the Manchester City first team he moved on to Gillingham and Southend; at the latter he lined up with ex-Norwich man and Hall of Famer Roy Hollis. On 26 September 1958 and no doubt after a good word from Hollis, Crossan joined Hall of Famer Archie Macaulay's revolution that was underway at Norwich.

A day after joining, Crossan made his Norwich debut in a 1–0 win at Doncaster and the following week he scored on his home debut in a 2–2 draw with Bournemouth. Crossan had made an instant impact on the side; the missing piece of the jigsaw, as he went on to play every game for the remainder of the 1958–59 season.

This run of games included the 11 in the FA Cup. The FA Cup campaign coincided with a rich vein of form in the League that saw Crossan score in five consecutive League games between 27 December 1958 and 7 February 1959. Not only was Crossan a goalscorer but he was the main provider in the Norwich side. He played out on the wing and would frighten defenders with his raw pace and direct approach. He became an important outlet for the Norwich team when under pressure, and he also had an end product – whether a shot on goal or a perfectly weighted cross.

Crossan's style of football summed up a Norwich team that played with an attacking flair during that Cup run. His first telling contribution came in the second round replay when he curled a delightful effort into the top corner to seal a 1–0 win over Swindon and bring Manchester United to Carrow Road for the third round.

Norwich and Crossan coped better with the icy conditions than Manchester United; they attacked United at will. Leading 1–0, Crossan reacted quicker than anybody to score the killer second goal and give Norwich some much needed breathing space. After despatching United, Cardiff were next up in the fourth round. Norwich found themselves 0–1 down at half-time, before a low shot by Crossan equalised. Then, as a replay looked likely, Crossan nicked the ball off a Cardiff defender and got to the byline, before pulling the ball back for Hall of Famer Terry Bly to finish.

Tottenham were shocked in the fifth round as the city became gripped by Cup fever. Tickets were at a premium and supporters were travelling away in huge numbers. The team were carried along by their ability, their team spirit and the support. Crossan was central to the team bond. He was the dressing room prankster, the joker that lightened the mood and helped ease the nerves.

Crossan not only entertained the team but he could also play; he scored a crucial equaliser in the quarter-final game against Sheffield United after earlier having an effort ruled out for offside. Then, in what was Norwich's biggest game in their history, the semi-final versus Luton Town, Crossan ripped the Luton defence apart only to see his efforts fall agonisingly wide. One did hit the net, but it was harshly disallowed for a foul.

As the glorious Cup adventure came to an end, in the semi-final replay on 18 March 1959, Norwich brought their Cup form into the League. They lost only two more games and finished fourth in Division Three South. Crossan, helped by his four goals in the FA Cup, finished the season with 16.

In Norwich's promotion season, 1959–60, Crossan continued to petrify defences throughout the League. He again finished on double figures (13) but was credited for many more assists. Crossan had deserved his opportunity in a higher division, but was to play only 23 games for Norwich in the Second Division before a mid-season move to fellow Second Division side Leyton Orient.

His move to Orient had earned Norwich a £10,000 transfer fee and a new player, George Waites. Unfortunately Crossan failed to settle at Orient and after only two months he had returned to Canada. Crossan remained in Canada and was elected to the Canadian soccer Hall of Fame in 2000.

Errol Crossan made 116 appearances for Norwich scoring 32 goals.

Sandy Kennon

November 1933, South Africa   Player 1959–65

Sandy Kennon is the second player born overseas and the second goalkeeper in the Norwich City Hall of Fame. As a Goalkeeper his career was sandwiched between Hall of Famers Ken Nethercott with 416 appearances and Kevin Keelan with 673. Kennon himself kept goal in 255 games for Norwich which spanned a successful period in the club's history.

Kennon was born in South Africa and played both Football and Rugby as a sports-mad youngster. He progressed through the ranks locally to represent South Africa in an exhibition game against Wolverhampton. Wolves were at the time one of the best sides in England and gave Kennon plenty of work to do. A confident performance led to a bid from Charlton Athletic that was turned down by Kennon's parents, who felt at 16 years he was too young to leave home.

Fortunately for Kennon further exhibition games, including two against an FA XI select team, kept him in the shop window and, aged 23, he signed for Second Division Huddersfield.

After two and a half uneventful seasons at Huddersfield Kennon was signed by Norwich manager and Hall of Famer Archie Macaulay on 5 February 1959, just ten days before the FA Cup fifth round tie against Tottenham. At the time Macaulay needed cover for his experienced number one, Ken Nethercott, with fixtures coming thick and fast and the recent transfer of Nethercott's long- suffering understudy Ken Oxford.

Macaulay's decision to bring in Kennon as cover was soon justified when Nethercott suffered a dislocated shoulder in the FA Cup quarter-final at Sheffield United. Four days later, on 4 March 1959, Kennon was selected to make his debut in the replay; it was Norwich's biggest game for years, possibly the biggest in the club's history. Kennon had only been at Norwich for a month on trial and had not even signed full-time.

Kennon had to fight his nerves as he walked out for the first time on the Carrow Road pitch to the roar of 38,000 passionate supporters engulfed by the excitement of the Canaries' Cup run. His confidence would not have been helped when he pushed a low shot into the path of the oncoming Sheffield forward to bring Sheffield United back into the

game. To his credit, Kennon did not let this error affect him and he played his part in a resolute second half display, seeing Norwich through to their first semi-final.

First Division Luton Town awaited in the semi-final at White Hart Lane. 63,500 were packed in the terraces, creating an electric atmosphere, while Kennon's opposite number in the Luton goal, Roy Baynham, was an experienced 'keeper with three England caps to his name. Undaunted, Kennon had a superb game for Norwich as Luton made the early running. Twice he made low saves to his left to keep out near post headers while at 0–1 to Luton, he kept Norwich in the game with a fine save from a low shot across the six-yard box. In the second half, after Norwich had equalised and were pushing for a winner, Luton broke on the counter attack. Kennon kept City in the Cup, diving to his right to keep out a shot from just past the penalty spot.

In the semi-final replay Kennon further enhanced his growing reputation with a commanding performance as he met cross after cross. He was beaten just once but it was enough to end Norwich's Wembley dreams.

In a run that saw Norwich lose only twice, Kennon played the remaining 17 games of the 1958–59 season. So good were his performances that Norwich's legendary 'keeper Nethercott never played again for the first team, despite regaining fitness from the injury that had given Kennon his big break. Despite their rivalry for the 'keeper's jersey, the two men remained friends and had tremendous respect for each other. So much so that Kennon stated that if Norwich had made it to Wembley he would have given his medal to Nethercott.

Kennon missed only one game in the promotion year of 1959–60, keeping an impressive 16 clean sheets. He further excelled in the Second Division in 1960–61 against higher quality attackers. He kept five clean sheets in the first seven games including two in two games versus Charlton.

Norwich's undisputed number one for the next three seasons, Kennon only briefly lost his place to the emerging Keelan. He was a cultured 'keeper who always looked to keep possession and launch counter attacks by throwing the ball out to a team mate. Ironically, it was this part of his game that ultimately led to him losing his place, with new manager and Hall of Famer Ron Ashman favouring a longer distribution direct to the forwards. Keelan was applying pressure and Kennon played his last game on 4 November 1964, fittingly in a Cup competition, against Workington.

Kennon moved on to Colchester, where he gained a reputation for saving penalties, before returning to Norfolk. He played minor counties cricket and was a regular at Carrow Road. Recently he returned to attend the '59ers' reunion. He was also in the dugouts as a guest manager in May 2011 for a Football Aid charity game.

Sandy Kennon made 255 appearances for Norwich.

Bill Punton

May 1934, Scotland   **Player 1959–66**

Bill Punton is recognised in the Norwich City Hall of Fame not only for his exceptional performances for Norwich in the early 1960s, but also for what he has contributed to local Norfolk football at the grass roots level.

The first Hall of Famer from after the 1959 FA Cup adventure, Punton was signed by Norwich manager and fellow Hall of Famer Archie Macaulay in July 1959.

After the euphoria of the FA Cup, Norwich were aiming to build on their fourth place finish in Division Three, targeting promotion in the following season of 1959–60.

The ideal man to help Norwich achieve their ambitions, Punton had earned top flight experience at Newcastle who he signed for in 1954 after scoring 38 League goals for Irish club Portadown. He played 23 games for Newcastle in the First Division in the same team that included Newcastle legend Jackie Milburn. Also in the Newcastle squad during his time there was Norwich Hall of Famer Jimmy Hill. Another Norwich Hall of Famer that Punton had played with was Errol Crossan after they appeared briefly together for Southend at the start of the 1958–59 season. These associations helped Punton to settle into a close knit squad for the beginning of the 1959–60 season.

He made his debut in the fourth game of the 1959–60 season, a 0–0 draw at Tranmere. He was a pacey, direct winger; a like for like replacement for the aging Norwich hero and Hall of Famer Bobby Brennan. As the season progressed Punton became first choice winger, missing only five games from mid-October to the end of the season. His defining moment came in the penultimate game of the season at home to his former club Southend. The equation for Norwich was simple – a Norwich win would see them promoted to the Second Division for the first time in 21 years. A large Carrow Road crowd of 34,905 witnessed a thrilling game in which Punton played his part. He scored the Norwich equaliser to settle the nerves before keeping the Southend defence on the back foot with his skill and energy as Norwich played the game

at a high tempo. Two goals from Punton's opposite winger Crossan, helped settle the game 4–3 to Norwich.

Punton's experience was to play an important part in Norwich's first season back in the second tier. He played in every game of the 1960–61 season as unfancied Norwich shocked the pundits with a fourth place finish. During the season Punton scored in a 2–0 win at Luton Town – the first game between the two since the 1959 FA Cup semi-final. He enjoyed a goal at Anfield, home to Liverpool; unfortunately it was a consolation in a 1–2 loss. However, his five other goals that season all came in Norwich wins – most of them convincing – including Lincoln 5–1, Middlesbrough 4–1 and, on the last game of the season, Southampton 5–0. Norwich's fourth place finish saw them end the season in good company, one place below Liverpool and for the first time ever above some of English football's biggest clubs such as Sunderland, Leeds and Stoke.

Punton missed some matches in the following season (1961–62); possibly a reason why Norwich had slipped to a sixth from bottom finish. He managed six goals in 29 games including another against Southampton, having scored against the Saints in the previous two seasons. Punton also scored a goal in the 3–1 League Cup Final first leg victory over Rochdale which set Norwich up for their first trophy since 1933–34.

After another sporadic season in 1962–63 (although there was one more goal against Southampton!) Punton had a good run of games in 1963–64. He scored six goals including one in Norwich's record victory in the League Cup: 7–1 at Halifax.

Again, Punton found himself in and out of the side over the next couple of seasons, as Norwich became an established Second Division club. His final Norwich game came on 24 September 1966 when he was substituted in a 1–1 draw at Preston North End.

Punton moved to Sheffield United but was reluctant to leave a settled life in his adopted Norfolk. He attempted to commute, as he did when he moved to Scunthorpe, but in practice this was proving difficult. In June 1969, keen to get involved in local football, he became player-manager and then manager at Yarmouth where he was to remain for the next 21 years and 1,085 games. During that period he also found time to manage the Norfolk County team and in 1994 he led Diss Town to the greatest moment in their history, winning the FA Vase at Wembley.

When not in the dugouts of the region's grounds, Punton can be regularly heard on Radio Norfolk. Most recently, in 2011, he was in the manager's hot seat for the very same Football Aid game that saw Hall of Famer Sandy Kennon managing the opposition.

Bill Punton made 256 appearances for Norwich scoring 29 goals.

Ollie Burton

November 1941, Wales   **Player 1961–63**

Ollie (real name Alwyn) was an exciting prospect when he joined Norwich in March 1961. He became a real fans' favourite during his short career at Carrow Road, before enjoying many successful years at Newcastle United.

As a youngster growing up on the Welsh/English border, Burton was destined to reach the very top of the game. He represented Wales at schoolboy level and made his League debut for Third Division Newport aged just 17 years old.

Burton's performances were soon attracting interest from beyond the Third Division, and it was to Norwich manager and Hall of Famer Archie Macaulay's credit that he secured Burton's signature despite competition from Southampton and Arsenal. At £11,000 Burton became the most expensive teenager in Norwich's history, but it would prove to be money well invested.

Signed in March 1961, Burton came straight into the team in a 4–1 win over Middlesbrough, but went on to make only one further appearance that season as he adjusted to his new surroundings. An injury meant that it was a while before Norwich supporters got to see the best of the exciting teenager; his first run of games came in the second half of the 1961–62 season, almost a year after joining.

Burton's run in the first team coincided with Norwich's League Cup success. He scored his first Norwich goal in the fifth round in a remarkable 4–1 win against a Sunderland team that finished third in Division Two. Burton also played in the fifth round of the FA Cup as Norwich supporters were beginning to dream of another 1959. As in 1959, their opponents were First Division Sheffield United but, unfortunately, there was no repeat performance. Norwich lost 1–3 in front of 49,304 at Bramall Lane.

Norwich and Burton enjoyed better fortune in the League Cup. Burton played in both legs of the semi-final

versus First Division Blackpool as Norwich clung on to achieve a 4–3 aggregate win. Burton also played both legs in the Final; a much more comfortable 4–1 aggregate victory over Rochdale gave Burton his first winners' medal aged just 21.

The next season, 1962–63, Burton was a regular in the Norwich defence where his consistency was earning him much praise. He scored in the opening fixture to earn a 2–2 draw away at Preston and went on to score a further seven League goals – an impressive return for a full-back. Burton was also part of the Norwich team enjoying another FA Cup run, playing in every game through to the quarter-final clash against Leicester. The visit of First Division high-fliers Leicester attracted a record Carrow Road crowd of 43,984, a gate unlikely to ever be beaten in today's all-seater ground. Despite holding his own against higher level opponents, Burton could not prevent Norwich suffering a 0–2 defeat and Cup exit.

Burton was to play a total of 10 Cup games (FA and League Cup) that season in addition to 41 League games. He also made his international debut for Wales in 1963 in the home international against Northern Ireland. Burton went on to win another Welsh cap during his time at Norwich and was only the second Norwich player to represent Wales after Hall of Famer Noel Kinsey in the early 1950s.

Perhaps Burton's best game for Norwich in the 1962–63 season came in the 5–0 thrashing of Newcastle United in the FA Cup fourth round. His performance made an impression on the Newcastle hierarchy and in June 1963 they made a bid, believed to be around £35,000, as they looked to try and regain their First Division status. At the time this was a lot of money, and on accepting the offer Burton became the first Norwich player to be sold for a fee exceeding £30,000, much to the disappointment of the Norwich support.

Burton went on to enjoy a long and successful career at St James' Park. He spent just under 10 years at Newcastle until injury forced him to retire in October 1972. He helped Newcastle return to the First Division, winning the 1964–65 Division Two title, and spent the rest of his career as a First Division player. Burton was part of the Newcastle side that went on to win the European Fairs Cup (The predecessor to the UEFA Cup); it was a Cup run that saw him test himself against some of the best in Europe including Feyenoord, Sporting Lisbon and a 'Battle of Britain' clash against Rangers.

After retirement Burton received a testimonial in May 1973 against local rivals Sunderland, just weeks after they had lifted the FA Cup at Wembley as a Second Division side. He then moved back to Norfolk where he had fond memories in spite of his success in the North East. Settled in Diss, South Norfolk, Burton still had good relations with Norwich Football Club and often attended games in the directors' box.

Ollie Burton made 73 appearances for Norwich scoring nine goals.

Tommy Bryceland

March 1939, Scotland   **Player 1962–70**

Tommy Bryceland became Norwich's record signing in September 1962; it was the first time Norwich had spent £20,000 on a player and signalled the club's intent to reach the promised land of Division One.

£20,000 was to prove a sound investment by new Norwich manager George Swindin, who was acting on the advice of his predecessor Willie Reid. Prior to his short spell as Norwich manager, Reid had been manager at Scottish First Division side St Mirren and had signed Scottish schoolboy international Bryceland as a 17-year-old.

Bryceland went on to become a star at St Mirren with 47 goals in 105 appearances. He played in two Scottish Cup Finals, scoring the opener and winning his first Final versus Aberdeen in 1956, and finishing a runner-up in the 1962 Final against Rangers.

Only four months after the 1962 Final, Bryceland completed his move to Norwich. He made his debut on 29 September 1962 and helped his new side to a 2–0 win against Derby. He scored his first Norwich goal the following week in an away win at Rotherham. Bryceland's first home goal came on 10 November 1962 in a 5–0 victory over Swansea; a date better remembered for the departure of manager Swindin, after an ill-fated six months in charge. Bryceland had been one of Swindin's few signings but he was to keep his place in the side after Bryceland's teammate and Hall of Famer Ron Ashman was appointed as Swindin's replacement.

Under Ashman, Bryceland was an ever-present in the League during the 1963–64 season and missed only one competitive game, a 2–0 League Cup win against Birmingham. He finished the season second top goalscorer with his 13 goals helping to fill the void caused by injury to goal machine and Hall of Famer Terry Allcock. In the League Bryceland scored 12 goals which contributed to seven Norwich victories, in a season where they won only 11 games in total. With many of his goals proving to be match winners he played a large part in Norwich's fight against relegation, eventually finishing sixth bottom, only three points off the drop zone.

While Bryceland was to score just five goals the following season (1964–65) he played his part in an improved sixth place finish, level on points with Ipswich. As a clever attacker with a low centre of gravity he became a provider as much as a goalscorer, bringing others into play with his intelligent football. Again the goals he scored proved crucial with Norwich winning four and

drawing one of the League games that he scored in. In the draw Bryceland scored the equaliser against eventual champions Newcastle.

Bryceland continued to play regularly, missing only two League games in 1965–66 season. He again finished second top goalscorer, behind Hall of Famer Ron Davies. Of his nine goals, the pick of the bunch was the winner in a 1–0 home win against Ipswich on 25 September 1965. The victory helped Norwich finish above their Suffolk rivals for the first time since the 1952–53 Division Three South campaign 13 seasons ago.

For the third and final time, Bryceland finished second top goalscorer with another nine goals in the season 1966–67. That season he played in one of Norwich's greatest ever FA Cup giant-killings when Norwich rocked the football world by beating First Division champions elect Manchester United – a United side including Best, Charlton and Law – 2–1 at Old Trafford.

The Cup shock earned Norwich a fifth round trip at home to another First Division side Sheffield Wednesday. This time there was no surprise, with Wednesday prevailing 1–3. Norwich's consolation in front of 41,000 was scored by Bryceland. His goal marked a significant landmark as it was the first for Norwich seen on the national institution that is the BBC's *Match of the Day*.

For the third season in a row, 1967–68 Bryceland ended the campaign with nine goals, although by the end of the season he was becoming less involved in the first team. Becoming more of a squad player, Bryceland made his last Norwich appearance on 8 November 1969 against Huddersfield. The game saw him score his only goal of the season before being substituted.

In March 1970 Bryceland turned down an offer to coach at Norwich, instead prolonging his playing career at Fourth Division Oldham Athletic where, in his first season, he completed a double of promotion and the Player of the Season award. After 18 months at Oldham, Bryceland returned back to his first club St Mirren as player-manager. In 2007 he was inducted into the St Mirren Hall of Fame.

Tommy Bryceland made 284 appearances for Norwich scoring 55 goals.

Dave Stringer

October 1944, Norfolk

Player 1963–76
Manager 1987–92

With over 30 years' association with Norwich City, Dave Stringer is a true City great. His achievements as a player alone would have been enough to warrant a place in the Hall of Fame but he is also remembered as one of Norwich's most successful managers.

A look at Stringer's playing and managerial career provides an overview of Norwich's history over an exciting and successful period for the club.

A local boy, he stood out in his youth team as a player of potential. He was in his local senior side (Gorleston) at the age of 15, had trials at Arsenal and was called up by England schoolboys. Rejected by Arsenal, a determined Stringer broke into the Norwich B side before signing professional terms in May 1963.

After a couple of seasons developing his game in the reserves, he made his senior debut in the 0–3 defeat to Coventry in April 1965. The following season (1965–66) saw Stringer establish himself as the first choice full-back, where he offered balance and a high work ethic in a relatively uneventful Division Two campaign.

The 1966–67 season was Stringer's first of four where he played every game. This included the experience of beating Busby's Manchester United at Old Trafford and the opportunity for Stringer to test himself against the best.

In his second season as an ever-present, 1969–70, Stringer scored his first goal for the club in a 1–1 draw versus Huddersfield in February 1970 on his 215th appearance. This was his first

goal of 22 that he scored for Norwich. Stringer's tally included two crucial goals that are forever ingrained in the club's history. The first of these goals came in Norwich's Championship season of 1971–72. He was an ever-present again, and had switched to central defence to form a formidable partnership with Hall of Famer Duncan Forbes. Earlier in the season his winner at Bristol City had sent Norwich top of Division Two. However, it was his equaliser some seven months later in the final game of the season at Watford that clinched Norwich's first ever Division Two title. It was the icing on the

cake following the promotion party the previous week. To top off the season for Stringer he was awarded the Player of the Season in May, a great achievement in a year of many contenders.

Stringer played in Norwich's first ever Division One game and went on to make 38 appearances in that historic first top flight season of 1972–73. His second crucial goal ensured that Norwich were to enjoy the experience again when he scored a last minute winner, a header from a corner, against relegation rivals Crystal Palace. Stringer's goal in the 2–1 win meant that Norwich survived the drop at Palace's expense.

1973–74 was Stringer's fourth ever-present season, a season where he captained every game but unfortunately could not prevent City from being relegated. Stringer played a big part in Norwich's subsequent promotion in 1974–75, but by this time he was no longer a first choice. Stringer finished his Norwich playing career at the very top, marking Footballer of the Year Kevin Keegan in a narrow 0–1 loss at champions Liverpool on the opening day of the 1976–77 season.

On his move to Cambridge, in September 1976, Stringer had completed 13 years with Norwich, 11 as a first-team regular. He had made 499 appearances – the third highest, and the most for a Norfolk born Norwich player. He had experienced a Division Two title, a promotion, two League Cup Finals and a testimonial versus West Ham.

Stringer returned to Norwich in 1980 and progressed from Youth team coach to assistant manager, and eventually manager following Hall of Famer Ken Brown's departure in November 1987. The sacking of the popular Brown, in hand with Norwich's poor League form, meant it was a baptism of fire for the novice manager. However, Stringer rose to the task, guiding Norwich to safety and a respectable 14th in Division One.

In the following season, 1988–89, Norwich were expected to struggle, especially after the sale of star striker and Hall of Famer Kevin Drinkell. However, under Stringer's management, with a combination of clever signings, good coaching and good man-management skills, Norwich confounded the critics to finish a record fourth in Division One and reach their first FA Cup semi-final since 1959.

While Norwich could not repeat these heights over the next couple of seasons Stringer did maintain Norwich's First Division status, despite continuously losing his best players as the hierarchy looked to profit from the club's talent. The 1991–92 season proved to be the most challenging, with Norwich facing the threat of relegation. After seeing Norwich to safety and another FA Cup semi-final, Stringer decided it was the right time to leave to allow for a fresh start in the first ever Premiership season.

In his five seasons he had become one of Norwich's best managers, with a record League finish and two FA Cup semi-finals. His win ratio of 38.9 per cent, while bettered by some of his fellow Norwich managers, was achieved entirely in the top Division.

Dave Stringer made 499 appearances for Norwich, the third highest in the club's history, and scored 22 goals. He also managed Norwich for 229 games.

Kevin Keelan

January 1941, India   Player 1963–80

No other player in the history of Norwich City Football Club has pulled on the green and yellow jersey more times than Kevin Keelan. On 673 occasions he was Norwich's number one, their goalkeeper for 571 League games, 31 FA Cup, 57 League Cup and 14 Texaco Cup games.

Keelan's journey into the Norwich record books began on 24 August 1963 when he made his debut in a 1–3 defeat at Cardiff. Keelan had signed a month earlier in July 1963 for £6,500 from Third Division Wrexham. He was signed by manager and Hall of Famer Ron Ashman, a man whose appearances record he would later beat.

During the 1963–64 and 1964–65 seasons Keelan faced competition for the 'keepers jersey from Hall of Famer Sandy Kennon and it was only after Kennon's retirement in November 1964 that Keelan finally made the position his own. The 1965–66 season was his first season as an ever-present; despite a 13th place finish in Division Two Norwich conceded only 52 goals, four fewer than second place Southampton. Keelan's other seasons where he played every game (not including Texaco Cup) came in 1971–72, 1972–73, 1973–74 and 1975–76. This included a run of 133 consecutive League games between August 1971 and September 1974, ending only when he missed the 0–4 defeat at Fulham. The first game of this run came in the opening match of the 1971–72 season which was to end in Norwich's first ever promotion to the top Division. The promotion was based on the bedrock of a solid defence with only 36 goals conceded, the lowest ever by a Norwich team. Keelan as goalkeeper played a huge part in this record, keeping 18 clean sheets as he enhanced his reputation as an agile shot stopper with sharp reflexes.

Keelan was the only player to appear in every game in Norwich's first season in Division One. He kept eight clean sheets against the best strikers in the land, including one against high-flying Ipswich and one against relegation rivals WBA, both earning Norwich valuable points in their quest to avoid an immediate relegation. Keelan even managed to get himself on the score sheet that year when he netted in a penalty shoot-out victory over Leicester City in the second round of the newly formed Texaco Cup. Such was Keelan's contribution to Norwich's survival that he was voted 1972–73 Player of the Season.

Unfortunately, Norwich did not improve in the next season (1973–74). They finished their second in Division One a disappointing bottom place, their first since re-election in 1956–57. Keelan's performances stood out in an ultimately poor season and he was again awarded with the Player of the Season trophy, becoming the first player to win the award in two consecutive seasons.

The 1973–74 season ended with Keelan's testimonial against Ipswich – normally the swansong of a player's career. Keelan went on to play in the Norwich first team for a further six seasons. The first of these seasons, 1974–75, again included some personal triumphs for Keelan. He played in all bar four League games (giving his long suffering understudy Roger Hansbury some action) and kept 19 clean sheets as Norwich bounced back winning promotion to Division One at the first attempt that season. Keelan also enjoyed a bittersweet moment in the 1975 League Cup Final against Aston Villa. In front of 100,000 at Wembley he became the first Goalkeeper to save a penalty in a Wembley Cup Final when he dived to his right to push a Ray Graydon penalty onto the post. Unfortunately Graydon followed up to score the rebound and win the Cup for Villa.

Back in Division One, Keelan played in all of Norwich's competitive games in the 1975–76 season. Now more streetwise, and with a few additions to the squad, Norwich enjoyed their highest ever finish (10th in the First Division). Keelan proved his class with clean sheets against top five sides Derby and Leeds.

Despite suffering injuries to his hands and wrist which forced him to miss some games, Keelan was still the number one 'keeper during a period of First Division consolidation during the late 1970s. In the summer of 1978 he began to think of his career beyond Carrow Road, joining New England Tea Men for the North America Soccer League summer season where he was voted best goalkeeper.

Back at Norwich, Keelan's last season was in 1979–80. He played his last derby game on Boxing Day 1979 in an exhilarating 3–3 draw. This was Keelan's 23rd competitive match against Ipswich – the most for any Norwich player. He was involved in seven derby wins and kept six clean sheets in total versus Ipswich, at a time when they were one of the best teams in the country.

His final Norwich game was on 9 February 1980 in a 3–5 home defeat to Liverpool, a game better remembered for Hall of Famer Justin Fashanu's goal of the season. At the end of that season, aged 39, Keelan moved to the US permanently with Tampa Bay Rowdies, first as a player then later as a coach. His move to the US ended a 17 year playing career with Norwich, second only to fellow Hall of Famer Bernard Robinson.

Kevin Keelan made a record 673 appearances for Norwich.

Ron Davies

May 1942, Wales   **Player 1963–66**

Later described as one of the greatest centre-forwards in Europe, by none other than Sir Matt Busby, Ron Davies was certainly one of Norwich's most prolific strikers ever.

After an early set back when he was turned down by Blackburn Rovers, Davies emerged at perennial Fourth Division strugglers Chester where 44 goals in 94 games earned Davies a move to Second Division Luton Town.

Davies spent only one season at Luton, scoring 21 goals for a side that eventually finished bottom. Included in his 21 goals in the 1962–63 season were four scored in one game which was to define his career. The victims that day (13 April 1963) were Hall of Famer Ron Ashman's Norwich. Ashman himself was run ragged by the young Davies, whose four goals clinched a 2–4 Luton win.

Six months later, with Davies' star performance still in the forefront of Ashman's thoughts, Norwich broke the bank to sign Davies for £35,000, a record buy for Norwich (the first exceeding £30,000) and record sale for Luton. Davies signed on 5 September 1963 and made an instant impact, scoring on his debut to earn Norwich a 2–1 win over Scunthorpe and arrest an alarming start to the season that had seen Norwich lose the first four games.

Davies went on to score in the next three League games and then consistently throughout the season. His arrival coincided with a run of 31 consecutive games in which Norwich scored before eventually drawing a blank in a 0–4 defeat at Rotherham. During this club record run Davies contributed 20 goals including a double away to eventual champions Leeds and a hat-trick against his fellow Welshmen Cardiff. He ended the season with 30 goals in all competitions, ending Hall of Famer Terry Allcock's domination of the top scorer position that he had held over the last four seasons. Allcock himself had spent much of the season injured and Norwich therefore relied on Davies' goals to keep them in the Second Division, eventually finishing 17th. Davies became the last Norwich player to score 30 in a single season, until the milestone was achieved by Grant Holt in 2009–10. Davies' total of 26 League goals in one season was second only to Hall of Famer Ralph Hunt.

Davies was rewarded for his goals with his international debut for Wales on 15 April 1964, in a 2–3 defeat to Northern Ireland. In total he was to win five Welsh caps during his time at Norwich. All five games ended in defeats, including two against World Champions Brazil.

Davies struggled to match the heights of his debut season but still managed 14 League goals in 35 games in an improved sixth place finish for Norwich. His tally included his first in the East Anglian derby which Norwich won 2–1, and two doubles versus South Coast rivals Southampton and Portsmouth. A large percentage of Davies' goals came from headers which were rapidly becoming his trademark, with his ability to rise above defenders and get power and accuracy behind each header.

More than just a big centre-forward, Davies had quick feet and a superb shot on him. He was a star player in the 1965–66 season with his 21 goals – 18 in the League helping him to another club 'golden boot'. As in 1963–64 his goals undoubtedly ensured that Norwich avoided being sucked into the relegation dogfight. The second top goalscorer that season finished on just nine.

Davies ended the season playing an international friendly versus Brazil. He was seen as a key player to spearhead a promotion challenge for 1966–67; therefore there was much

disappointment and frustration when he was sold to Southampton (managed by former Norwich apprentice Ted Bates) for £55,000 on 5 August 1966 – a record fee received by Norwich. Davies had been a fans' favourite, a relationship which had started when the supporter's club donated £20,000 towards his transfer to Norwich and was cemented by his goals and performances.

Norwich supporters had to watch in dismay as Davies netted 37 goals in Southampton's first season back in Division One while Norwich succumbed to another mid-table finish in Division Two. Davies' 37 won him the country's golden boot award and national recognition, as he finished eight clear of World Cup hero Geoff Hurst.

Davies went on to score 134 goals in 240 games for Southampton, all in the First Division. He went on to win another 24 Welsh caps scoring nine times for his country. He became such a hero at Southampton that their supporters even forgave him after a season at rivals Portsmouth. After a brief spell at Manchester United, Davies emigrated to the USA.

At Norwich Davies' 66 goals left him joint 10th in the all-time goalscorers listing, while his ratio of 0.52 goals per game is one of the best of any Norwich striker, comparable with fellow Hall of Famers Roy Hollis and Ralph Hunt.

Ron Davies made 126 appearances for Norwich scoring 66 goals.

Hugh Curran

September 1943, Scotland   **Player 1966–69**

Hugh Curran signed for Norwich in January 1966. He was one of manager and Hall of Famer Ron Ashman's last, and also one of his best, signings. A goalscorer first and foremost, he soon became a firm fans' favourite with an all-action approach that tormented Division Two defenders, reminding City supporters of his fellow Scot and Hall of Famer Tom Johnston some 12 years earlier.

Ashman paid £12,000 for the Scot who had proven himself in a single season at Millwall, where he topped the scoring charts as Millwall won promotion to Division Three. The following season Millwall were on their way to back to back promotions with Curran's tally up to 26 goals in just 57 games when Ashman pounced.

Curran made a scoring debut in a 2–0 win over Carlisle on 29 January 1966. The other goal was scored by Hall of Famer and legendary goalscorer Ron Davies. It appeared that Norwich now had a forward line capable of firing them into the promised land of Division One, but they would play only 11 more games together before Davies' controversial transfer to Southampton.

With Davies' departure the goals burden fell on Curran during the 1966–67 season. However, his appearances were restricted by injury and he ended the season with just seven goals in 31 League and Cup games.

If the 1966–67 season was something of an anticlimax for Curran, the following 1967–68 season was one of the best in his career. It got off to a good start with his winner against newly relegated Aston Villa in a 1–0 home win. Injury free, he went on to play in every game that season, the only ever-present in a side that included Hall of Famers Dave Stringer and Kevin Keelan.

Curran finished the season with 18 goals, including a quick-fire hat-trick to give Norwich a 4–0 half-time lead over Birmingham (in a game Norwich eventually won 4–2) and a Portman Road double on 3 February 1968 in a thrilling derby that unfortunately ended in a 3–4 defeat (to an Ipswich side that went on to win the Championship).

On 27 January 1968 Curran scored his first FA Cup goal for

Norwich as they took First Division Sunderland to a third-round replay which Norwich won at Roker Park. This set up a fourth round against another First Division opponent, high- flying Chelsea. Again, Curran did himself proud in a narrow 0–1 defeat in front of 57,987 at Stamford Bridge.

Curran's 18 goals in 1967–68 meant that he topped the Norwich goalscoring charts. He was also awarded the Player of the Season trophy in recognition of his popularity on the terraces. He became only the second ever winner of the award, to cap off a superb season.

Curran picked up where he left off, scoring on the opening day of the 1968–69 season in a 2–1 win over Birmingham. An incredible run followed, leaving him with 17 League and Cup goals by the end of September. A ratio of 1.30 goals per game put him well on target to beat the goals scored in a single season record: Hall of Famer Terry Allcock's 37 in 1962–63. Curran's hot patch included scoring two goals in three consecutive League games against Bury, Sheffield United and Carlisle.

Sandwiched between the Bury and Sheffield United games came a League Cup second-round hat-trick at Portman Road. The hat-trick that was to confirm his legendary status among Norwich fans, with the 4–2 victory made all the sweeter by the fact Ipswich were a division higher than Norwich. Curran's treble meant he had the honour of being the only Norwich player to score a hat-trick at the home of local rivals Ipswich Town.

Curran's blistering start to the 1968–69 season had alerted scouts from the First Division; talk of a transfer was rife in the media and there was inevitable concern among Norwich supporters who remembered the Davies transfer just two and a half years earlier. Despite manager Lol Morgan's claims that Curran was not for sale at any price he was eventually sold to Wolverhampton for £60,000 on 30 January 1969.

Fittingly Curran scored in his final game on 18 January 1969, taking his season total to 22. Despite missing a third of the season it was enough to leave him Norwich's top goalscorer for the second successive season.

At Wolves, Curran finished top goalscorer in his first full season. He went on to score 40 in 82 games, playing in the 1972 UEFA Cup Final and scoring at Wembley for Scotland against England. On leaving Wolves, Curran played for Oxford and Bolton before a knee injury ended his career. He had been the top goalscorer for a least one season for every club that he had played for.

Hugh Curran made 124 appearances for Norwich scoring 53 goals.

Ken Foggo

November 1943, Scotland   **Player   1967–73**

'One nil Foggo' was the cry often heard from the Barclay end terrace and in the City pressroom, as Norwich's goalscoring winger Ken Foggo spearheaded Norwich's charge to the Division Two Championship and the reward of First Division football for the first time in the club's history.

Foggo was one of the experienced members of Norwich's Championship winning squad of 1971–72. He had started his professional career some 12 years previously when he signed for WBA in November 1960 after he had shone as a Scottish schoolboy international.

He made an instant impact at First Division WBA, setting up two goals on his debut in a 6–1 rout of Fulham. Foggo played a total of 129 competitive games for WBA, all League appearances were in the First Division, where WBA spent much of the 60s as a mid-table team. In spite of his 29 WBA goals he was often underrated at the club and on 6 October 1967 he looked to progress his career by signing for Norwich.

The Norwich manager at the time was Lol Morgan, Hall of Famer Ron Ashman's replacement and the man briefed to get Norwich out of the Second Division. Morgan invested £10,000 in Foggo and put him straight in the side for his debut, a 1–0 win over Blackburn. Foggo played in every game except one for the rest of the season, contributing six goals in a campaign that saw Norwich finish ninth in Division Two, 15 points off a promotion place.

After settling into his new surroundings and adapting to the physically tougher environment of the Second Division, Foggo's class began to shine through during his first full season 1968–69. He ended the season with nine goals, although he failed to find the net on his return to the Hawthorns in the FA Cup third-round defeat to WBA. His overall old fashioned wing play with pace and ability made him a big hit with the fans who voted him their Player of the Season.

He continued to find the net as a regular occurrence during the 1969–70 season, with his 11 goals proving important after the sale of Hall of Famer Hugh Curran. He missed only one League game, a defeat

at Millwall, and ended the season on a high with a double in the 6–0 thrashing of Birmingham in the penultimate game of the season. Foggo's tally of 11 was enough to see him finish as Norwich's top goalscorer.

The next two seasons saw Foggo establish himself as a winger with an eye for goal. An improved total of 17 in 1970–71 was a career best for Foggo and gave him a personal double of top scorer and Player of the Season, becoming the first player to win the award twice. Foggo played a key role the following season 1971–72, the year that Norwich finally fulfilled their ambition of First Division football. He played every game in the best ever start to a season made by a Norwich side; 13 matches undefeated until the 1–2 reversal at Millwall on 23 October.

Missing only four games of the promotion campaign, Foggo continued his impressive scoring rate as he operated on either wing. As a senior member of the team his experience was crucial as nerves were tested in the run in. He scored one and set up two from pin crosses in a 5–1 win over Blackpool on 25 March 1972; an important victory after Norwich had lost two of the last four games.

Foggo also scored the first goal in the game that finally confirmed Norwich's promotion. On a Monday evening in East London Norwich fans travelled to Leyton Orient 'en masse' knowing a win would confirm their place in the top flight next season. With the score 0–0 at half-time and into the second half, Foggo collected a pass on the edge of the area, controlled, turned and shot low into the corner. Foggo's goal broke Orient's resistance, Norwich went on to win 2–1 and with it promotion.

He ended that most momentous of seasons, 1971–72, as the club's top scorer with 14 goals and his third Norwich golden boot in a row. He scored a total of 57 goals for Norwich, 15th in the all-time listing and the highest scoring winger.

Surprisingly, he would play only two First Division games for Norwich, both as substitute, before moving back into Division Two with Portsmouth. After a couple of seasons at Fratton Park, Foggo ended up at Southend before retirement from League football in 1976.

Ken Foggo made 201 appearances for Norwich scoring 57 goals.

Max Briggs

September 1948, Norfolk   **Player 1967–74**

As with Hall of Famers Terry Bly and Bryan Thurlow in the 1959 FA Cup run, Max Briggs was a local lad in a successful Norwich side as they went on to win the Second Division title and bring top flight football to Norfolk for the first time.

Born just outside Norwich, a short jog from Carrow Road, Briggs more than anyone could appreciate what Norwich's success meant to their supporters and how the team's achievements on the pitch raised spirits and uplifted a whole community.

Briggs was one of four Norfolk born players, including Hall of Famer Dave Stringer, that gave the Championship winning side a local heartbeat. He had represented South Norfolk schools, the County team and Norwich juniors but it looked as if his future lay in insurance when he joined the Royal Exchange Insurance Company on leaving school. As his career in insurance was taking off he continued to play at a decent level and, after impressing with the Norwich B team, Briggs was offered professional terms in December 1967 aged 19.

It wasn't until the following season, 1968–69, that Briggs made his first team debut a 2–2 draw at home to Bury. This began a spell of nine games over September and October, including the 4–2 League Cup victory at Portman Road, that Briggs played in before injury intervened. He played only one further game that season away at Oxford on 1 February 1969. Norwich won 2–0 and Briggs scored his first and only Norwich goal, unfortunately witnessed by just 9,305 at the Manor Ground.

The next couple of seasons, 1969–70 and 1970–71, saw Briggs appear in approximately half of Norwich's League games as a combination of injury and team selection prevented a consistent run in the team. In the Championship winning season of 1971–72, Briggs had played in only four games of the 13 match unbeaten run at the start of the season. However, as the season progressed, Briggs was to play a central role in Norwich's title charge.

Playing mostly in central midfield, Briggs provided energy and defensive know-how, supplementing the flare of Hall of Famers Graham Paddon and Ken Foggo. His work ethic epitomised Hall of Famer Ron Saunder's team and their determination to succeed that season. Briggs played in 27 League games including the last six games of the season, as Norwich were pushed all the way to the title by rivals Birmingham and Millwall.

Briggs played in Norwich's first ever First Division game on 12 August, a 1–1 draw at home to Everton. He went on to make 34 appearances, his most to date, in that historic season of 1972–73. In just five years he had gone from insurance clerk to the highest level of English football.

In addition to the League, Briggs played 17 Cup games, including Norwich's debut in the recently formed Texaco Cup. The Cup was designed to cash in on the increasingly popularity of European football, pitting sides from England, Scotland and Ireland against each other. Briggs captained the side in Norwich's first game in the competition; despite a 1–2 defeat at Dundee, Norwich progressed after the second leg. Briggs was the only Norwich player to play every game in the competition which eventually saw Norwich lose 2–4 on aggregate to rivals Ipswich in a two-legged Final, with the home leg at Carrow Road attracting a Cup record crowd of 35,798.

Briggs also played every game of Norwich's League Cup run that ultimately ended in their first trip to the home of English Football. It was Norwich's first Wembley Final and the first time Norwich had played before a crowd of 100,000. Unfortunately a late Ralph Coates goal gave Tottenham the Cup, but this disappointment was to be later replaced with joy as Norwich clinched First Division survival. Briggs played his part in a tense 2–1 win over relegation candidates Crystal Palace.

After relegation survival and two Cup Final appearances, the 1973–74 season was an anticlimax for Briggs as Norwich struggled to build on the momentum of the previous season. Briggs played 24 League games and another five in the Texaco Cup in a Norwich side that struggled. His last game for Norwich came on 5 February 1974 when he featured in Norwich's only away win of the season, a 2–1 against an up and coming QPR side.

Troubled by injuries, Briggs moved to Second Division Oxford United where he made 97 appearances before eventually retiring with cartilage and ligament damage.

Max Briggs made 170 appearances for Norwich scoring one goal.

Duncan Forbes

June 1941, Scotland   **Player 1968–80**

Norwich City's very own 'Captain Marvel' Duncan Forbes was the inspiration behind the Norwich side of the early 1970s. A natural leader, Forbes became the first man since Hall of Famer Stan Ramsey in 1933–34 to lift a League Championship Trophy, the first man to lead Norwich out at Wembley and the first man to skipper Norwich in the top Division.

When Norwich manager Lol Morgan signed Forbes in September 1968 for £10,000 he was purchasing a player with proven experience. Forbes had left his native Scotland in 1961 and settled at Colchester United where he spent seven years, racking up 270 appearances as Colchester yo-yo'd between the Third and Fourth Divisions.

Forbes made his Norwich debut on 9 October 1968 in a 0–1 home defeat to Crystal Palace and soon became a regular in the Canaries back line. In his first full season, 1969–70, he played every League game. He captained Norwich for the first time on 15 November 1969 in the hostile atmosphere of Millwall's Old Den, and would hold the armband for five of the next six seasons. His totally committed displays at the heart of the Norwich defence, where he was prepared to put his body on the line for City's cause, made him a hit with the fans and won him the 1969–70 Player of the Season award.

1969 had seen the arrival of new Norwich manager and Hall of Famer Ron Saunders; Forbes became Saunders' voice and represented his character on the pitch. Before Saunders' appointment, Morgan had switched Hall of Famer Dave Stringer from full-back to centre-half and under Saunders this was to develop into one of Norwich's best ever centre-back partnerships. Both Stringer and Forbes were tough, uncompromising defenders, with each instinctively knowing the other's game. Forbes would be the man to harass the opposition number nine, challenging in the air and on the ground, while Stringer would provide the cover.

The Forbes-Stringer partnership really came together in the 1971–72 Championship winning season, with Norwich's success based around a solid defence. A

record start to the season of 13 unbeaten games saw only seven goals conceded and seven clean sheets, at the time the best defensive record in the country. After the record was ended at Millwall, Norwich suffered a dip in form that coincided with Forbes missing 15 games with a hamstring injury. Forbes' return to the team on 11 March 1972 was welcomed by all, as it followed a run of five without victory including a 0–4 loss to promotion rivals Birmingham.

The skipper's return proved crucial as he came up with winning headers in two consecutive home games – both 1–0 wins, over Sheffield Wednesday and Swindon – that ultimately saw Norwich over the finishing line for promotion and Forbes holding aloft the Second Division trophy during a civic reception at City Hall.

On 12 August 1972 Forbes led his team out for the first time in Division One, and went on to captain the club at venues such as White Hart Lane, Anfield and Old Trafford. He had another spell out injured, returning to fitness just in time to lead Norwich out for their first ever Cup Final at Wembley on 3 March 1973. After a disappointing performance and a 0–1 defeat to Tottenham on the biggest of stages, Forbes rallied his teammates for the relegation battle that Norwich faced. Again, Forbes inspired the team to success, this time securing their First Division status.

With a new Norwich manager – Hall of Famer John Bond – at the helm, Forbes lost the captaincy for the 1973–74 season. With Norwich relegated at the end of the season, Forbes was identified as the man to lead the team back from Division Two. The Forbes-Stringer partnership was once again the bedrock behind another promotion, with only 37 goals conceded and 20 clean sheets. The season also saw a return to Wembley in the 1975 League Cup Final. Forbes is still one of only two Norwich players to have led his team out at Wembley and the only player to have done it twice.

The 1975–76 season was the last for Forbes as a first team regular and captain. Missing just three League games he captained Norwich to their best ever finish, 10th in Division One, as Norwich for once enjoyed a low-key end of season run in.

Now in his mid-30s, Forbes made only 19 League appearances over the next three seasons as Norwich established themselves in the top flight. He was awarded a testimonial on 11 April 1978; the 1971–72 champions reunited to beat the current first team 3–0.

Forbe's testimonial appeared to signal the end of a great Norwich career but on 30 August 1980, at Anfield, home of champions Liverpool, he made a first-team appearance just under 18 months after his 'last' game. He played another two games in the 1980–81 season; the last was on 11 October 1980, a 1–1 home draw with Wolverhampton. Aged 39 years and 114 days, Forbes became Norwich's second oldest player and the oldest to have played in the top Division.

On retirement Forbes stayed at Carrow Road working in the club's commercial department, as well as keeping a hand in playing matters through scouting.

Duncan Forbes made 357 appearances for Norwich, 15th in the all-time listing, scoring 12 goals.

Ron Saunders

November 1932, Merseyside   Manager 1969–73

On his appointment as Norwich manager in July 1969, Ron Saunders' brief was simple; to get Norwich promoted to the First Division. In just three years Saunders had completed his objective and in doing so became the first manager to bring First Division football to Norwich in the club's 64-year history.

Saunders had already had a distinguished playing career scoring 156 goals, mostly for Portsmouth. On retirement he successfully made the transition to manager, first with Yeovil and then in 1968 with Oxford. At Oxford he had taken over a side adrift at the foot of Division Two and led them to a third bottom finish which, in those days, was enough to avoid relegation.

At Norwich meanwhile, manager Lol Morgan had been in charge for three seasons. Despite some high profile signings, Norwich were unable to progress beyond mid-table finishes. The 1968–69 season saw another disappointing 13th place finish which was reflected in crowds falling below 10,000 for the last two home games. A change was needed; chairman and Hall of Famer Geoffrey Watling fought a tough battle with Oxford before eventually unveiling Saunders in July 1969.

Saunders' first season, 1969–70, was a transitional period as he began to stamp his mark on the squad. He brought in Hall of Famers Graham Paddon and Peter Silvester to add some flair to the team, and despite another mid-table finish the signs were good, as Norwich finished the season unbeaten in their last 12 League games.

Disappointingly, Norwich failed to build on their fine end to the 1969–70 season, finishing 10th in 1970–71. Fortunately chairman Watling did not panic and Saunders was allowed to continue a project that all came together in 1971–72, culminating in the Second Division Championship.

The 1971–72 Championship winning side was a testament to the hard work and organisational skills of Saunders. Under him

Norwich, as they were some 12 years earlier under Hall of Famer Archie Macaulay, were the fittest team in the League. Stories of intense training sessions on Mousehold Heath became part of the legend. Norwich used their high fitness levels to play a high tempo game, constantly pressing the ball and never letting their opponents settle. Saunders organised the team with every player knowing his job. He also fostered a team spirit that was to become particularly important during a couple of periods where results went against Norwich.

As well as a good man-manager, Saunders was an effective coach who would improve a player. Six members of the Championship team were part of a Norwich side that preceded Saunders and had consistently finished mid-table. He added to that core with some wise signings made at the right times, none more so than the additions of Hall of Famers David Cross and Jimmy Bone during the 1971–72 season. Under Saunders Norwich became difficult to beat, especially at Carrow Road where they went through the whole 1971–72 season unbeaten, having lost only two home games the season before.

Norwich would need all their team spirit and high fitness levels to survive their first season among the elite of the First Division in the 1972–73 season. Saunders' first season as a First Division manager saw him pit his wits against some of the game's greatest managers including Bill Nicholson, Brian Clough, Don Revie and Bill Shankly.

In a difficult season Saunders did achieve the dream of every manager when he led his side out at Wembley, for the League Cup Final in March 1973, the first Norwich manager to experience this. Meanwhile in the League, Saunders again demonstrated his managerial abilities, bringing in the experienced and functional Trevor Hockey at the expense of the more flamboyant Bone. Hockey was more suited to a relegation dogfight and he played the last 13 games of the season that ended with Norwich avoiding an instant return to Division Two.

Norwich got off to a poor start in the 1973–74 season and had won only two matches by the time Everton arrived at Carrow Road on 17 November 1973. After a 1–3 defeat to Everton, Saunders' boyhood club, Saunders resigned after a tense boardroom meeting. By the end of the week Saunders was the new Manchester City manager.

Saunders had just one season at Manchester City where he again reached the League Cup Final, before switching to Aston Villa. At Villa Park Saunders became an Aston Villa legend, beginning with promotion back to Division One in his first season and a unique hat-trick of three consecutive League Cup Finals with three different teams. This time Saunders was a winner at the expense of his old club Norwich!

Six seasons later, Saunders won the big prize with Aston Villa when they won the League in 1980–81, their first Championship since 1909–10. However, he left Aston Villa before they were crowned champions of Europe the following season. Staying in the West Midlands Saunders also managed Birmingham and WBA before leaving the game in 1987.

Ron Saunders managed Norwich for 221 games.

Peter Silvester

February 1948, Berkshire   **Player 1969–74**

When new Norwich manager and Hall of Famer Ron Saunders was appointed in July 1969, he was tasked with taking Norwich into the promised land of Division One. With a limited transfer budget, Saunders had to spend wisely – something he did when he spent £20,000 on striker Peter Silvester.

Silvester was Saunders' first signing when he joined Norwich in September 1969, the first signing in the Saunders revolution that was to end in promotion. He was signed from his home town club Reading where he had made 79 appearances since signing professional terms in February 1966. After scoring 26 goals in the Third Division he was ready to make the step up to the Second Division.

When he joined Norwich, the club were in a bit of a rut; the supporters were beginning to lose patience after a number of false dawns and were still coming to terms with the sale of crowd favourite and Hall of Famer Hugh Curran. Silvester was therefore under pressure to produce from the start.

Silvester made his debut on 16 September 1969 in a 1–3 loss at Birmingham. This was followed by a 0–4 at Bristol City as Norwich's promising start to the 1969–70 season came to an end. He did score on his home debut in a 2–0 win over Oxford and scored one in the 6–0 thrashing of Birmingham (the first 6–0 since Stoke in 1963) in the penultimate game of a season that Norwich finished strongly. Silvester scored 10 goals in his debut season, Norwich's second top scorer, one behind Hall of Famer Ken Foggo.

In his first full season, 1970–71, Silvester went on to outshine his more famous striking partner, Albert Bennett. He scored a total of 16 goals in another season where Norwich struggled to challenge at the top of the table. Silvester missed only three games that season and scored three doubles in games against Orient, Birmingham and Sunderland. On 16 September 1970, exactly a year after his debut, he scored his lone Norwich Cup goal in a low-key second round replay win over Chester. Meanwhile, the FA

Cup was less memorable; Silvester was part of the Norwich side knocked out 1–5 in the third round to Wolverhampton.

Silvester's 16 goals were enough to finish second in the top goalscorer listing, again behind Ken Foggo who had scored just one more. Both players enjoyed a good start to 1971–72, a season that would end in mixed emotions for Silvester. In Norwich's record 13 game unbeaten start to a season Silvester scored six goals, all coming in wins. He scored in the 1–2 defeat to Millwall on 23 October 1971 when the run finally came to an end. By this time Silvester had a new striking partner, Hall of Famer David Cross, as Norwich looked to keep up their momentum at the top.

Silvester scored another five goals with Norwich winning four and drawing one, the draw coming against promotion challengers Birmingham where Silvester's goal was to earn a vital point. Then on 22 January 1972 disaster struck when Silvester suffered a serious knee injury in the 1–1 home draw with Preston. The injury kept him out for the rest of the season as he watched Norwich go on to win the Second Division title from the touchlines. Despite missing the last 16 games he played a significant role in Norwich's first ever promotion to Division One and his 12 League goals meant he was second top scorer, behind Ken Foggo for the third successive year.

Unfortunately Silvester's knee injury was to keep him out for 18 months as he required surgery on his cartilage. A skilful forward with a clever footballing brain and good movement, he would surely have gone on to become a success in the First Division. However, he missed the whole of Norwich's 1972–73 First Division debut season.

Silvester eventually made his top flight debut almost two years after that fateful game versus Preston, playing in a 2–4 defeat to West Ham on 1 January 1974. He played just two more Division One games for Norwich; the last was a 0–1 loss to champions Liverpool.

With a new manager and new strikers at Norwich Silvester moved first on loan to Colchester and then permanently to Southend. While at Southend he made a career for himself in the more laid back environment of the North America Soccer League where he represented four different clubs as well as the NASL all-star team. In the US he showed he had not lost his scoring touch with 14 goals in 18 games in his first season, while back in England he netted 32 in 81 games for Southend before his eventual retirement following more knee injuries.

Peter Silvester made 113 Norwich appearances scoring 37 goals.

Graham Paddon

August 1950, Manchester   **Player 1969–73 and 1976–81**

Graham Paddon is the third Hall of Famer to have appeared for Norwich in two separate spells as a player. His 12 years at Norwich, divided by a successful period at West Ham, saw him become an integral part of the club in the 1970s. He was a player held in high esteem by both Norwich and West Ham fans alike.

Paddon started his career as a highly talented youngster at First Division Coventry. His potential was spotted by Norwich manager and Hall of Famer Ron Saunders and reflected in the £25,000 transfer fee to secure his services.

Signing in October 1969, Paddon fitted the profile of the type of player Saunders wanted; he was young, hungry and had something to prove after failing to break into the Coventry first team. Paddon also had a tremendous work ethic that, coupled with silky skills, a great shot and range of passing, meant he was soon to become a regular fixture in Saunders' Norwich side. He played every game of the 1969–70 season after making his debut on 4 October 1969.

Paddon continued to command a first team place in 1970–71 and played a major role in the Championship winning team of 1971–72. Missing only two games of the title winning season, Paddon scored eight League goals, all from midfield. He scored four goals in games that finished 1–1, earning Norwich valuable points in the days of two points for a win.

One of the more creative members of the promotion team, Paddon had a sweet left foot and a fierce shot. This was particularly evident when he scored the pick of the bunch – a 30-yard effort that curled away from the 'keeper into the top corner – in an important 5–1 win over Blackpool on 25 March 1972. It was a win that set the impetus for the final promotion push; promotion to the First Division was sealed at Orient on 24 April 1972 when a Paddon penalty helped Norwich to a 2–1 win.

The talented Paddon made the step up to First Division football with ease, playing in 38 of Norwich's 42 League games in 1972–73 and scoring seven League goals. He flourished in the

First Division environment where he was allowed more time on the ball which he could use to influence a game. He took Norwich's free-kicks, penalties and long throws and many of the team's attacking moves came through him. He scored important goals that season including the winner in Norwich's first ever top flight home win, 1–0 against Derby on 26 August 1972, and goals in victories over Norwich's relegation rivals Crystal Palace (2–0) and WBA (2–0). On 17 March he scored Norwich's first ever penalty in the First Division earning a valuable point in a 1–1 draw against Leicester.

It was in that season's League Cup that Paddon was to enjoy his greatest game in a Norwich shirt. He topped his two goals in a third round win at Hull with a hat-trick in the fifth round at Highbury, home to the mighty Arsenal. Arsenal were riding high in the League (eventually finishing second) and a Cup side of some pedigree. Paddon's hat-trick stunned the home crowd; it is still to this date the only hat-trick scored by a Norwich player against Arsenal and was the catalyst for Norwich reaching Wembley for the first time in the 1973 League Cup Final.

Paddon's exploits at Highbury had put him on the footballing map. In December 1973, the following season, he was transferred to West Ham in exchange for Hall of Famer Ted MacDougall as Norwich looked to solve a goalscoring crisis. Arriving at a West Ham side deep in relegation trouble he helped the team to a 2–1 win over leaders Manchester City and eventually to First Division safety. The run to safety included two Paddon goals in a 2–4 victory on his return to Carrow Road on New Year's Day 1974.

Paddon went on to achieve much success in a West Ham midfield that included Trevor Brooking, Billy Bonds and Frank Lampard. He won an FA Cup-winners' medal in 1975 and runners'-up medal in the European Cup-winners' Cup before he made a welcome return to Carrow Road in November 1976.

Despite breaking his leg in his third game back with Norwich, Paddon went on to make another 143 appearances in a Norwich side that had settled in Division One. He captained the side for the first time in March 1978 – at Ipswich of all places – and had his first season as an ever-present in 1980–81. Unfortunately Norwich were relegated that season and Paddon's last ever Norwich game, a disappointing 1–2 home defeat to Oldham, was back in the Second Division where it had all started 12 years ago.

Graham Paddon made 340 appearances for Norwich scoring 37 goals.

Doug Livermore

December 1947, Merseyside   **Player   1970–75**

Doug Livermore was an important member of the Norwich team that won the 1971–72 Division Two Championship and went on to play in the First Division and at Wembley both firsts for Norwich, the following season.

Livermore began his career at the best in the land when he joined local club and League champions Liverpool in November 1965. Managed by the legendary Bill Shankly, the Liverpool team of the time included many stars such as Ian St John, Roger Hunt and Tommy Smith. With such talent ahead of him in the pecking order Livermore found opportunities limited in the first team. He did appear to make a breakthrough towards the end of the 1969–70 season, playing the final 13 games and helping Liverpool to a fifth place finish.

The stiff competition at Liverpool was Norwich's gain when the promising Livermore was signed by manager and Hall of Famer Ron Saunders in November 1970. It was a tough decision for Livermore with Liverpool challenging for the title, but Norwich offered him games and the chance to make a name for himself.

Having been a fringe player at Liverpool, Livermore immediately established himself in the Norwich team; he went on to play in all 25 remaining games of the 1970–71 season. Saunders had converted Livermore from a striker at Liverpool to a central midfielder, where Norwich benefitted from his energy and inventiveness. Playing in a more defensive 'anchor' role, Livermore provided the platform for the attacking flare of his fellow midfielders and hall of Famers Ken Foggo and Graham Paddon.

In his first full season at Carrow Road (1971–72), Livermore became a main component of Saunders' hard working side that was to sweep all before them to win the Second Division Championship. Livermore missed just one League game that season (only three players played every game). His consistent performances, allied with his big game experience, proved particularly valuable in the big games towards the end of the season, as Norwich were pushed all the way by Birmingham and Millwall.

Norwich's debut season in the First Division in 1972–73 coincided with Livermore's peak footballing years. He was in the Norwich midfield for the opening First Division League game versus Everton and kept his place for the next 31 consecutive League games. Initially, Norwich were comfortably in the top half of the table, but a slump in form saw a run of 19 games without a victory which left them deep in relegation trouble.

Sandwiched within that poor run was a much better run in the League Cup. Livermore played in six out of the seven League Cup games and was instrumental in Norwich reaching Wembley for the first time. He impressed in the 3–0 fifth round win at Arsenal and also in the dramatic semi-final versus Chelsea. Taking an impressive 2–0 lead into the home leg, Norwich were within touching distance of Wembley, leading 5–2 on aggregate before fog caused the game to be abandoned. Fortunately Norwich came through the rearranged game 1–0 and Livermore got to play his first game on the hallowed Wembley turf.

Livermore missed five games towards the end of the 1972–73 season, which included an away trip and 1–3 defeat to his old club Liverpool on 24 March 1973. His return on 14 April 1973 was a boost for Norwich in their relegation battle starting with a 1–0 win against Chelsea, Livermore played in further wins against WBA and Crystal Palace as Norwich won three out of the last five games to finish third bottom and another season in Division One.

A serious knee injury was to limit Livermore's appearances over the next two seasons, 1973–74 and 1974–75. He played just 18 games before eventually joining Cardiff in August 1975. An injury free run saw him help Cardiff to promotion to Division Two in 1975–76; however, Livermore knew his injuries would limit his future as a player and he began to take his coaching badges.

After retiring as a player, Livermore enjoyed a successful coaching career with Cardiff before returning to coach the Norwich reserves. He had spells at Swansea and Tottenham where at Spurs he even held the caretaker manager role briefly in 1987. In the mid-90s he was Roy Evans' assistant manager at Liverpool before taking the same role back at Norwich under Bruce Rioch, Bryan Hamilton and Hall of Famer Nigel Worthington. Livermore can be credited for the development of several Norwich youth players that were to break into the first team during that period.

Doug Livermore made 139 appearances for Norwich scoring six goals.

Russell Allison

October 1957, Hampshire   **Groundsman 1970–80**

Beginning with his father, followed by himself and now his son, Russell Allison's family have been connected with Norwich Football Club for much of the club's existence. All three have served the club with distinction in the role of groundsman.

First Allison senior looked after the pitch at the Nest, the Canaries' first home. The Nest was built inside an old quarry with steep, chalk walls and limited space; not an ideal home for the players, or for the groundstaff who would have had to look after the pitch with the most basic of equipment.

Allison's father moved with the team to Carrow Road in 1935 where he was heavily involved in the laying of the new pitch; the ground was built in just 82 days. During his time at Carrow Road, he would involve his son Russell, teaching him the trade that would set him up for future years.

Carrow Road was gradually developed over the next few decades including work on the stadium and the introduction of the floodlights that nearly bankrupted the club. On the pitch, the biggest challenge facing the Allisons was ensuring that the ground was playable during the harsh winter months; a combination of poor weather and overuse due to the number and frequency of games was a constant challenge.

Particularly challenging seasons were 1958–59, where the FA Cup run would mean a period of 17 games in just 47 days, and 1962–63 where, following the winter snow, it took the Groundstaff 11 attempts to get the FA Cup third round match against Blackpool on (the tie eventually took place on 4 March 1963).

Russell Allison finally succeeded his father as head groundsman in the summer of 1970, while his brother took over responsibilities at the Trowse training ground. Allison's promotion coincided with the beginning of a golden period for Norwich, where the Carrow Road pitch hosted First Division football and the team got to play on the most famous turf of all at Wembley.

The First Division debut season in 1972–73 was a test for Allison and his team; Norwich played 60 games in total that season, a club record. The season also included Norwich's highest profile abandonment when the League Cup semi-final second leg at Carrow Road was called off with just six minutes to go, although this was due to fog rather than anything Allison could control with the pitch.

The 1970s and 80s would become renowned for the mud bath pitches that made a mockery of many a game. The pitch at Carrow Road, thanks to the efforts of the team, tended to be one of the better pitches in the League. The state of the pitch during this time would prove to be important as Norwich were developing a passing brand of football under Hall of Famers John Bond and Ken Brown that was reliant on a good playing surface.

It was during this era, and because of the problems of costs associated with pitch maintenance and postponements, that some clubs began to turn to plastic pitches. The first was at Loftus Road, QPR, followed by Kenilworth Road, Luton, in 1985. Norwich would play many games on both of these pitches but, as with many away clubs, their record was poor with the unnatural bounce of the ball difficult to adapt to. This advantage, and the increasing risk of injury, led to the banning of such pitches and a return to grass.

In 1984 a fire destroyed the main stand but one of the key features, the original clock, was saved by Allison and looked after by his family until it was restored in the new Geoffrey Watling stand just before the 2009–10 season.

The next challenge faced by Allison after the fire was the installation of a new pitch and, for the first time, under soil heating. This was a revolutionary introduction to prevent postponement of games because of frost, which often left pitches unplayable and the risk of injury high.

Over the next few decades, during which Allison's son took over the reins under the guidance of head groundsman Gary Kemp, the Carrow Road pitch would be relaid twice. Each time, more sophisticated techniques were used, resulting in the carpet-like pitch that we see today.

Allison himself was honoured with the naming of the Russell Allison Lounge, providing facilities for the boisterous Barclay Enders.

David Cross

December 1950, Lancashire   **Player 1971–73**

David Cross' arrival as a Norwich City player was made very public when his club record £40,000 transfer was announced via the club's tannoy system on 6 October 1971, during the League Cup third round tie at home to Carlisle.

The half-time announcement ended much speculation about Norwich's search for a striker, which had been manager and Hall of Famer Ron Saunders' priority for many months.

Ironically, Cross had actually played most of his 59 games for his first club Rochdale as a right-winger. However, he had shown his potential as a forward, scoring 21 goals in his two seasons at his local club.

Although only 21 when he signed for Norwich, Cross had the potential and hunger to succeed at the higher level. He joined a Norwich squad that were top of Division Two and at that point unbeaten in the League. Despite this lofty position Norwich had struggled for goals, scoring 13 in the first 10 games with the unbeaten run including three 0–0 draws. There was a reliance on goals from Hall of Famers Peter Silvester and Ken Foggo, and a risk that injury or loss of form for either could derail Norwich's promotion challenge.

David Cross made his debut on 9 October 1971 in a 1–1 draw at Sunderland. A further three games without a goal, in hand with his high profile arrival, had begun to increase the pressure on Cross before he scored in a 2–1 win over Cardiff. Another goal followed in the next match – another 2–1, this time against Hull – as Cross settled into Saunders' hard working, organised team.

He went on to score eight goals in the Championship winning team. He, like all players in that side, constantly harassed the opposition, never giving his defensive marker a moment's peace. Cross complemented his striking partners; he was an expert at holding up the ball and bringing the midfielders into the attack. His eight-goal total included a crucial goal in the top of the table clash at home to Millwall where a 2–2 draw in front of 34,000 kept Norwich top. He scored twice over the important Easter period with one in the 2–0 away win at Charlton and another to secure a point at home to Bristol City – both goals kept the momentum going at a vital time in the season.

Cross played in Norwich's first game in the First Division in the 1972–73 season, but he had to wait 10 matches before scoring his first top flight goal in a 3–2 win in Norwich's first ever League game versus Arsenal. During the season Cross proved that he could make the transition to the First Division, scoring 11 League goals in his debut season at that level.

In what was to be a difficult season for Norwich, Cross scored some critical goals, earning important points. He scored a double on 14 October 1972 in a 2–1 win against Tottenham, and another double in April 1973 where Norwich earned a point in a 2–2 at Goodison Park, Everton. Two weeks after Norwich's first League visit to Everton, Cross scored the winner in the home match versus Chelsea, where the 1–0 victory ended a barren spell of 19 games without a win.

Chelsea were also Norwich's opponents in the 1973 League Cup semi-final; Cross scored in the first leg at Stamford Bridge to set Norwich on their way to a first ever visit to Wembley. Cross had earned his day at Wembley, playing in all seven League Cup games with a return of three goals.

Back in the relegation dogfight, Cross scored the winner in a tense 'four pointer' at bottom club WBA with the two points gained ultimately securing Norwich's First Division status. Cross ended the season with 17 goals in total – Norwich's top goalscorer in a historic season.

The following season, 1973–74, got off to a bad start for Norwich, winning just one in their first 13 games. Cross' form was also suffering, scoring only two goals during this run. Cross made his last Norwich appearance on 10 November 1973 in a 0–2 defeat to Stoke. He was sold to Coventry for £150,000 Norwich's first sale over £100,000 just a week prior to manager (and his mentor) Saunders' Carrow Road exit.

Cross struggled initially at Coventry and took a while to win over the Coventry support, but 30 goals in 91 games represented a good return. In 1976 a short spell at WBA was followed by four and a half happy years at West Ham. Like Hall of Famer Graham Paddon before him, Cross enjoyed success at West Ham, which included an FA Cup-winner's medal in 1980, a hat-trick in the European Cup-winners' Cup, and being top scorer in the promotion winning side of 1980–81 where his 34 goals won him the Second Division golden boot.

After leaving West Ham, in August 1982, Cross played for another seven League clubs before eventually retiring in 1987. Since then, Cross has remained in football with coaching roles at Oldham Athletic.

David Cross made 106 appearances for Norwich scoring 30 goals.

Jimmy Bone

September 1949, Scotland   Player 1972–73

A member of the 'Hot Cross Bone' partnership (as it was once dubbed in the local press) Jimmy Bone, along with his strike partner and Hall of Famer David Cross, helped fire Norwich to the Division Two title, First Division football and a first Wembley appearance.

Just like Hall of Famer and member of the 1959 FA Cup team Matt Crowe, Bone had started his career in Scotland with First Division club Partick Thistle.

The highlight of his early career was a shock 4–1 League Cup win over Celtic in 1971 with Bone himself scoring the fourth goal of an incredible Final. Bone's performance in that shock Cup win alerted scouts in England but it was Norwich manager and Hall of Famer Ron Saunders that won the race for his signature, signing Bone for £30,000 on the leap year day of 29 February 1972.

Norwich were top of the Second Division in the 1971–72 season when Bone signed, but they had just lost leading scorer and Hall of Famer Peter Silvester to a long term injury. Without Silvester's goals there was a risk that all the good work that season could be undone. In fact, Bone made his debut in a traumatic 0–4 defeat to Birmingham on 4 March 1972 that saw the Midlands side replace Norwich at the top of Division Two, a position Norwich had held for the last 23 weeks.

Bone opened his account the following week in his home debut, to earn a point in a 1–1 draw against high-flying Sunderland. Bone went on to score another three goals as Norwich regained and kept top spot. He formed an instant understanding up front with Cross, the two of them scoring in the same game on three occasions. Whereas Cross' game was more suited to playing with his back to goal holding up the ball, Bone was happier attacking defenders and running with the ball at pace. He would read Cross' flicks and terrorise defenders with his work rate and persistence.

At the end of the season Bone was rewarded for his performances with his first Scotland international cap when he played in a 2–2 friendly against Yugoslavia in June 1972. Bone became the first player to win a Scottish cap while playing for Norwich.

His most defining moment in a Norwich shirt came on the opening day of the 1972–73 season, Norwich's first ever game in the First Division. The opponents at Carrow Road on 12 August 1972 were Everton, a fitting team for Norwich's big day as they were founder members of the Football League and, along with Arsenal, had spent most of their history in the First Division. A crowd of 25,851 gathered at Carrow Road with a mix of excitement and fear in the air. Norwich started brightly and a three man move saw Bone collect a chipped pass into the box. Bone controlled the ball and beat his man, before dinking the ball with the outside of his boot into the net to score Norwich's first ever First Division goal.

Everton's second half equaliser saw the points shared but Norwich did not have to wait long for their first ever top flight victory, which came at Portman Road of all places. Again, Bone was among the goalscorers in a 2–1 victory in front of 29,828 on 15 August 1972.

The autumn of 1972 was a prosperous time for Bone, scoring two in the League Cup second round that would set Norwich on the journey to the Final. He scored two in the Texaco Cup as Norwich overcame Dundee in the first round. In the League, Bone scored in an important 2–0 win over Crystal Palace. Finally, on 18 October 1972, he scored his first international goal, helping Scotland to an impressive 4–1 World Cup Qualifying win in Denmark.

Bone would only score another two League goals for Norwich (although he did score an important goal in the League Cup semi-final), before he was controversially sold to fellow Division One team Sheffield United. Bone was exchanged for Midfielder Trevor Hockey as Norwich looked to adapt their formation and style for the relegation battle that lay ahead.

Jimmy Bone played his last Norwich game on 10 February 1973, a home loss to West Ham, this final game coming just under a year after his debut. In his short time at Norwich he had endeared himself to the Norwich supporters who loved his energy and positive play, while his infectious personality had helped lift spirits for the final promotion push.

His time at Sheffield United was short and after just 31 games he moved back to Scotland with Glasgow giants Celtic. He spent the rest of his career playing for a number of clubs in Scotland, as well as spells overseas in Canada and Hong Kong, before coaching and eventually rising to become manager of St Mirren.

Jimmy Bone made 51 appearances for Norwich scoring 15 goals.

Colin Suggett

December 1948, County Durham   **Player 1973–78**

Colin Suggett was the first Hall of Famer to join Norwich City as a First Division club when he signed in February 1973 for a club record at the time of £75,000.

For his money, Norwich manager and Hall of Famer Ron Saunders was getting an experienced attacking midfielder who had succeeded in the professional game since representing England Under-15s, Under-18s and England Youth as a youngster growing up in the North East.

Suggett's first breakthrough was with his local club Sunderland. He made his debut in 1966 in the First Division aged just 18 and finished the following season as top goalscorer. In 1969 he became WBA's first £100,000 signing; he played 69 games for the Baggies, all in the top flight.

When Suggett left WBA for Norwich on 16 February 1973 he was swapping one relegation battle for another, with both clubs at the wrong end of the League. Norwich, in their first season 1972–73 among the elite, were in a period of free-fall. Prior to Suggett's arrival they had lost their last four and were 11 without victory. Suggett's transfer was overshadowed by the sale and exchange of Hall of Famer Jimmy Bone for Trevor Hockey, as Saunders looked to add some steel to the Norwich midfield. Both Suggett and Hockey made their debuts on 24 February 1973 in another defeat, this time 0–1 at home to Newcastle.

Hockey and Suggett played in the last 10 games of the season and while Hockey took much of the credit for Norwich's survival through his swashbuckling displays, Suggett also played his part, adding some invention and quality to Norwich's attacking line-up. In the 'winner takes all' encounter at home to Crystal Palace on 24 April 1973, Norwich were struggling after conceding a first-half penalty. Suggett equalised and calmed the nerves, setting the platform for

Hall of Famer Dave Stringer's late winner. The win spared Norwich from relegation, sending Palace down instead in front of Carrow Road's second highest ever League attendance of 36,688.

Suggett took his good form into the next season, 1973–74, when he scored in the opening day defeat at Wolverhampton. Suggett was an ever-present in the League that season scoring five goals. He scored an equaliser at high-flying Derby County and hit two in two games in March 1974, helping Norwich to back to back victories over Birmingham and Stoke. Despite these wins Norwich were in another relegation scrap and this time there was no happy ending. They finished bottom of Division One with 29 points; their lowest total since the 28 obtained in 1946–47.

Colin Suggett's close control and natural ability on the ball was to stand out as Norwich embarked on a season (1974–75) back in Division Two. He was credited with many of the assists for free scoring forwards and Hall of Famers Ted MacDougall and Phil Boyer, as well as scoring eight goals himself. He got off to a good start, scoring in consecutive 1–1 draws in August – both away games, at Aston Villa and Southampton – in a campaign where Norwich would lose only five away games, a joint club record.

He also played his part as Norwich reached another League Cup Final at Wembley. He played in all 11 games in an exciting League Cup campaign, including knocking out his old club WBA in the third round and scoring against rivals Ipswich in the quarter-final. In a tense semi-final versus Division Two leaders Manchester United, Suggett's goal in the second leg was enough to edge Norwich to Wembley 3–2 on aggregate.

While Norwich were beaten in the League Cup Final by Aston Villa, both clubs ended the season with the main prize of promotion; for Norwich it was at their first attempt after last season's relegation. Suggett missed only one game in the promotion season and was voted Player of the Season, a great achievement considering the number of candidates.

Back in Division One for the 1975–76 season, Suggett played 38 League games; again, he was the creative spark behind the goals scored by the Norwich front two. The pick of Suggett's four goals came in a shock 3–1 win at champions elect Liverpool, as Norwich proved they could live with the best with a 10th place finish.

Suggett's appearances were hampered by injury in 1976–77 but he enjoyed a consistent run in the 1977–78 season where he played 38 League games in a 13th place finish. He was made captain for the first three games of the season, in which Norwich were unbeaten. He also repeated his trick of the 1975–76 season, scoring against champions Liverpool in a 2–1 victory on 10 December 1977. Suggett also scored in a thrilling 3–3 draw against Brian Clough's champions elect Nottingham Forest proving that he was a man for the big occasions.

Suggett's last appearance for the club was on 29 April 1978 against his old club WBA. In August 1978 he joined Newcastle United. As injuries restricted his playing appearances with Newcastle he moved into the club's coaching set up that saw the emergence of England's greatest player of his generation: Paul Gascoigne.

Colin Suggett made 243 appearances for Norwich scoring 29 goals.

Arthur South

June 1914, Norfolk   **Chairman 1973–85**

One of only two Hall of Famers born within the boundaries of the City of Norwich and the only Hall of Famer to be knighted, Sir Arthur South's legacy stretches way beyond his beloved Norwich City Football Club.

South had always been a public figure looking to serve the people of Norwich, representing them and their needs as he strove to improve all aspects of public service in Norwich.

In 1935, at the age of 21, he became the youngest councillor in the country when he was elected to Norwich City Council. His spell as councillor was only broken by World War Two when he served his country in the RAF.

South's first involvement with Norwich Football Club came during the crisis of 1957. With Norwich in dire financial straits following the purchase of new floodlights, coupled with falling gate receipts and an increasingly out of touch board, the club's very existence was at stake. South had been Sheriff and was now Lord Mayor and the ideal candidate to turn to in the club's hour of need.

After hosting a meeting of prominent local businessmen, South was elected chairman of an appeals committee tasked with raising £25,000, while the other Norwich born Hall of Famer, Geoffrey Watling, became chairman of the football club. Under South's guidance the appeals committee raised the target funds and South was made club vice-president as a mark of gratitude by the club.

While the role of vice-president was very much a figurehead position, South became more involved in the day to day running of the club when he joined the board as a director in 1966. When chairman Watling decided to step down in the summer of 1973, South was the natural candidate for the role and on the 30 August 1973 he was appointed chairman.

Watling had resigned after finally fulfilling his dreams of seeing First Division football at Carrow Road as well as seeing his team at Wembley. South was therefore walking straight into the top job at a First Division club. In fact, during his 12-year tenure, Norwich were in the First Division for all but two years. South's appointment also represented a time when football clubs were run by local men; far removed from the foreign investment common in the top two divisions today.

On the pitch, Norwich got off to a poor start under South's stewardship in the 1973–74 season, with things coming to a head on 17 November 1973 when manager and Hall of Famer Ron Saunders resigned immediately after a defeat to Everton. With Norwich struggling after two years of success under Saunders, South's first managerial appointment was to be important in shaping Norwich's future in the First Division. South showed great insight when he appointed Hall of Famer John Bond as manager in November 1973. Bond's only managerial experience had come in the Third Division at Bournemouth and his appointment was to cost Norwich £10,000 in compensation.

South had got the biggest decision of his chairmanship right, as Bond brought a new brand of football to Norwich and a style which the team is still associated with to this day. Under Bond, Norwich enjoyed a period of consolidation in the First Division, while the books were balanced with two £1 million transfers under South's stewardship.

Off the pitch, South received his knighthood in 1974 and was made freeman of Norwich in 1977. The South Stand at Carrow Road was named after him, and in 1975 it was turned into a modern all-seater stand complete with a roof. The River End was also developed from an open terrace to a two tier stand complete with Norwich's first fully functional executive boxes.

Another revenue stream that was developed under South was income from sponsorship with advertising boards introduced, and shirt sponsors were seen for the first time in 1983. South ensured that the extra income generated was used for the benefit of the football club, with the redevelopment of the Trowse training centre providing Bond with First Division quality facilities. South's commercial mind would no doubt have appreciated the redevelopment of the South Stand in 2003 and its rebranding as the Jarrold Stand.

It was a dispute over a stand that was to end South's association with Norwich. On 25 October 1984 a fire destroyed the City Stand, and following allegations surrounding the building of the new stand the Norwich board, including South, resigned on 25 November 1985.

In South's 12-year stewardship he had managed to balance development of the ground with success on the pitch, while many aspects of the modern game such as sponsorship were also started under him. One aspect of modern football not evident under South was the high turnover of management. South never sacked a manager, with only three working under him in 12 years.

Arthur South was Norwich chairman for 12 years. All three managers that worked under him are in the Hall of Fame.

John Bond

December 1932, Essex   **Manager 1973–80**

Brian Clough, Bobby Robson, Don Revie, Bob Paisley, Bill Nicholson, Ron Greenwood and Malcolm Allison, the 1970s were littered with personalities and characters, the good and great of football management. John Bond was at home among this illustrious group, establishing Norwich as a permanent fixture in the First Division through an attractive footballing philosophy and excellent man-management.

Bond had spent his entire playing career as a full-back at West Ham United, winning an FA Cup-winners' medal in 1964. He played over 400 games for the Hammers between 1950 and 1966, in a defensive unit that included England's greatest captain: Bobby Moore.

During his 16 years at Upton Park, Bond had been schooled in the famous West Ham 'academy'. Throughout all levels at the club the emphasis was on a short passing game, with footballers trained to be comfortable on the ball. The 'West Ham way' of playing football became renowned in England and it was something that Bond took with him as he embarked on his managerial career at Fourth Division Bournemouth.

Bond guided Bournemouth to promotion to Division Three in his first season as manager in 1970–71. He almost made it consecutive promotions the following season, 1971–72, but Bournemouth's third place finish came at a time when only the top two were promoted. At Bournemouth, Bond was developing a side of bright young talent that Norwich were to benefit from in the near future.

Bond joined Norwich in November 1973 after the sudden resignation of manager and Hall of Famer Ron Saunders. Under Saunders Norwich had enjoyed a rapid rise, first with the long awaited promotion to Division One then survival in the first season and a first Wembley Final. Saunders' success was based primarily on hard work and an organised team with an inner toughness and determination to succeed. Bond's arrival marked a

distinct change in focus to Saunders' resolute defence with more emphasis on ball work, pass and move and adding an overall attacking flair to the side. Off the pitch they were chalk and cheese; Saunders kept matters private and rarely spoke to the press while Bond was more outgoing, actively encouraging the media to sound his opinions and becoming a journalist's delight.

It took a while for Bond's influence to be felt at Norwich and he could not prevent relegation at the end of the 1973–74 season. Bond's solution was to raid his former club Bournemouth for players he knew and had helped develop. Hall of Famers Ted MacDougall, Phil Boyer, Mel Machin and Tony Powell all arrived from the south coast and all played their part in Norwich's instant return to the big time after finishing third in Division Two in 1974–75. Bond also became only the second manager to lead a Norwich team out at Wembley in the 1975 League Cup Final, but like his predecessor Saunders he could not lead his team to victory; they were defeated 0–1 by Aston Villa.

After the hard work of getting back in to Division One, it was crucial that Norwich remained there. This they achieved comfortably with a record high finish of 10th in the 1975–76 season. A key player in the success that season was Hall of Famer and World Cup winner Martin Peters. His signing in March 1975 was a major coup for Norwich and only made possible through Bond's reputation and his West Ham links.

Under Bond, Norwich spent the next four seasons comfortably in Division One. They were playing an attractive style of football which, like West Ham, they were to become associated with nationally. During this period Bond gave his son Kevin his debut in April 1976. He went on to make 161 appearances for Norwich, was an ever-present in the 1978–79 season and won Player of the Season the following year in 1979–80.

Norwich got off to a poor start in the 1980–81 season. Bond's record signing, Yugoslav international Drazen Muzinic had failed to fulfil his potential, and the pressure was on. Bond had always enjoyed a great working relationship with his chairman and Hall of Famer Arthur South, but in October 1980 he decided to take on the challenge of managing Manchester City. The Manchester side were struggling but had just bought two £1 million players, including Norwich Hall of Famer Kevin Reeves who had been with Bond as a youth player at Bournemouth. Reeves had been bought by Norwich for just £50,000 in 1977.

Bond had an instant impact at Manchester City, leading them to a mid-table finish and the 1981 FA Cup Final. The Cup run included a 0–6 thrashing of Norwich in the fourth round, Norwich's joint heaviest Cup defeat. Bond stayed at Manchester City until February 1983 before managing Burnley, Swansea, Birmingham and finally Shrewsbury.

John Bond managed Norwich for 340 games in just under seven years; he is the second longest serving Norwich manager.

Ted MacDougall

January 1947, Scotland　　　　　　　　　　　　　　　　　　　**Player 1973–76**

Ted MacDougall was an out and out goalscorer, a striker who achieved a number of 'firsts' during a distinguished playing career that finished with 256 goals in 535 games. Of these goals, 66 were scored for Norwich playing under manager and Hall of Famer John Bond, a man who always got the best out of MacDougall.

MacDougall first played under Bond at Bournemouth after starting his professional career with an impressive 34 goals in two seasons at struggling Fourth Division York.

His goals helped Bournemouth to promotion to the Third Division in the 1970–71 season. However, it was in the FA Cup first round the following season (1971–72) that MacDougall came to national prominence when he netted nine goals in Bournemouth's 11–0 win over non-League Margate.

Still a record in the famous old competition, the feat made MacDougall the most talked about striker in the country and eventually he got a big money move to the First Division with Manchester United. MacDougall's time at United coincided with the famous old club going through a transitional period and struggling on the pitch. After new manager Tom Docherty was appointed, MacDougall moved to West Ham and after just eight months he was reunited with John Bond at Norwich.

When he signed on 7 December 1973 he became Norwich's first purchase to exceed the £100,000 mark, costing a club record £140,000 that also saw Hall of Famer and fans' favourite Graham Paddon move in the other direction. Obviously under pressure, MacDougall got off to

a great start with the fans, scoring his first goal against Ipswich and a double against old club West Ham. Unfortunately, both games ended in defeat in a season that saw Norwich relegated, although on a personal front MacDougall finished the 1973–74 season top scorer with 13 goals.

Reunited with his old strike partner from the York and Bournemouth days, Hall of Famer Phil Boyer, MacDougall was an ever-present in the 1974–75 season playing an impressive 57 games and scoring 17 League goals as Norwich bounced straight back up. He proved a

point to his old employers Manchester United, scoring two in Norwich's 2–0 win over the eventual champions. He also got a goal in the return fixture at Old Trafford on 15 March 1975 to earn Norwich a valuable point.

MacDougall scored another important goal at Manchester United in 1975, this time in the League Cup semi-final first leg where he scored a late equaliser to silence the 58,010 home crowd and give Norwich the slight advantage for the second leg. Norwich progressed to the Final where MacDougall made his first Wembley appearance in the 0–1 defeat to Aston Villa.

He finished the 1974–75 season Norwich's leading goalscorer again, with 23 in all competitions, and was awarded with his first Scotland cap. He made, and scored in, his international debut in a 1–1 friendly with Sweden. MacDougall won seven Scottish caps in total, the most for any Norwich player and at a time when the Scotland national team was relatively strong on the world stage.

Carrying his form into 1975–76, MacDougall became the first Norwich player to hit a hat-trick in the top division when he scored three in an exciting 5–3 win over Aston Villa. His second top flight hat-trick came just a fortnight later in the next home game, on 6 September 1975, with Norwich beating Everton 4–2.

By the end of September MacDougall had scored 12 League goals; more than one a game. An uncomplicated player and a tough character, he was the focal point in Bond's attack-minded team, operating solely around and within the penalty area. Specialising in the near post run, he was a prolific finisher of chances. He finished the season with 23 League goals.

His 23 goals were enough to land him the prestigious First Division golden boot, awarded each year to the country's leading goalscorer. He became Norwich's first – and to date, only ever – winner of the award and had proved he could perform at the highest level after the doubts following his spells at Manchester United and West Ham. Naturally he also finished the season as Norwich's top goalscorer with 28 in all competitions, the third season in a row where he had finished as the club's leading scorer.

MacDougall missed the opening game of the 1976–77 season away at Liverpool, breaking a run of 124 consecutive League and Cup games. Despite success on the pitch and his popularity in the stands MacDougall was keen to return to the south coast. He played just three more games for Norwich, the last coming on 11 September 1976 in a 0–2 loss at Coventry, before moving to Southampton for a bargain £50,000.

MacDougall was top scorer in his first season at Southampton and led them back to Division One the following season. He went on to play and coach a number of clubs both on the south coast and overseas before settling in the USA.

His 66 goals for Norwich, coming in just three seasons, have put him joint 10th in the all-time listing. His goals to appearances ratio of 0.47 goals per game is comparable with the best City strikers and perhaps even more impressive when you consider that many of these goals were scored in Division One against the best defenders in the land.

Ted MacDougall made 138 appearances for Norwich scoring 66 goals.

Mel Machin

April 1945, Staffordshire   **Player 1973–77**

Mel Machin was a respected and talented player and coach during his 14-year association with Norwich City. He was the second (signing just five days after Hall of Famer Ted MacDougall) of Norwich manager and Hall of Famer John Bond's Bournemouth old boys to swap Dean Court for Carrow Road and became an integral part of Bond's new revolution of entertaining football.

Machin continued to preach this pleasing brand of football during his spell as coach and assistant manager, as Norwich's reputation for good football grew throughout the country.

Prior to moving to Norwich, Machin had spent his career in the lower Leagues with Port Vale, Gillingham and Bournemouth. His signature was a major coup for both Bond and Norwich as Tottenham were also interested, but he chose Norwich and joined in December 1973. Machin's transfer saw Clive Payne, an ever-present full-back in the 1971–72 Championship winning team moving in the other direction. Although previously a striker it was the vacant left-back slot that Machin would fill.

Machin's debut was a baptism of fire with the visit of champions Liverpool on 15 December 1973. Despite a credible 1–1 draw that day, Norwich ended the 1973–74 season bottom of Division One. Machin played 15 League games which included four wins (Norwich won only seven in total that season) and impressive draws at Ipswich and Tottenham.

Bond's influence began to show the following season, 1974–75, as Norwich began the season with just one defeat in the opening 15 games. Machin had established himself as the first choice left-back and epitomised Bond's style of football. He was comfortable on the ball with quick feet and a footballing brain. Many Norwich attacks would start through him as they looked to play the ball patiently out from defence.

While happy to join the attack, Machin was not renowned for his goalscoring; therefore it came as quite a surprise when he scored his first, second and third Norwich goals all in a 3–1 victory at Nottingham Forest on 12 October 1974. Machin's second half hat-trick were his only goals that season. In fact he was to score just once more for Norwich, over two years later in a 2–0 win versus QPR.

Machin played in 10 of the 11 League Cup games that ended with Norwich's second Wembley appearance in three seasons. Machin was part of the Norwich starting XI and played a part in Aston Villa's winning penalty, when he instinctively dived to his right to keep out a Chris Nicholl header that was going into the top corner; a save that Machin's colleague and Hall of Famer Kevin Keelan would have been proud of.

He had been carrying an injury during the League Cup Final which subsequently kept him out of the last 13 games. Norwich finished third and were promoted along with their League Cup conquerors Aston Villa.

Having regained fitness, Machin was back in the starting line-up for the 1975–76 season. He was involved in some exhilarating games, including a 5–3 (Aston Villa), 4–2 (Everton) and 4–4 (Burnley) that kept the Carrow Road crowd entertained. Again injury intervened, but Machin still played over half of the League games in what was Norwich's best ever season.

It was a similar story in the 1976–77 season with 28 appearances and that one solitary goal against QPR. Just three matches followed in 1977–78, the last a 0–3 defeat at Everton on 17 September 1977 before Machin retired to start a new chapter in his career as reserve coach.

He progressed to become assistant manager to Hall of Famer Ken Brown. The two worked well together during a period of mostly highs for Norwich. Machin was a very 'hands on' assistant, getting involved in the first team coaching. Technically strong, his sessions were innovative and he was widely respected by the players.

Machin had built up a reputation within the game for his knowledge and coaching abilities. In May 1987 he took the opportunity to become a manager when, following a path set by Hall of Famers Ron Saunders and John Bond, he was appointed by Manchester City in May 1987.

Machin built a side around a core of promising young players at Second Division Manchester City, while at Norwich his departure had an instant negative impact. Norwich won just three of the first 15 games of the 1987–88 season and were bottom by November. Back at Maine Road, Machin guided Manchester City to promotion in 1988–89 and then, going well in the First Division, a famous 5–1 derby drubbing of Alex Ferguson's Manchester United. Just nine weeks after Machin's team had destroyed their neighbours he was sacked, a victim of an impatient board.

Machin was appointed Barnsley manager, and in his four seasons there kept he kept them in mid-table safety in Division Two, despite the sale of key players. Eventually frustrated at losing his best players, Machin resigned from Barnsley and management in general. He did some scouting for Liverpool, Tottenham and West Ham before returning to Bournemouth as a member of the board.

Mel Machin made 117 appearances for Norwich scoring four goals.

Phil Boyer

January 1949, Nottinghamshire   Player 1974–77

Phil Boyer was part of the legendary Boyer/MacDougall partnership that excited Norwich's supporters over two memorable seasons in the club's history.

The partnership was first born in the Fourth Division at York City with Boyer arriving in summer 1968, almost a year after Hall of Famer MacDougall had joined them. It was then developed by Hall of Famer John Bond at Bournemouth.

Together they fired Bournemouth to promotion to Division Three in 1970–71 and narrowly missed out on back to back promotions with a third place finish in Division Three in 1972–73. That season they scored 50 goals between them representing 68 per cent of Bournemouth's total goals tally.

By February 1974, with Bond and MacDougall both at Norwich, it was only a matter of time before Boyer would join them. When he signed on 6 February 1974 he became Norwich's record signing at £145,000 beating the £140,000 spent on MacDougall just a couple of months earlier.

Lining up alongside MacDougall, Boyer made his Norwich and First Division debut on 9 February 1974 in a 2–1 home win versus Sheffield United. His first goal came in memorable circumstances, earning Norwich an unlikely 1–1 draw away to high-flying Ipswich. With Boyer in the team Norwich won four and drew five of their last 15 games, a considerable turnaround but not enough to avoid relegation at the end of the 1973–74 season.

The 1974–75 promotion year saw the Boyer/MacDougall partnership really take off. They complemented each other's games; Boyer worked hard running the channels and dropping deep to link play while MacDougall was the predator in the box, exploiting the space and time created by Boyer's unselfish running. Together they scored 33 League goals; Boyer scoring 16 and MacDougall 17 (although strangely they only scored in the same game on three occasions).

Boyer scored four doubles in his 16 goals tally, including one in the 3–0 home win against Nottingham Forest on 19 April 1975. This was Norwich's penultimate home game and, with second place Aston Villa next up at Carrow Road, the win was vital to keep Norwich ahead of fourth place Sunderland in the race

for third spot. The following week the race was won when Norwich completed a 3–0 win at Portsmouth with Boyer again on the score sheet.

Boyer also played in 10 of the 11 League Cup games that season including the League Cup Final at Wembley. He had contributed towards Norwich's second visit to the national stadium with important goals in the earlier rounds against Bolton and WBA.

While there was disappointment at the 0–1 Cup Final loss, the season was to end on a personal high for Boyer when he was voted into the Professional Football Association (PFA) Second Division team of the season. The PFA team of the year had only been established the previous season; Boyer (along with Hall of Famer Mel Machin) had been selected for the Third Division team while at Bournemouth. Selection for the team was a great honour as it was voted for by fellow footballers and indicated the value Boyer added to the Norwich team.

In the 1975–76 season, with Norwich back in Division One, Boyer was to win an even greater accolade when he was selected to play for England in March 1976. Called up by Don Revie, Boyer played the full 90 minutes in a 2–1 victory in a friendly against Wales. Boyer's cap represented a landmark moment for Norwich as he became their first ever Norwich player to represent England.

In the League Boyer scored 11 goals but could be credited for many assists, as partner MacDougall won the First Division golden boot. He scored some big goals for Norwich including one in a 3–1 home win against Tottenham, an equaliser at home to Manchester United and the third in a crucial 3–2 win against an exciting QPR side that effectively ended QPR's title challenge in front of 30,895 at Carrow Road.

With his England cap and Norwich's 10th place finish, the following 1976–77 season looked to be full of promise; however, injury restricted Boyer to 24 games and just six goals. After playing in just two of the last 22 League games Boyer moved that summer to Southampton for £135,000.

At Southampton he was reunited with MacDougall and rediscovered his goalscoring touch, first as top scorer in their promotion season back to Division One and then finishing with the First Division golden boot in 1979–80 season. Boyer eventually left Southampton after the dramatic signing of twice European Footballer of the Year and England captain Kevin Keegan.

Like most footballers of the period, Boyer did a stint abroad. He went to Hong Kong before a short spell at Manchester City, which was followed by a manager-coach role at the non-League Spalding.

Phil Boyer made 140 appearances for Norwich scoring 40 goals.

Tony Powell

June 1947, Bristol   **Player 1974–81**

Tony Powell was a Norwich City regular during the club's first sustained period of First Division football as Norwich consolidated their place among the elite after an up and down period in the early to mid-70s that included two promotions and a relegation.

Powell was another member of the Bournemouth squad who learnt his trade on the south coast before making the step up at Norwich. He had joined Bournemouth in April 1968 – after turning his back on a potential career as a bantamweight boxer – and played 219 games, mostly in midfield in front of the full-back and Hall of Famer Mel Machin.

Powell's manager, first at Bournemouth and then at Norwich, was Hall of Famer John Bond. Bond appreciated the high level of consistency that Powell delivered to the team along with his defensive capabilities. Norwich had just been relegated, conceding 62 goals, and Bond was keen to reinforce his team prior to the new season back in Division Two. The experienced Powell signed in August 1974, with first team fringe player Trevor Howard moving in the other direction.

He made his Norwich debut just a day after signing in the opening game of the 1974–75 season, scoring in the 2–1 win over Blackpool to get Norwich's season off to a winning start. This proved to be his only League goal of the campaign, although he did manage one more goal that season in the big League Cup semi-final clash at the 'Theatre of Dreams', Old Trafford. A Second Division side themselves that season, Manchester United fell behind to Powell's opener only to come back to draw the game 2–2. Norwich eventually prevailed in the second leg and Powell became another Hall of Famer to appear in the 1975 League Cup Final at Wembley.

Powell settled instantly during his first season as a First Division player when Norwich returned to the top division in 1975–76 after a one year absence. He made 31 League appearances including three as captain. His first game with the armband came on 31 March 1975 in the pressure pot atmosphere of the East Anglian derby. Powell skippered the team to a 1–0 win in front of the first 30,000 plus home gate of the season.

The away game at Birmingham on 28 February 1976 marked the start of a remarkable run of consecutive games for Powell which was to span three seasons as an ever-present in the Norwich team. The run covered 150 League and Cup games and was particularly impressive coming in an era where uncompromising tackles and poor pitch conditions were common. The run finally ended when Powell sat out a 4–0 record win against Tottenham on 22 August 1979.

Powell's run of games coincided with Norwich establishing themselves as a First Division side with 16th, 13th and 16th place finishes during the seasons where he played every game. He became a dependable player whose commitment made him popular with manager and fans alike.

Of his three seasons as an ever-present, the 1978–79 season was his most memorable. It was a season where he switched to left-back and held the captaincy for four games, the first of which was in the derby against Ipswich. This time he led his troops away from home to a commendable 1–1 draw against Bobby Robson's talented FA Cup winning side.

Powell scored a rare goal that season, his first since the opener at Manchester in 1975. It came on 11 November 1978 in a 2–2 draw versus Southampton. All together that season Norwich drew a record breaking 23 League games, a record since equalled but not yet beaten. This included a sequence of seven draws in a row, ended by a 0–6 loss at Liverpool. Norwich failed to win a single away game but, with two points for a win, the 23 points gained from those draws were enough to keep Norwich clear of the relegation zone. For Powell the season ended on a personal high when he was voted the Player of the Season.

For so long a permanent fixture in the Norwich first team, it was strange to see Powell missing during parts of the 1979–80 season as he picked up a few injuries. He made 28 appearances in all competitions, including another League Cup win (4–1) against Manchester United. The Player of the Season award this time went to Powell's defensive partner Kevin Bond.

The 1980–81 season was Powell's last in the yellow jersey. In March 1981, like many players of his generation, he crossed the Atlantic to play in the razzmatazz of the North America Soccer League. He played for San Jose Earthquakes and Seattle Sounders alongside Manchester United icon George Best. On retirement Powell remained in the USA.

Tony Powell made 275 appearances for Norwich scoring five goals.

Martin Peters

November 1943, London   **Player 1975–80**

World Cup winner and scorer of a World Cup Final goal, Martin Peters is one of a few players worldwide to have played at the very pinnacle of international football. This fact alone makes him almost certainly the most famous player ever to represent Norwich and he is often acknowledged as the club's greatest player in supporter polls.

By the time Peters signed for Norwich in March 1975 he had already amassed nearly 500 League games, all in the English First Division with West Ham and Tottenham, in a career spanning 14 years. His transfer from West Ham to Tottenham in March 1970 was a British record at the time of £220,000. He had won 67 England caps and had played in European and League Cup Finals, as well as the big one at Wembley in July 1966.

When Peters signed for Norwich he was still a household name, a genuine star signing that was testament to Norwich manager and Hall of Famer John Bond's influence and ability to sell his vision for Norwich to Peters. Even more impressive was that Norwich were a Second Division side at the time of the £50,000 transfer. His arrival was a major boost to the team as they looked to gain promotion back to Division One at the first attempt.

Peters made his Norwich debut on 15 March 1975, helping Norwich gain a point in a 1–1 at League leaders Manchester United. He went on to play the remaining nine games of the 1974–75 season with Norwich losing just twice, scoring in crucial late wins over Nottingham Forest and Portsmouth that finally sealed promotion for Norwich over fourth place Sunderland.

Despite his transfer exciting the Norwich public, at 31 years old, Peters' long-term commitment to the cause caused skepticism among supporters. This fear was soon dispelled as Peters went on to become an ever-present for two consecutive seasons. In fact he played 105 games in a row after making his debut.

In the first of his ever-present seasons, 1975–76, Peters' quality stood out as Norwich more than held

their own back in the top League. He scored 13 goals that season, including a memorable strike in the shock 3–1 win away at top of the table Liverpool in Norwich's first ever League win at Anfield. Later in the season Peters scored a double in a 3–1 win against Arsenal and, more importantly in the eyes of Norwich fans, the winner in a 1–0 victory over Ipswich in their first League win over their rivals since August 1972.

Peters' performances in Norwich's record high 10th place finish earned him the Player of the Season and he won the award again at the end of the 1976–77 season, this time as team captain. He again scored a winner against champions Liverpool as well as a winner in a 1–0 win over his old club West Ham.

His final tally of eight goals in 1976–77 was again impressive for a midfielder. Initially a left midfielder, Bond had moved him into the centre where he became pivotal to Norwich's free flowing attacking football. Like all quality players he found space and time on the ball and was impossible to mark. His high standards set the bar for his teammates and went a long way to consolidating Norwich in the First Division.

After missing the first five games of the 1977–78 season, Peters returned on 17 September 1977 to captain the side in a 0–3 defeat at Everton. Four goals in three games were soon to follow, including one in a 1–1 draw against Brian Clough's Nottingham Forest side that were to storm to the Championship that season. Peters celebrated a goal in yet another home win against Liverpool and he also scored in the incredible 4–5 defeat at Coventry.

The 1978–79 season was a landmark year for Peters. He was awarded an MBE for services to football while back at Norwich he was given a testimonial in recognition of his efforts at the club. On 18 October 1978 Norwich welcomed the 1966 World Cup squad to Carrow Road and beat the World Cup winners 4–2. Back in the First Division Peters captained Norwich, playing 43 games that season scoring 12 goals enough to win him the club's golden boot. He also played an important role in nurturing the next generation of stars: Hall of Famers Kevin Reeves and Justin Fashanu.

In his final season, 1979–80, Peters still managed 48 games despite turning 36. He helped Norwich to yet another comfortable mid-table finish, signing off on 3 May 1980 with a 4–2 win versus Derby.

In August 1980, Peters decided to try his hand at management with Third Division sleeping giants Sheffield United. After an unhappy year in Sheffield, culminating in United's relegation to the Fourth Division, Peters returned and settled in Norfolk. He has since been a board member at Tottenham as well as working in match day hospitality at White Hart Lane. In 2006 he was inducted into the English Football Hall of Fame to add to his membership of both the Tottenham and Norwich Hall of Fames.

Martin Peters made 232 appearances for Norwich scoring 50 goals.

Jimmy Neighbour

November 1950, Essex   **Player 1976–79**

Essex boy Jimmy Neighbour is the first Hall of Famer to have spent his whole Norwich career in the top Division of English Football.

Neighbour started his playing career at Tottenham Hotspur. He progressed steadily through the youth ranks and signed professionally in 1968 with his League debut coming in 1970.

At Spurs he became the provider for Tottenham legends Martin Chivers and fellow Norwich Hall of Famer Martin Peters. Although not a regular in the Tottenham starting line-up, Neighbour did play in the 1971 League Cup Final where he won a winners' medal as Tottenham beat Aston Villa 2–0.

Neighbour also experienced European football with Tottenham. He was part of the team that won the first-ever UEFA Cup Final against fellow English side Wolverhampton 3–2 on aggregate, after knocking out Italian giants AC Milan in the semi-final. He was also part of the Tottenham squad that won the League Cup again in 1973, this time at the expense of Norwich. During this successful period for Tottenham, Neighbour became a fans' favourite with his own terrace chant acclaiming his position on the Tottenham right wing.

Despite his popularity Neighbour was in and out of the Tottenham team. This was spotted by Norwich manager and Hall of Famer John Bond and, with the help of Neighbour's ex-colleague Peters, he managed to sign him on 30 September 1976 for £75,000. Neighbour arrived at Norwich just five days after they had gained a point in a 1–1 draw against Tottenham. His move continued the connection between the two clubs that had started in the 1950s through Hall of Famers Roy Hollis, Johnny Gavin and Maurice Norman and was further grown in the 1980s.

An experienced First Division player, Neighbour came straight into the Norwich team for his debut on 2 October 1976, a 3–2 home win against Newcastle. His arrival helped kick-start Norwich's season after they had lost four and drawn two in the first eight

games. He went on to miss only two games (both defeats) in the rest of the 1976–77 season and scored three goals.

His first Norwich goal will live long in the memories of the 25,617 at Carrow Road on 22 January 1977. A great individual effort, Neighbour beat three men before applying a confident finish. The solo effort came against some of the country's finest defenders and was a fitting winning goal in a 2–1 win against the champions Liverpool.

Later in the season Neighbour scored against his old club Tottenham. Despite Norwich losing on the day 1–3, it was Tottenham that would eventually finish the season bottom and be relegated to Division Two for the first time in 27 years. Tottenham's downfall indicated the importance of Neighbour to the Tottenham team and vindicated his decision to join Norwich who finished the season 16th.

Norwich meanwhile were consolidating their position among the top sides. Neighbour played an important role in Norwich's progress at that time. While he failed to score in 1977–78 his job was to supply the ammunition for the forwards to finish. An out and out winger, Neighbour had pace, control, skill, and an excellent delivery. As a traditional winger he always aimed to attack the full-back, get to the byline and put in a cross, something he did consistently.

Neighbour made 36 League and Cup appearances in 1977–78. Norwich again performed well in the League finishing 13th, but fell at the first hurdle in both Cups. The FA Cup defeat was particularly disappointing; Norwich lost 0–1 at home to mid-table Second Division side Leyton Orient. After years of gaining a reputation as giant-killers Norwich now found themselves victims of a Cup shock.

The 1978–79 season was to be Neighbour's last full season in a Norwich shirt. He made 34 League appearances, in the year that Norwich became a Pools favourite with their record breaking 23 draws. He scored two goals that season including one in a rare win, 3–0 versus Bristol City on 24 March 1979.

After helping Norwich to a respectable 16th position in Division One he spent the now traditional footballer's summer in the USA playing for Seattle Sounders in the NASL. On returning to Norwich he played the first five games of the 1979–80 season before he was sold to Second Division West Ham for £150,000.

At West Ham Neighbour became the supply line for ex-Norwich striker and Hall of Famer David Cross. Together they played a part in West Ham's promotion in 1980–81 as well as a League Cup runners'-up medal in 1981. Neighbour retired as a player in 1983. He went on to take positions at both West Ham and Tottenham within the respective academies.

Jimmy Neighbour made 115 appearances for Norwich scoring five goals.

Kevin Reeves

October 1957, Hampshire   **Player 1977–80**

Kevin Reeves was Norwich's first million pound man. In fact he was only the fourth player in the history of English Football to command such a fee when he moved from Norwich to Manchester City in March 1980.

Reeves' £1 million day was a long way off from his first footballing experiences at Fourth Division Bournemouth. He had grown up in the area in a footballing family. His cousin, Derek, played for Southampton, holding the record for most goals scored in one season, while Reeves would watch and learn from strikers such as Hall of Famer Ron Davies at Southampton and later Hall of Famers Ted MacDougall and Phil Boyer at Bournemouth.

After finishing top goalscorer in his first professional season at Bournemouth aged just 18, he was offered a shot at the big time by Norwich manager and Hall of Famer John Bond. Initially on a one month loan, the switch happened very quickly with the young Reeves making an unexpected First Division debut on 15 January 1977 in a 0–1 loss away to Arsenal.

Bond was a big fan of Reeves and saw enormous potential in the youngster and this, coupled with a goal on his home debut in a 1–1 draw versus Stoke, sealed a permanent transfer for £50,000 as Reeves joined the long list of those who had swapped Bournemouth for Norwich.

Reeves' permanent arrival at Norwich started with a baptism of fire in a 0–5 embarrassment at Portman Road. However, both the team and Reeves recovered, winning the following match 3–0 against Coventry with Reeves on the score sheet. Reeves went on to score another five goals that season, 1976–77, ending with eight in total as Norwich's second top goalscorer.

In his first full season, 1977–78, Reeves was a regular in the Norwich team, playing with a number of partners. He was a talented player, with a low centre of gravity allowing him to twist and turn to create space. Reeves was a goalscorer too. He hit 12 goals in 39 games including doubles against Midlands trio Derby, Coventry and Wolverhampton as Norwich finished in an improved 13th place.

Reeves continued to improve as a player under Bond's management and Hall of Famer Martin Peters' guidance. The experienced World Cup winner finished the 1978–79 season top goalscorer with Reeves close behind on 10 goals. The season also saw the start of a young but hugely promising partnership with Hall of Famer Justin Fashanu, the two starting a game together for the first time on 13 January 1979 in a 1–1 at WBA.

1979–80 proved to be a defining season for Reeves. It got off to a great start with two goals in the second game of the season in a 4–0 against Tottenham; a win that took Norwich top of the First Division for the first time in the club's history (albeit after only two games). A further goal in a 3–1 against European champions Nottingham Forest ended Forest's 12 game unbeaten run and kept Norwich in touch with the early pace-setters.

The reward for Reeves' good form came with his first senior England cap in the European qualifier against Bulgaria at Wembley on 22 November 1979. Reeves had already earned 10 Under-21 caps before becoming only the second Norwich player to be capped by England. The other debutant that day was future England manager Glen Hoddle who scored in a 2–0 England win.

As an England player at just 22 and with Norwich flying high in the First Division, it was not long before Reeves generated transfer interest and the club faced a battle to keep hold of their star striker. In the days before a transfer window, it was Manchester City's incredible £1 million bid that proved too good to turn down. After scoring in his last Norwich game, a 2–2 against Brighton, Reeves joined Manchester City on 11 March 1980.

Despite the £950,000 profit that went towards the redevelopment of the River End stand, there was disappointment and protest among the supporters who felt that Norwich could have made the next step up with their promising young strike force. Meanwhile, weighed down by the price tag, Reeves' Manchester City career got off to a slow start before he was reunited with former manager Bond.

Reeves finished top scorer at Manchester City for two consecutive seasons, won a second England cap and scored in the 1981 FA Cup Final replay in the 2–3 loss to Tottenham after Ricky Villa's famous winner. Manchester City's relegation in 1983 saw Reeves follow Bond to Burnley before injury ended his career aged just 26.

Kevin Reeves made 133 appearances for Norwich scoring 42 goals.

Peter Mendham

April 1960, Norfolk   **Player 1978–87**

Peter Mendham was a true representative of Norfolk football. A dedicated one club career with Norwich City was followed by spells at numerous local sides, interspersed with community work and coaching of local children.

Mendham represented Norfolk and Norwich throughout his childhood. Growing up in King's Lynn he played for West Norfolk and Norfolk Schoolboys, and Norwich City Schoolboy, Youth and Under-15s. He even represented the County in cross-country running.

In June 1976 Mendham made the natural progression to apprentice at Norwich and eventually signed as a professional in April 1978. He made his debut the following season, 1978–79, in a 3–0 win over Derby. Despite a run of six games in which Norwich lost just once, the young Mendham spent most of the season on the bench or developing his game in the reserves.

It was in the second half of the 1979–80 season that Mendham began to establish himself in the Norwich midfield, playing alongside, and no doubt learning from, the master and Hall of Famer Martin Peters. His first Norwich goal came in the intensity of the traditional Boxing Day clash against Ipswich, Mendham scoring in a classic 3–3 draw. He also scored for Norwich in the

FA Cup that season, a 2–3 defeat in a fourth round replay against Wolverhampton. While in the League Cup he came up against the League's best midfield pairing, Graeme Souness and Jimmy Case, as Liverpool knocked out Norwich 1–3 in the fifth round.

A series of injuries limited Mendham to only 15 games in the 1980–81 season that finished in relegation to Division Two, ending a six season stint in the top League. By the start of the 1981–82 season Mendham was back to fitness and ready to play his part as Norwich looked to make an immediate return to Division One as per the 1974–75 season; an objective that Norwich achieved thanks largely to an inspired run of results late in the season. Mendham played his part in the successful promotion campaign, chipping in with six goals from midfield with three coming in tight 2–1 encounters.

Norwich's return to Division One marked another season interrupted by injury for Mendham, although there was one notable highlight when, on 27 December 1982, he scored twice at Portman Road to earn Norwich a thrilling 3–2 win in front of 29,596.

Mendham finally enjoyed a consistent run in the team during the 1983–84 season missing just one League game (Ipswich away) all season. He became an important component in a Norwich side that finished 14th in Division One. Mendham was the heartbeat of the team with boundless energy and stamina covering every inch of the pitch. Strong in the tackle, he provided his defence with important cover necessary for survival in the First Division.

1984–85 was a bittersweet season for Norwich and Mendham. He got off to a great start scoring in the opening day 3–3 draw against champions Liverpool. Mendham played 36 League games and 14 Cup games including all nine League Cup games that led to another Final appearance at Wembley. This time Norwich went one better than the teams of 1973 and 1975, winning 1–0 against Sunderland to lift their first major trophy. However, joy was soon followed by despair with another relegation to Division Two at the end of the season.

As the only Norfolk born player in that famous Cup winning side, Mendham became the focal point for the fans and media. He represented the club at many functions within the community. As a youngster growing up in south Norfolk, I spent many a summer at my local Peter Mendham Soccer Schools.

For the third time of asking Norwich bounced straight back up to Division One, this time in style as Division Two League champions. The 1985–86 season was one of Mendham's best yet; both his and the team's First Division quality and experience stood out. Mendham contributed eight League goals and one in the League Cup. His League Cup goal on 29 October 1985 inflicted Luton's first ever defeat on their controversial plastic pitch as Norwich won 2–0. In the League, Mendham scored in a 1–0 win against Oldham in the opening game of the season to ensure Norwich got off to an important winning start.

With a Division Two champions' medal following a League Cup-winners' medal, the 1985–86 season marked the high point in Mendham's career. In 1986–87 he played just three games, although they were three of the biggest games in the fixture list (Liverpool, Tottenham and Manchester United) before injury finally forced him to retire in April 1987.

Norwich played a benefit match versus Spanish team Real Sociedad on Mendham's retirement from playing; he was aged just 27. Mendham continued his community work, becoming Norwich Football in the Community Officer while playing for various local sides. He did have one last shot at glory, scoring an extra-time winner back at Wembley as Diss Town won the 1994 FA Vase Trophy, nine years after his League Cup triumph at the national stadium.

Peter Mendham made 267 appearances for Norwich scoring 29 goals.

Justin Fashanu

February 1961, London   **Player 1978–81**

Justin Fashanu was a trail-blazer. He was the first black footballer to be sold for £1 million and the first and still, to date, the only professional footballer to be openly gay.

Fashanu had a tough start to life. His parents divorced and he was sent to a Barnardo's home before, as a six-year-old, being fostered by a couple from rural Norfolk. He was joined by his brother John who eventually went on to enjoy a successful playing career with Wimbledon's crazy gang. As a youngster Justin Fashanu was a keen boxer, reaching the finals as an ABA junior heavyweight, as well as a promising footballer. In 1978 he hung up his boxing gloves for good, signing professional terms for Norwich following a glowing reference from scout Ronnie Brooks, who believed Fashanu would eventually play for England.

In January 1979, as a 17-year-old, Fashanu made his full Norwich debut in a 1–1 draw with WBA. Such was his promise that he replaced former England international Martin Chivers for the remainder of the season. Fashanu was an extravagantly gifted footballer who had a delicate touch for a tall man. He excelled in the air and could hold up the ball allowing midfielders into attack. He finished the season with five goals in 16 appearances.

Fashanu continued to score regularly in his first full season, 1979 –80, but it was one particular goal that was to propel him into the national limelight and change his life forever. On 9 February 1980 Norwich welcomed League leader's Liverpool to Carrow Road. In an entertaining game Liverpool were leading 3–2 when a flowing five man Norwich move saw Fashanu receive a pass on the edge of the box with his back to goal. Twenty-five yards out and tightly marked by the defender, he flicked the ball up with his right foot before turning and hitting a volley with his left that flew into the net past the despairing dive of Ray Clemence. The goal was captured on the BBC cameras and featured on *Match of the Day*. Commentator Barry Davies screamed 'Ohhh what a goal, what a magnificent goal!' in contrast to Fashanu's modest almost nonchalant raised finger celebration. For the record, Liverpool went on to win the game 3–5 but Fashanu's goal won Goal of the Season and in days of limited football coverage on television was replayed regularly, featuring on the opening credits to *Match of the Day*. Fashanu finished the season with 13 goals, the joint top goalscorer, helping Norwich finish a respectable 12th in the First Division and winning his first of 11 England Under-21 caps.

It is often thought that Fashanu's goal of the season was the pinnacle of his career and it was even rumoured that he was signed by Nottingham Forest on the back of that goal alone. However, Fashanu continued to score regularly finishing the 1980–81 season as Norwich's top goalscorer. His 19 League goals in the 1980–81 season were only one short of Division One leading goalscorers Peter Withe and Steve Archibald. Fashanu's record was even more impressive when you consider that his goals were scored in a struggling side; Norwich were relegated at the end of the season.

With Norwich's relegation Fashanu was hot property, with a number of leading clubs chasing him. When he signed for Nottingham Forest he was part of an elite group whose transfer exceeded the £1 million mark. Great things were expected but a poor start was made worse when he fell out with outgoing manager Brian Clough. The relationship reached rock bottom when Clough banned Fashanu from the training ground. Unhappy with the very public fall out,

Fashanu left Forest and led a nomadic lifestyle, making only 13 appearances for seven clubs over the next 10 years.

By the late 1990s Fashanu finally seemed to be settled. He had publicly announced that he was gay and was coaching in the USA in Maryland. Suddenly though, he returned to London after accusations of assault, which were later dropped through lack of evidence, and in May 1998 in an isolated warehouse in East London, he committed suicide at the young age of 37.

It was a tragic end to a promising career. Today Fashanu's name lives on in the 'Justin Campaign' set up in his honour to challenge homophobia in football.

Justin Fashanu made 103 appearances for Norwich scoring 40 goals.

Mark Barham

July 1962, Kent   **Player 1980–87**

After a Norwich debut at 17 years old and two England caps by 21, the hugely talented Mark Barham could have gone on to become one of the country's top players were it not for bad luck with injuries.

Nurtured within the Norwich youth system Barham stood out among his teammates as he captained the youth side to the South East Counties League title in 1979–80.

Barham was so impressive in the youth team that manager and Hall of Famer John Bond took the unusual step of handing him his first-team debut on 24 November 1979 while still an amateur player. It was a further sign of Bond's faith in Barham's ability that the game happened to be against title challengers, and one of the World's most famous teams, Manchester United. It was a baptism of fire for the 17-year-old Barham with Norwich losing 0–5 in front of 46,540.

By the time of his second game some four months later in April 1980, Barham had signed professional terms and was now part of Bond's first team squad. Barham played the last three games of the 1979–80 season but it was in the following season, 1980–81, that he began to establish himself.

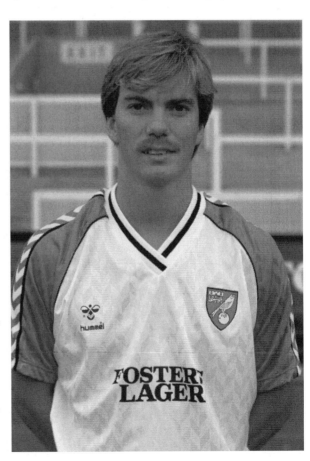

Barham's first full season proved to be a difficult one for Norwich as the team struggled during a transitional phase. Barham played 40 League and Cup games on the Norwich right wing and scored his only goal in a 1–3 defeat at Arsenal on 21 October 1980. A post-Christmas run of one win in 10 left Norwich in trouble with the season coming down to a final showdown at home to relegation rivals Leicester City. Despite Barham producing a classic display of wing play, including an important assist, Norwich fell short. They lost 2–3 and their relegation was confirmed.

Barham played in the first 14 games of the 1981–82 Division Two season, before injury struck. His next consistent run in the team started in the 5–0 home win versus Charlton on 10 April 1982 it helped maintain an upturn in form, with Norwich winning six out of the last seven games to snatch the final promotion place. Barham scored one goal during this run as Norwich extracted sweet revenge over promotion favourites Leicester with a thumping 4–1 win at Filbert Street.

Back in the big League, Barham flourished out on the wing. He was a creative winger with skill and pace who could beat a man. He scored in Norwich's first win back in Division One, a morale boosting 5–1 over Birmingham after what had been a difficult start to the 1982–83 season. Barham played 48 games that season. One personal highlight was an assist in the 1–0 FA Cup fifth round win against Ipswich, a win that maintained Norwich's proud record of never losing an FA Cup game to their Suffolk rivals.

Barham ended the season with a goal on 30 April 1983 to earn a 1–1 draw against Manchester United as Norwich finished well clear of the drop zone in 14th. To cap off a superb season Barham was selected for the England summer tour of Australia. He made his England debut with John Barnes on the other wing, on 12 June 1983 in a 0–0 against the hosts. Three days later Barham became the first ever Norwich player to win more than one England cap when he played in a 1–0 win, again against Australia.

Now an England international, Barham suffered his first serious knee injury in the home game against Tottenham in the 1983–84 season. Out for over a year, Barham did return just in time to play in the 1985 League Cup Final and collect a winners' medal. However, he would miss much of the run that eventually saw City relegated again.

The 1985–86 Championship winning season was Barham's last at the top of his game. Again his ability shone in the second tier, no more so than a goal and man of the match award in the top of the table clash versus Portsmouth on 18 January 1986 which Norwich won 2–0. Four goals in six games followed in March, including one in a 3–0 win over Shrewsbury that made it 18 unbeaten for Norwich as they eventually cruised to the Second Division title.

Alas, further injuries combining with the emergence of Hall of Famers Dale Gordon and Ruel Fox meant that Barham was restricted to just 14 appearances and two goals in the 1986–87 season. His final Norwich game came on 14 February 1987 in a 1–1 draw with Manchester City. At the end of the season Barham tried to revitalise his career with a move to Huddersfield and then Middlesbrough, but never managed to fully regain fitness or form.

Mark Barham made 223 appearances for Norwich scoring 25 goals.

Tim Sheppard

October 1950, Lancashire   Physio 1980–2001

The club physio is often the unsung hero of a football club and Tim Sheppard, Norwich's physio for 21 years, is no exception.

Part of the true fabric of Norwich Football Club, Sheppard spent more time in the Norwich dugout than any player, manager or coach, amassing over 1,000 games. Perhaps unusually for a physio he became a household name among Norwich supporters, as he served the club with dedication and distinction.

Sheppard began his medical career in the NHS at Coventry while working part-time for Coventry Rugby Club where he would have witnessed some shocking injuries. A transfer to Bolton hospital followed with Sheppard keeping his hand in sport, working part-time at the local sports injuries clinic.

Having decided to specialise in football, Sheppard got his first break when he was successfully interviewed for the Norwich physio job by Hall of Famer and then assistant manager Ken Brown. He made his debut with the magic sponge on 6 September 1980, a 0–3 defeat to WBA.

During his long association with Norwich, Sheppard would have seen hundreds of players come and go through his treatment room. As physio he was often the first face that new players would meet when arriving at the club for a medical. Not only was his assessment critical in ensuring the club's cash investment would be sound, Sheppard also created a good first impression of Norwich that could convince a player to sign or help a player to settle, making him and his family feel welcome.

A successful team is based on a settled side, with the physio's role important in ensuring that players are match fit and ready to perform to their maximum. The successful Norwich sides of 1988–89 and 1992–93 seasons illustrated this with nine players playing 30 or more League games; Sheppard worked tirelessly to ensure that the manager could select a consistent team.

During his time at Norwich Sheppard had to deal with some serious injuries. Hall of Famers Mark Barham, Bryan Gunn, Darren Eadie and Craig Bellamy all faced serious long term injuries, but all returned to play again under the guidance of Sheppard. One player that Sheppard could not help was new signing John O'Neill. Just 34 minutes into his Norwich debut on 18 December 1987 O'Neill suffered severely ruptured knee ligaments that were to end his career. It was, in his own words, the worse injury that Sheppard had to contend with during his time at Norwich.

A member of the Chartered Society of Physiotherapy, Sheppard was technically very knowledgeable but also had the ability to fit in and get on with the players, becoming very much part of the team. He earned respect through the quality of his work and a wider reputation within the game beyond Carrow Road. Sheppard also understood the psychological aspects to the job – players often faced a mental battle as well as a physical one during longer term injuries – and Sheppard proved to be an expert at maintaining motivation as well as being a good listener.

Sheppard's time at Norwich coincided with the best years in the club's history. He got to step out onto the Wembley turf in the 1985 League Cup Final as Barham required treatment. He also got to represent the club during the European adventure of 1993.

After 21 years of dedicated and loyal service, where Sheppard would often work seven day weeks as well as travelling the width and breadth of the country, he decided to retire from the dugout and treatment room to spend more time with his family. As a sign of the affection and respect that Norwich held for him, a testimonial was arranged with Celtic on 22 January 2001, a game attended by an impressive 15,000 supporters.

Sheppard was involved in the interview and selection process for his replacement, eventually appointing Neal Reynolds as the new club physio. Sheppard meanwhile went to work in his own physiotherapy practice in Norwich. He is still a fan of the team and still helps out any ex-players who have grown to know him over the years.

He returned to Carrow Road in 2002 to join in with the centenary celebrations and he finally got a game in the 5–4 victory over Harwich and Parkeston, City's first opponents all those years ago.

Ken Brown

February 1934, London   **Manager 1980–87**

For seven years and 367 games Ken Brown was in the hot seat at Norwich. He is Norwich's longest serving manager and one of the club's most successful.

During his tenure he guided Norwich to success on the pitch, and signed and developed more Hall of Fame players than any other manager as he laid the foundation which Hall of Famers Dave Stringer and Mike Walker would later build on.

Before management, Brown had a long career as a top class footballer. He played for West Ham in a career spanning 16 years, winning FA Cup and European Cup-winners' Cup finals. He won a single England cap and played alongside many greats of English football.

One of Brown's West Ham teammates was Hall of Famer John Bond. They formed a friendship off the pitch and shared the same footballing philosophy. Brown became Bond's assistant manager at Bournemouth before moving to Norwich with him in November 1973.

After almost seven years at Bond's side, learning the trade and earning respect in the dressing room, Brown was the natural candidate to take over as Norwich manager when Bond left for Manchester City in November 1980.

As manager, Brown continued the good work under Bond, ensuring that Norwich still played an attractive brand of football admired throughout the country. This would continue throughout Brown's time as manager. He remained true to his principles despite a tough start to his managerial career that saw Norwich relegated by the end of the 1980–81 season.

During his first season Brown had already demonstrated an eye for a player, first signing Dave Watson in November 1980 and then Chris Woods in March 1981. Both at the time were promising youngsters who would later go on to cement their places in Norwich folklore, become Hall of Famers, represent their country and move on for big money. Meanwhile, going out of the door was Hall of Famer Justin Fashanu for £1 million; the first of many players that Brown would lose for big fees.

Brown found himself under pressure in his first full season in charge (1981–82) with Norwich in mid-table by early spring. In today's environment Brown would have been fired, but thanks to a supportive Board and the wholehearted backing of the dressing room he kept his job and turned Norwich's season round. He made two inspired signings, Hall of Famers Martin O'Neill and John Deehan, kick-starting a late surge up the table culminating in a dramatic promotion.

Over the next couple of seasons Brown blended a mix of experience and youth into a successful team. He signed Hall of Famers Mick Channon, Asa Hartford and Steve Bruce who, together with the core of his promotion winning squad, he led to Norwich's first ever major domestic honour at Wembley: the 1985 League Cup. In doing so Brown became the first Norwich manager to win at Wembley and would have become the first Norwich manager to take his team into Europe were it not for the Heysel disaster and subsequent ban on English clubs.

The 1984–85 season ended in disappointment with Norwich's relegation to Division Two, but to Brown's credit he rebuilt a side that returned instantly and in style, winning the 1985–86 Division Two Championship. It was the second time he had got Norwich promoted at the first time of asking.

The 1986–87 season was expected to be a struggle but Brown's Norwich surpassed all expectations with a record fifth place finish in Division One. Again, the success was based on Brown's activity in the transfer market and his ability to create a happy environment for his players to work in. Brown was a popular man with an infectious character and his players were prepared to run through the proverbial brick wall for him.

One member of that record breaking team was full-back Kenny Brown, Brown's son, who would play 28 games in total for Norwich with 21 appearances coming that season.

The 1987–88 season got off to a bad start for Norwich. Suffering from the loss of coach and Hall of Famer Mel Machin, Norwich lost seven of their first ten games. The final straw came on 7 November. After a 0–2 defeat at Charlton and with Norwich bottom of the First Division, Brown was sacked by the Board. He left the club with dignity, and such was the esteem that he was held in by the Norwich supporters that despite the club's lowly position, there was sympathy and vocal support for him during the next League game.

In his time at Norwich Brown had won a League Cup, two promotions and achieved a top five finish. He had signed or brought through the youth ranks an incredible 18 Hall of Famers.

After a well-earned break from football Brown returned as manager at Plymouth before doing some scouting for England. He returned to Carrow Road as guest of honour in February 2004 when the new Jarrold stand was formally opened.

Ken Brown managed Norwich for 367 games, making him the club's longest serving manager.

Dave Watson

November 1961, Merseyside   **Player 1980–86**

With six England caps and two winners' medals achieved during his Norwich career, Dave Watson is one of Norwich City's most decorated players and one of their most respected captains.

He was Norwich manager and Hall of Famer Ken Brown's first signing and certainly up there with the best.

Plucked from the reserves of champions Liverpool, where first team opportunities were limited, Watson was supplementing his reserve team income with a job as a sheet metal worker.

The initial transfer fee was £50,000 but Liverpool obviously realised Watson's potential; they inserted a clause in the transfer where an England cap would trigger an additional payment of £100,000. In the end, the final fee totalled £200,000 but it was still an absolute steal.

Signed in November 1980, Brown demonstrated his faith in his young defender by giving him his debut in the white hot atmosphere of an East Anglian derby. Norwich lost the game on Boxing Day 1980 0–2, but Watson had made an impression, keeping his place in the team for the rest of the season at the heart of the Norwich defence.

Unfortunately, despite some strong performances and three goals by Watson, Norwich ended the 1980–81 season third bottom and were relegated to Division Two. They conceded 73 goals, their worst tally in the First Division (11 more than when they finished bottom in 1973–74). However, in his first full season (1981–82) Watson proved to be the answer to Norwich's defensive issues. He played 38 League games in a defence that conceded just 50 goals and in a season that saw Norwich promoted back to Division One at the first time of asking.

The 1982–83 season saw Watson begin to establish himself as a top-class defender. He was a tough, uncompromising centre-back with excellent positional sense. He was very much in the Hall of Famer Duncan Forbes' mould and, like Forbes, Watson was handed the captaincy. His first game wearing the armband was on 5 February 1983. Aged just 21, he commanded the respect of an experienced Norwich dressing room which included seasoned internationals and Hall of Famers Martin O'Neill and Mick Channon.

Watson's appointment as captain kick-started an excellent run of form in the League with Norwich losing just two of their last 16 games, dispelling any fears of relegation with a 14th place finish. In his second game as captain he led Norwich to a 1–0 FA Cup fifth round victory against Ipswich in front of the highest gate of the season of 28,001. Watson ended the season being honoured by the supporters, winning the 1982–83 Player of the Season award.

The 1983–84 season proved equally successful for Watson with the Norwich defence conceding just 49 goals, one better than the promotion year, as he captained Norwich to another comfortable mid-table finish. Watson's attributes in the Norwich defence were recognised when he was selected for the England summer tour of South America. On 10 June 1984 Watson made his England debut against the World's best international side, Brazil, in the world famous Maracana stadium. In a game still remembered for John Barnes' individual goal, the England defence kept a clean sheet in a famous 2–0 win.

Watson played in another two games of the tour and returned to America in summer 1985, playing a further two internationals. His total of six England caps is the most of any player while playing for Norwich.

Watson picked up another record in the following 1984–85 season when he became the first and, to date, only Norwich player to lift a major trophy at Wembley after he captained the side to a 1–0 League Cup win versus Sunderland. In spite of Watson's commanding and consistent performances at the back, Norwich were relegated again to Division Two after a short two year spell in the top flight.

At the end of the 1984–85 season Watson could have had his pick of First Division clubs, but he stayed loyal to Norwich playing every League game – all as captain – of the 1985–86 season in Division Two. He was rewarded for his loyalty as he lifted the Second Division Championship trophy after a 4–0 win over Leeds in the final game of a season that had seen Watson dominate the division's centre-forwards.

In August 1986, as Norwich prepared for life back in Division One, Watson made a big money move back to Liverpool, this time to the blue half of Merseyside. In a transfer that eventually exceeded the £1 million mark (an Everton record at the time), Watson had an immediate impact; Everton won the League title in his first season (1986–87). Norwich fans could not begrudge Watson's moment of glory as the title was sealed after a 0–1 win at Carrow Road in the penultimate game of the season.

Watson went on to become an Everton legend, making over 500 appearances, becoming captain and winning the FA Cup in 1995 to complete a personal treble (League Cup, League and FA Cup). He is also a member of the Everton Hall of Fame.

Dave Watson made 256 appearances for Norwich scoring 15 goals.

Martin O'Neill

March 1952, Northern Ireland   **Player 1981–83**
                                                             Manager 1995

A student of Law, and a footballing intellectual, Martin O'Neill enjoyed a glittering career both as a player and manager with a number of clubs.

Norwich City was the only one of these clubs that saw O'Neill feature in both roles. Both his spells at Carrow Road, as player and manager, were short lived. However, both left an equal mark on Norwich and their supporters.

Born in Northern Ireland, O'Neill's break in English football came in 1971 at Nottingham Forest. Relegated in his first season, Forest were an average Second Division side until the arrival of Brian Clough. Clough made O'Neill his midfield general and together they enjoyed a golden era for the club, winning the League title in 1977–78, two League Cups and two European Cups, the biggest prize in club football.

Norwich manager and Hall of Famer Ken Brown therefore got himself a bargain when he signed O'Neill in February 1981 for £250,000 to help spearhead Norwich's fight against relegation. With over 300 games' experience behind him, O'Neill was immediately selected as captain and got off to a winning start beating Brighton 3–1 on 28 February 1981. O'Neill's impact was instant; the win was Norwich's first in eight games and ended a slump of six consecutive defeats.

O'Neill remained captain for the remaining ten games of the season, scoring one goal in an important 3–2 away win at Tottenham. Despite an upturn in form, with Norwich winning six out of the 11 games that he played in, O'Neill arrived just too late to help prevent Norwich's relegation from the top division.

A clever man and an expert negotiator, O'Neill had pre-empted the risk of relegation when signing for Norwich in February and had a clause in his contract allowing him to leave if Norwich were to go down. This clause was activated on 2 May 1981 when Norwich's demise was confirmed after the 2–3 defeat to Leicester. O'Neill would remain in the First Division with Manchester City.

For the first time in his career O'Neill struggled to establish himself and after just eight months he returned to Carrow Road signing for the second time for Ken Brown. This time he was joining a Norwich side struggling for form in the Second Division. O'Neill made his second Norwich debut on 3 February 1982, scoring in a 2–3 loss at home to Sheffield Wednesday.

It was not long before O'Neill's experience began to shine as he ran the midfield for Norwich with his tenacious approach and range of passing. He was a motivator and role model for his younger teammates and a senior member in the dressing room.

O'Neill's return to Carrow Road pretty much marked the start of a remarkable run of games that was to see Norwich storm up the table into third place and ultimately promotion. The run included 10 wins in 11 games as Norwich played with confidence and momentum. O'Neill scored some important goals in the run, including one in a 4–2 win over second top Watford (my first ever Norwich game) and a late winner at Bolton. In his 20 League games that season, Norwich won 14 and drew one in a sequence of games that was testament to the positive influence he had on the team.

A successful season ended on a high for O'Neill as he captained Northern Ireland, the 1982 World Cup surprise package. In front of a live TV audience of millions Northern Ireland stunned hosts Spain, winning 1–0 on their way to the second Group stages before losing to eventual semi-finalists France. In total O'Neill won 18 caps while at Norwich and his role in the 1982 World Cup earned him an MBE.

Back in the top division for the 1982–83 season, O'Neill continued to be an important player as Norwich comfortably avoided relegation. O'Neill played 43 League and Cup games scoring six goals. He scored in momentous wins at both Ipswich and Liverpool. The Liverpool result was particularly symbolic as Norwich became the only team to double the eventual champions that season.

O'Neill's last game for Norwich was a 2–1 win on 14 May 1983 against Brighton, the team he had made his debut against back in 1981. After negotiating his contract directly with the Board he decided to leave for Notts County in August 1983.

O'Neill would return to Norwich 12 years later when he was appointed as manager in June 1995, just after Norwich had lost their Premiership status. He had been successful in his first managerial job at Wycombe and was just the boost that the supporters and team needed.

As in his playing days, O'Neill's presence inspired another winning run. By the end of November 1995 Norwich were second after a 2–0 win at Watford and having lost just four games all season. O'Neill, aware that he had a side that could go up, was ambitious and keen to strengthen the squad. However, he came into conflict with chairman and Hall of Famer Robert Chase. To the surprise and disappointment of Norwich fans, O'Neill resigned on 17 December 1995 just hours before Norwich lost 2–3 in the televised clash at Leicester.

A week later O'Neill was appointed Leicester manager and took them up that season via the Play-offs, leaving Norwich fans wondering what might have been. O'Neill then enjoyed a successful time at Leicester, before moving on to Celtic, Aston Villa and Sunderland.

Martin O'Neill made 75 appearances for Norwich scoring 13 goals. He also managed Norwich for 26 games with an impressive win ratio of 46.2 per cent.

Chris Woods

November 1959, Lincolnshire　　　　　　　　　　　　**Player　1981–86**

Chris Woods was Norwich's undisputed number one during his five seasons at Carrow Road. He missed only five games in 267 appearances; Norwich had finally found a goalkeeper of record appearance holder and Hall of Famer Kevin Keelan's calibre.

Woods was a naturally gifted sportsman playing both squash and basketball at County level as well as football for Nottingham Forest schoolboys.

Progressing through the ranks at Forest, his entry to the first team was blocked by England international Peter Shilton. Woods' opportunity came in the 1977–78 League Cup; with Shilton Cup-tied he played in every game as Nottingham Forest progressed to the Final versus Liverpool. In the Final itself Woods enhanced his growing reputation by keeping a clean sheet in both the 0–0 at Wembley and then the 1–0 win in the replay at Old Trafford. That was 210 minutes without conceding against the League champions, and all before Woods had even made his League debut.

With opportunities limited at Forest, Woods signed for QPR and was a regular in their Second Division side before Norwich manager and Hall of Famer Ken Brown captured him for £225,000 in March 1981. He finally made his Division One debut in a 0–3 defeat to Wolverhampton on 14 March 1981. Although he impressed with four clean sheets, including one against Ipswich, he could not prevent Norwich's relegation at the end of the 1980–81 season.

From his debut in March 1981 Woods played in the next 171 League and Cup games before missing a run of three games in October 1984. He was an ever-present between the sticks for four seasons. The first of these ever-present seasons was the promotion year of 1981–82, Woods' first full year at Norwich, where he soon became a fans' favourite.

Back in the First Division Woods was guaranteed to get plenty of action as Norwich looked to ensure that they avoided a swift return to Division Two. Woods proved more than a match for the country's top strikers; Norwich conceded 58 goals, Norwich's second best total in the First Division. Notable highlights for Woods in the 1982–83 season were two clean sheets against high-flying Tottenham and, even more impressively, a further two clean sheets against champions Liverpool with Norwich winning 1–0 and 2–0 to become the only club to 'double' Liverpool that season. So good was Woods' display in the 2–0 win at Anfield on 23 April 1983 that he received loud applause from the infamous Kop terrace, after he had repelled everything that the Liverpool forwards could throw at him during a second half onslaught on his goal.

Woods maintained the high standards he had set throughout the following 1983–84 season. His performances instilled confidence throughout the team. He commanded his box well and was comfortable coming for and collecting crosses. In his third season as an ever-present, Norwich conceded just 49 goals comfortably beating the previous season and only four more than third place Nottingham Forest. Woods was voted the 1983–84 Player of the Season.

Woods finally missed four games in the 1984–85 season, with aging ex-England 'keeper Joe Corrigan providing the cover. He played in eight League Cup games as Norwich reached Wembley including an excellent display in the semi-final first leg at Portman Road on 23 February 1985, where Norwich came under sustained pressure in a 0–1 defeat. In the Final itself, versus Sunderland on 24 March 1985, Woods kept a clean sheet. He would have been credited with a penalty save had Clive Walker's second half penalty not brushed the outside of the post, as Woods had the shot covered.

In the League things were not so good, but Norwich's ultimate relegation did not prevent Woods from making his England debut on 16 June 1985. Playing behind Norwich teammate and Hall of Famer Dave Watson, in the friendly versus the USA, it was the first and only time an England side had featured two Norwich players in the starting XI. Woods would go on to earn four England caps in total, all as a Second Division player, as he became Norwich's second most capped England player.

Woods stayed at Norwich to help rectify the disappointment of the 1984–85 relegation. He played every game in the 1985–86 Championship winning season. Norwich conceded just 37 goals (less than one a game on average) and recorded 17 clean sheets.

The Championship was followed in the summer by Woods' £600,000 move to Scottish giants Rangers. Woods was the first of Graeme Souness' high profile English signings, and his time at Rangers coincided with a golden period for the club with four Scottish Championships. Woods also achieved a new British record when he went 1,196 minutes (13 games) without conceding a goal.

He was later inducted into the Rangers Hall of Fame after leaving in 1991 when he joined Sheffield Wednesday for £1.2 million. At Wednesday he played in the 1993 FA Cup Final defeat that saw Norwich clinch a place in Europe thanks to Arsenal's victory.

Chris Woods made 267 appearances for Norwich.

John Deehan

August 1957, West Midlands   **Player 1981–86**
                                                    Manager 1994–95

No player has scored more goals for Norwich City in the English top division than John 'Dixie' Deehan, with 48 League goals scored over three seasons in the First Division.

Before signing for Norwich in December 1981 Deehan had played in the First Division with his first club Aston Villa, where he scored 40 goals in 110 games while also winning England youth and Under-21 caps.

His career had stalled after a £500,000 move to WBA, providing Norwich manager and Hall of Famer Ken Brown with the opportunity to add a quality striker to a squad that was struggling for form in the 1981–82 season, Norwich's first season back in Division Two. Initially Deehan arrived on a one month loan, but after scoring four in a friendly versus Ipswich his move was soon made permanent in December 1981.

Deehan made a scoring start to his Norwich career with a goal in a 1–3 loss to League leaders Luton on 28 December 1981. The defeat had left Norwich isolated in mid-table. Deehan's arrival, along with the return of fellow Hall of Famer Martin O'Neill, ignited Norwich's season as they embarked on a late surge up the table that ended with promotion. Deehan scored 10 goals as Norwich stormed up the table, including a hat-trick in a 5–0 win over Charlton. In his 22 League games that season Norwich lost just seven.

The first of Deehan's 48 top flight Norwich goals came in the opening match of the 1982–83 season in a 1–2 defeat to Manchester City. Deehan continued to score in what was a difficult start to the season for Norwich; his winner against Aston Villa on 23 October 1982 earned only the second win for Norwich in 11 games.

Thanks to Deehan's goalscoring instincts Norwich improved to finally finish 14th. Deehan missed only two games that season and finished top scorer with 21 goals. He scored the winner in a 1–0 victory over champions Liverpool and scored a double in three consecutive games, in wins against Birmingham, Sunderland and Arsenal.

His fine form continued in the 1983–84 season where he scored 17 goals in all competitions to again finish top scorer, despite missing a run of six games through injury. Four of his season's tally came in one match on 7 April 1984 when he scored four in a 6–1 home win against Watford. The win set two club records, it was Norwich's biggest win in the top division, and the first time a Norwich player had scored four in one match in the top division.

Deehan's second First Division hat-trick followed the next season (1984–85); again, Watford were the victims in Norwich's 3–2 win on 22 September 1984. With two hat-tricks in the First Division, Deehan joined Hall of Famer Ted MacDougall at the top of the list for most top flight hat-tricks.

Deehan also scored two in a shock 4–2 win over an Everton side that were to run away with the Championship that season. His most important goal was to come later in the season against Ipswich in the second leg of the League Cup semi-final. Norwich lost the first leg 0–1 and the second leg on 6 March 1985 was a tense, tight affair. Nerves were finally settled when Deehan levelled the tie on aggregate with a shot on the turn after some exquisite chest control. The goal set the platform for a famous victory and a trip to Wembley.

In the Final at Wembley, Deehan played his part in the winning goal; he chased down what appeared to be a lost cause before nutmegging the Sunderland defender and putting a low cross into the box that led to the winner.

The 1985 League Cup win proved to be the high point in Deehan's Norwich career, for despite finishing the season top scorer again – for the third year in a row – his goals could not prevent Norwich's relegation to Division Two.

A combination of injury and the signing of Hall of Famer Kevin Drinkell limited Deehan's role in the 1985–86 Championship winning side, and in the summer of 1986 he crossed the Norfolk/Suffolk divide to play for newly relegated Ipswich.

After seeing out his playing days at Portman Road, Deehan got involved in coaching with Hall of Famer and ex-Norwich coach Mel Machin at Manchester City and Barnsley, before returning to Carrow Road as Hall of Famer Mike Walker's assistant. After two seasons of almost continual success Deehan stepped into the vacant manager's position after Walker's shock exit in January 1994.

Deehan began his Norwich managerial career with seven consecutive draws before his first win on 21 March 1994, 3–0 in Walker's much hyped return to Carrow Road with Everton. Deehan did a great job to steady the ship after the disruption caused by Walker's departure. However, the club policy of selling players for high transfer fees, combined with injury to key players saw Norwich struggle in the 1994–95 season. After a run of one win in 14 and a 0–3 defeat to Newcastle Deehan resigned, hoping that a new man could save the club from relegation.

Deehan later found managerial success at Wigan before being involved in a number of coaching, scouting and assistant roles at various clubs, the latest as Director of Football at Plymouth.

John Deehan made 199 appearances for Norwich scoring 70 goals leaving him seventh in the all-time goalscoring listing.

Mick Channon

November 1948, Wiltshire   **Player 1982–85**

Aged 34 and playing at Third Division Bristol Rovers, Mick Channon was to become an unlikely Canary hero. At Norwich he was to experience a late resurgence in his career, scoring goals in the First Division and winning another major trophy.

A player of undoubted pedigree, Channon had enjoyed a long and successful career at Southampton. For 14 years he had led the Southampton front line, winning an FA Cup-winners' medal, the First Division golden boot in 1973–74 and 46 England caps including two as captain. He scored a club record 227 goals for Southampton, and 21 for England, the joint 12th highest England goalscorer.

It was understandable therefore, that the perception when Channon signed for Norwich in December 1982, was that his best footballing days were behind him. Signed by Hall of Famer Ken Brown, Channon was on a rolling month to month contract, designed to provide Norwich with some much needed cover after a poor run of only four wins in 19 games at the start of the 1982–83 season.

Channon had an instant impact, with his big game experience proving crucial in a 3–2 win at neighbours Ipswich on his debut. This was followed by a further two wins in the next three games with Channon scoring the winners in 1–0 victories against Luton and Swansea respectively. He was to score one further goal that season in another win, this time 2–1 against Brighton on 14 May 1983 to guarantee a comfortable 14th place finish, a clear seven points above the drop zone.

For a man on a rolling contract, Channon played an incredible 48 League and Cup games in the following 1983–84 season. That season Norwich fans got treated to the famous arm swinging 'windmill' celebration a total of 11 times, including six goals as Norwich enjoyed good runs in both Cup competitions. In the FA Cup he scored in the third round replay against Aston Villa in a 3–0 win and then on 1 February 1984 in a fourth round replay against

Tottenham, Norwich winning 2–1. These were two large scalps before Norwich lost 1–2 to struggling Second Division Derby in the fifth round.

In the League Cup Channon was named captain for the second round first leg trip to Cardiff, while in the second leg he scored his only Norwich hat-trick in a 3–0 win. Only 9,887 witnessed the hat-trick but two rounds later, on 30 November 1983, 25,570 saw Channon score the winner to knock out Ipswich 1–0.

Channon was proving to be equally valuable in the League as Norwich again comfortably avoided a relegation battle. He was an influential figure in the dressing room, and an entertainer both on and off the pitch. Players looked up to him and his advice was respected.

On the pitch, Channon had not lost any of his striking instincts, scoring in the famous 3–3 draw versus Manchester United on 1 October 1983, a game in which Norwich completed a remarkable comeback after finding themselves 0–3 down after 56 minutes. As in the FA Cup, he also scored in wins against Aston Villa and Tottenham in the League.

The 1984–85 season kicked off on 25 August 1984 with another cracking 3–3 draw, this time against champions Liverpool, and again Channon was on the score sheet. He scored eight League goals that season, including one as captain in a 2–2 draw with QPR and a double on 30 March 1985 in a 2–1 win over Coventry.

Channon's Coventry double came a week after he had made his final appearance at Wembley in the League Cup Final. He was by far and away Norwich's most experienced player at Wembley, and the familiar surroundings inspired a great performance from him in the 1–0 win over Sunderland. Channon had also played a key role in Norwich's route to the 1985 Final, scoring in the third and fourth rounds as well as inspiring the team with a passionate team talk when under the cosh in the semi-final first leg at Ipswich.

Channon finished the 1984–85 season with 44 appearances at the age of 36. He did miss most of the final run in that ended with Norwich's relegation, and in the summer of 1985 he made his final club move. Surprisingly, for a Southampton legend, he went to Portsmouth. He eventually retired in 1986 to focus on his love of horse racing, obtaining his horse trainer's licence.

Mick Channon made 112 appearances for Norwich scoring 25 goals.

Jeremy Goss

May 1965, Cyprus   **Player 1983–96**

'Gossamania' hit the nation during the 1993–94 season as Norwich City's Jeremy Goss became a national institution, a star who was rarely off the back pages for his goalscoring exploits.

For a time in 1993 Goss was arguably the most famous footballer in the country, yet his journey to national fame was a long and at times frustrating affair.

After suffering rejections from Aston Villa and Southampton, Goss was given his opportunity at Norwich, joining the Government backed YTA apprentice scheme. Goss made an instant impression at Carrow Road as part of the successful 1983 youth side that won the South East Counties League in 1982–83 without losing a single game. The Youth Cup was added to the title with Goss scoring in the 6–5 aggregate win against Everton, to complete a unique League and Cup double.

Prior to the Youth Cup Final, Goss signed professional terms in March 1983 and made his first team debut a year later, on 12 May 1984, in a 1–2 defeat at Coventry. This was the penultimate game of the 1983–84 season, and at the start of the 1984–85, he found himself a regular on the Norwich bench.

Over the next seven seasons Goss would make just 68 appearances as he found himself a fringe player in a talented Norwich squad. He was in danger of becoming a 'nearly' man before making 44 appearances in the 1991–92 season. These included all six FA Cup ties as Norwich made it to their second FA Cup semi-final in four years. This time Sunderland were the opponents with the game ending in a 0–1 defeat, the same scoreline as in 1989.

By now Goss was also playing regularly for the Welsh national team, having made his debut in May 1991 in a 1–0 friendly win over Iceland. Goss would go on to win nine caps while with Norwich and was part of the Welsh squad that narrowly missed out on the 1994 World Cup.

In sync with his international career Goss' club career was also on the up, after the promotion of assistant manager and Hall of Famer Mike Walker to manager in the summer of 1992. Under Walker,

Goss played 25 games in the 1992–93 inaugural Premiership season, helping Norwich finish a historic third, their highest ever League finish.

Norwich continued their fine form in the 1993–94 season with Norwich playing some scintillating attacking football. Goss was the heartbeat of the team, closing down, chasing and winning the ball. He also supported the forwards, timing his runs into the box which, coupled with a devastating shot, produced some fantastic goals.

The first of Goss' dream strikes that season came in the third game at Leeds. A flowing move ended with a powerful Goss volley from the edge of the box that went in off the underside of the crossbar, and had even the home fans clapping as Norwich comfortably won 4–0. A not so spectacular but equally important goal followed a week later in the 1–0 win against Ipswich.

However, it was in Norwich's debut European campaign that Goss came to the nation's attention. He was a goalscorer in Norwich's first ever European game versus Vitesse Arnhem, but even that was eclipsed by a stunning volley on 20 October 1993 at the Olympic Stadium, Munich. Against the three times European Cup winners Bayern Munich, and live on national television, Goss' goal set Norwich up for a famous 2–1 victory as Norwich became the only English club side to beat Bayern in Munich.

Goss was at it again in the second leg at Norwich; this time it was a trademark late run into the box to connect with Hall of Famer Chris Sutton's near post flick to send Carrow Road wild. The game finished 1–1 and Norwich went through. In the two games Goss had gone toe to toe with Germany's most capped player, Lothar Matthaus, and more than held his own in the midfield battle.

Goss almost scored in the UEFA Cup third round against Inter Milan, but this time his long distance effort hit the crossbar and Norwich eventually went out losing both legs 0–1. With his three goals Goss finished, and is still, Norwich's top European goalscorer.

Back in the League Norwich's season tailed off following the departure of manager Walker, but there was one last highlight for Goss. On 30 April 1994 he scored the last ever goal in front of the standing Kop at Anfield. Norwich won 1–0, with Goss' first half wonder goal a fitting strike for such an occasion, and capped off a wonderful and well deserved season for Goss, a season that ended with his testimonial against Genoa on 9 May 1994.

The 1993–94 season was the peak for Goss. For the 1994–95 season injury restricted him to 25 League games and two goals, including one in the last game of the season in a 1–1 draw with Aston Villa which would prove to be Norwich's last Premiership game for nine seasons.

Goss played just 16 games in the 1995–96 season, including seven as sub as his career seemed to have gone full circle. His last Norwich game was on 27 April 1996, a 1–2 home defeat to Watford 12 years after his debut.

After a short spell at Hearts Goss returned to Carrow Road where he worked for the club in the community, sales and hospitality departments.

Jeremy Goss made 238 appearances for Norwich scoring 23 goals.

Dale Gordon

January 1967, Norfolk   **Player 1984–91**

'Disco' Dale Gordon was one of the most exciting talents to emerge out of Norfolk for many a generation. A skilful winger, his performances alone were worth the admission fee, as he became a firm fans' favourite during one of the most successful eras in Norwich City's history.

Gordon, born in Yarmouth, progressed rapidly through all levels, from Norwich youth to schoolboy and apprentice. He represented England under 15's and was being sought after by both Manchester United and West Ham, but chose to stay at his local club Norwich where he signed professional terms on 17 January 1984.

Gordon made his first team debut in the opening game of the 1984–85 season, a 3–3 at home to champions Liverpool. Aged just 17 at the time, Gordon went on to play in a further 23 League and Cup games before turning 18, a Norwich club record. During this run of games he scored two goals, including one against champions elect Everton in a convincing 4–2 victory, the first goals Everton had conceded in five games.

The return of winger and Hall of Famer Mark Barham from injury restricted Gordon's game time; he missed most of the remaining games in 1984–85 and in the following 1985–86 Championship winning season, although he did score the equaliser in a 1–1 draw against Stoke on 19 April 1986 that secured the Division Two title for Norwich, after promotion had been celebrated the week before.

Former Ipswich fan Gordon got his opportunity in the 1986–87 season with Barham again suffering a long term injury. The exciting winger took the opportunity with both hands, playing 51 League and Cup games. Gordon's exciting wing play mirrored the attractive football played by Norwich that season as they won many plaudits for the way they attacked their opposition. Gordon scored in two games that ended with Norwich scoring four, a 4–3 versus Southampton and a 4–1 versus Aston Villa. Gordon's role was more to supply the ammunition for leading scorer and Hall of Famer Kevin

Drinkell, something he did with regularity, beating his opposing defender with a trick, shimmy and turn of pace.

Gordon was rewarded for his consistent performances with England under 21 caps but injuries and loss of form resulted in a disappointing 1987–88 season. The following 1988–89 season was to be a different story for both Gordon and Norwich. The season started with a record breaking four successive wins, Norwich's best start to a top flight season, with Gordon's strike in the 2–0 win at Newcastle sealing the fourth of those wins.

Norwich continued to produce a high level of performance, leading the First Division table up to Christmas, and were rewarded for their entertaining football with their first ever live televised League game. On 27 December 1988 the nation watched Gordon round West Ham 'keeper Allen McKnight to score Norwich's first live televised League goal in a 2–1 win.

Norwich were also enjoying a good run in the 1989 FA Cup. Gordon scored a late winner in a 3–2 fifth round victory over Sheffield United to evoke memories of 1959. The following quarter-final against West Ham was a tight affair, going to a replay at Carrow Road, where on 22 March 1989 another late Gordon goal sent Norwich into the FA Cup semi-finals, for the first time in 30 years.

Unfortunately Norwich fell just short in both Cup and League, but an excellent season for Gordon was topped off with the Player of the Season award. He was only the second, and, to date, last Norfolk born recipient of the award.

The 1988–89 season may have been Gordon's best in a yellow shirt, yet he continued to shine on regular occasions, including a goal in a 2–0 win at Manchester United on the debut of Gary Pallister, who at £2,300,000 was Britain's most expensive defender. In the 1990–91 season he played 48 games, again scoring against Manchester United, this time in a 2–1 FA Cup fifth round tie.

After five seasons in the First Division, Gordon decided it was time to make a career move to win some medals. On 4 November 1991 Norwich received £1.2 million for their former apprentice when he was transferred to Rangers. Despite scoring on his debut and winning League and Cup medals, Gordon soon returned south of the border. He joined West Ham for £750,000 where his claim to fame was scoring the Hammers' first ever Premiership goal in a 1–1 against Coventry.

Since retiring from Football, Gordon has been focusing on his work in the local community and particularly on coaching youngsters through his academies. His son Remy is in the Norwich academy.

Dale Gordon made 261 appearances for Norwich scoring 43 goals.

Steve Bruce

December 1960, Tyne and Wear   **Player 1984–87**

Steve Bruce is often referred to as the finest player never to have been capped by England. It is a valid statement when you consider that Bruce has captained every side that he has played for, winning numerous trophies and awards, including the much coveted League and Cup double, twice, with Manchester United in 1993–94 and 1995–96.

A Geordie, Bruce was a product of the Wallsend Boys' club, a club with a reputation for producing future professional footballers. He appeared at Wembley in 1976, but as a ball boy for Newcastle and just two years later at Third Division Gillingham, he got his professional break.

In six seasons at Gillingham Bruce developed into a fine central-defender playing 205 games, winning the Player of the Season twice and captaining the team while still in his early 20s. He first came onto the Norwich radar in September 1979 when he scored two at Carrow Road in the League Cup second round, but it would be five years before he would return permanently when he was signed by Norwich manager and Hall of Famer Ken Brown in the summer 1984.

Like his fellow Hall of Famer and Norwich central-defender Stan Ramsey, Bruce began his Norwich career with an early own goal. It came in an exciting 3–3 draw against Liverpool on the opening day of the 1984–85 season. Despite this setback, Bruce recovered to form a formidable central defensive partnership with Hall of Famer Dave Watson; a partnership not seen by the Norwich faithful since Hall of Famers Dave Stringer and Duncan Forbes ruled the roost in the 1970s.

Similar in many aspects to Watson, Bruce was a commanding, brave defender. Not only could he tackle but he was comfortable bringing the ball down, particularly on his chest, and distributing out to the midfield. He was exceptional at heading the ball and therefore a threat from set pieces. This threat was illustrated in Norwich's biggest game of the season, the League Cup semi-final second leg against massive rivals Ipswich.

In front of Carrow Road's largest gate of the season, 23,545, the tie was poised at 1–1 on aggregate. As the game entered the final minutes, a corner from Hall of Famer Mark Barham at the Barclay end was met perfectly by Bruce who powered a header into the roof of the net to send the Norwich crowd into ecstasy. Bruce's header proved to be the winner, Norwich progressed to the Wembley Final, and ultimately lifted the trophy after a 1–0 win over Sunderland which gave Bruce his first major medal after he was voted Man of the Match in the Final.

Bruce was also a goalscorer in the FA Cup that season. His winner on 28 January 1985 finally settled the third round tie with Birmingham after the first game and two subsequent replays all finished 0–0. Taking four games to beat Birmingham set a new club record.

After the highs of the League Cup success, Bruce marked his debut season with the 1984–85 Player of the Season award.

The 1985–86 season saw Norwich back in the Second Division but the Bruce/Watson partnership was certainly First Division class. Bruce was an ever-present that season as Norwich kept 17 clean sheets on their way to the Second Division title. Bruce also chipped in with eight League goals, including three in the first six games and one in the end of season promotion party, a 4–0 win over Leeds.

The summer of 1986 saw the partnership break up with the sale of Watson to Everton. On Watson's departure Bruce took the armband for the 1986–87 return to the top flight. With two new partners that season Bruce was the rock at the back. A clean sheet in the opening 0–0 versus Chelsea was followed by a goal in the 4–3 win against Southampton as Norwich and Bruce got off to a great start.

Bruce missed just one game that season. He played in all four games in the newly formed Full Members Cup. There were two clean sheets in the League games versus Manchester United, and twice in the season Norwich kept three clean sheets in a row. The final fifth place finish was comfortably Norwich's highest ever finish, beating the previous high of 10th in 1975–76.

After captaining Norwich to such heights, Bruce became a sought after man and after 22 games in the 1987–88 season (all as captain) Bruce got his big money move to Manchester United. At United Bruce enjoyed unparalleled success, winning FA Cup, League Cup and Premiership titles. He famously scored two late headers against Sheffield Wednesday to set Manchester United up for their first title in 28 years and captained them to two doubles, the first club in English football to achieve this.

Since his playing days ended in 1998, Bruce has enjoyed a successful transition into management, managing Wigan, Birmingham and Sunderland among others.

Steve Bruce made 180 appearances for Norwich scoring 21 goals.

Asa Hartford

October 1950, Scotland   Player 1984–85

An experienced and classy midfielder, Asa Hartford's short period at Norwich City will always be synonymous with the Canaries' League Cup triumph at Wembley on that famous day in March 1985.

Hartford's appearance in the 1985 Final was his third as a player having played for WBA in the 1970 Final and later for Manchester City in 1976. He became the first player to play in three League Cup finals with three different clubs.

Prior to Norwich's big day, Hartford had already enjoyed a long and distinguished playing career beginning at WBA in 1967. Although missing out on a starting place in the 1968 FA Cup Final, Hartford went on to become a regular at the Hawthorns where he made a total of 214 appearances. During his time at WBA his performances attracted the attention of the leading First Division clubs, but a move to Division One runners-up Leeds United fell through after a heart condition was identified during the medical.

Leeds' loss was to be Manchester City's gain when Hartford signed in August 1974 just three months after he had been voted in the Second Division PFA Team of the Season. Hartford went on to star in a City side that enjoyed a League Cup win as well as a European campaign and two top four finishes.

During his time at Manchester, Hartford was a regular in the Scottish international team after making his debut against Peru in 1972. He was a member of Ally MacLeod's famous 1978 World Cup squad that fell at the first hurdle despite the abundance of talent available. Hartford also played in the 1982 World Cup with his final cap coming in the group game against Brazil on 18 June 1982. His final cap was also his 50th earning him a place in the Scotland Roll of Honour.

With over 500 competitive games behind him and career transfer fees totalling £1.5 million, Hartford signed for Norwich on a month to month contract in autumn 1984. Aged 34 Hartford would add valuable experience to the Norwich midfield, as manager and Hall of Famer Ken Brown was building an exciting squad combining youth and experience.

A talented midfielder with exceptional positional sense, Hartford became an important cog in the team, always making himself available for the ball. He made a goalscoring debut on 10 October 1984, scoring two in the comfortable 6–1 League Cup second round win over Preston. Hartford went on to play in every round of the League Cup through to the Final.

The Final on 24 March 1985 was Norwich's first trip to Wembley since 1976. Norwich's opponents on the day were fellow First Division strugglers Sunderland in a game that was to become known as the 'friendly Final' thanks to the refreshing, good-natured relationship between the fans.

On the pitch, the match was settled early in the second half when, after good work by Hall of Famer John Deehan, the ball fell to Hartford on the edge of the area. His calm side-footed shot was heading towards the far corner of the goal before a deflection off Sunderland defender Gordon Chisholm took it into the near corner. Although announced as an own goal in the stadium, Hartford has been credited with scoring Norwich's first ever and to date only goal at Wembley as Norwich held on to deservedly lift the Cup.

As well as being Norwich's first ever at Wembley, Hartford's goal was to achieve a couple of other firsts. It was the first goal scored in a Norwich game that was shown live on television and it was the first competitive Norwich goal to be scored on a Sunday.

In the 1984–85 League campaign Hartford played 28 games. He scored in his last game, helping Norwich to a 2–1 victory over Chelsea on the final game of the season. The win took Norwich to 49 points, eight clear of third bottom Coventry. Coventry won their last three games of the season, all coming after the official final weekend. The last was a controversial 4–1 win over champions Everton after their end of season party. Although no consolation to Norwich at the time, the League would change the rules for the future so that all final games had to be played at the same time.

Hartford's short but popular spell with Norwich ended in the summer of 1985. He has since undertaken a number of coaching and assistant manager roles, as well as a brief spell as Shrewsbury manager where his assistant was ex-Norwich manager and Hall of Famer John Bond.

Asa Hartford made 40 appearances for Norwich scoring five goals.

Mike Phelan

September 1962, Lancashire   **Player 1985–89**

Recognised now by many football fans for his media work and the television interviews as part of his role as assistant manager at Manchester United, Mike Phelan was a Norwich regular for four seasons during the 1980s, captaining the club to an almost unimaginable League and Cup double in 1988–89, debatably Norwich's finest ever season.

   Before making an impression at Carrow Road, Phelan began his professional career at his local club Burnley. Having attended summer soccer schools he signed professionally in 1980, making his League debut in 1981. Founder members of the Football League, Burnley had fallen on hard times with Phelan playing much of his football in the old Third Division.

   At Burnley Phelan experienced promotion and relegation, won six England youth caps and won Burnley's Player of the Season award before making the step up to Norwich in May 1985. Signing the day after the Heysel disaster had cost relegated Norwich their place in the UEFA Cup, Phelan joined Norwich at a low point in their recent history.

   Phelan made his debut in the opening game of the 1985–86 season as Norwich got the campaign off to a winning 1–0 start versus Oldham. Adding some quality in the centre of the Norwich midfield, Phelan was one of three ever-presents as Norwich comfortably won the title and promotion by a clear 11 points. Phelan contributed three goals, all coming in high scoring wins: 4–3 Crystal Palace, 4–0 Carlisle and 6–1 Millwall.

   The 1986–87 season was Phelan's first in the English top division; however, he looked at home with a number of consistent performances as Norwich got off to a flying start. The pick of the early season results was a 4–1 win at Aston Villa, in which Phelan grabbed the opener to send Norwich second.

   Thanks in part to Phelan's presence, versatility, and ability to find space and remain calm under pressure, Norwich managed to maintain their impressive start and finished the season fifth in the League. Phelan missed only two games and Norwich lost just eight times that season, the same number as champions Everton and three better than second place Liverpool.

Full of confidence going into the 1987–88 season Norwich never really recovered from three defeats in the opening four games, and by mid-October they had already registered as many defeats as in the entire 1986–87 season. With Norwich second bottom by December 1987 Phelan took over the captaincy from the departing Hall of Famer Steve Bruce and helped turn Norwich's season around. In his 18 League games as captain Norwich lost just seven, including a run of just one defeat in 11 which saw Norwich finish well clear of the relegation zone in 14th place.

The 1988–89 record breaking season was Phelan's first full campaign as captain. By this time an experienced member of the team in a midfield unit comprised of Hall of Famers Ian Crook and Andy Townsend, Phelan led Norwich to unprecedented success on the pitch. He scored in a well-deserved 2–1 win at Manchester United on 26 October 1988 as Norwich led the First Division table from 8 October until New Year's Eve; the longest ever period, at the time, that a Norwich team had held the top spot in English football.

As the season entered its final furlong, Norwich were still in contention for the League and Cup double until a run of three defeats in April 1989 ended hopes of a first Championship. Meanwhile in the FA Cup semi-final Phelan crucially failed a late fitness test to miss only his second match of the season; Norwich lost a nervous encounter 0–1 to Everton.

As the 1988–89 season finished Phelan broke into the England squad for the Rous Cup, but was not selected for either game against Chile or Scotland. With his international career in mind Phelan joined Sir Alex Ferguson's Manchester United revolution in June 1989 for £750,000 – another profitable transfer for Norwich.

At United Phelan went on to win FA Cup, European Cup Winners Cup and League titles as well as winning his first England cap against Italy in November 1989.

After hanging up his boots, Phelan returned to Norwich in 1995 as assistant manager and reserve team manager. However, as in his playing career, he ended up at Old Trafford, first as first team coach and then promoted to Sir Alex Ferguson's assistant manager.

Mike Phelan made 194 appearances for Norwich scoring 10 goals.

Dave Williams

March 1955, Wales   **Player 1985–88**

Signed on the same day as fellow midfielder and Hall of Famer Mike Phelan, Dave Williams' signature pretty much fell under the media and supporter radars; however, he would go on to become an unlikely fans' favourite who gave so much back to Norwich both as a player, coach and assistant manager.

Williams' arrival at Norwich on 30 May 1985 was low-key for a number of reasons. Firstly, as well as joining on the same day as Phelan, his arrival at Norwich came a week after the capture of Tottenham midfielder Garry Brooke. Brooke was approaching the peak age of his playing career, had 73 appearances for Spurs behind him and arrived with high expectation. His signing, rather than Williams, was the one that excited the fans, although Brooke would eventually make just 10 substitute appearances for Norwich.

Secondly, in contrast to Brooke, Williams had just turned the wrong side of 30 and had spent his entire playing career with Bristol Rovers, mostly in the Second and Third Divisions. A one club man for 10 seasons Williams started out at Rovers as an amateur, combining football with his job as a teacher. In his club total of 352 appearances he played in every position and is 14th in the all-time listing for Bristol Rovers appearances. In 1983 he was promoted to player-manager becoming, at the time, the youngest manager in the Football League.

His signing for Norwich was therefore a surprise to fans, but manager and Hall of Famer Ken Brown had done his homework and recognised Williams' talent (he had twice been voted in the PFA team of the season) and the experience that he could offer Norwich after the departure of Hall of Famers Mick Channon and Asa Hartford.

The oldest player in the Norwich squad for the 1985–86 season, Williams made a winning debut in Norwich's Division Two opener against Oldham. He soon settled into the Norwich midfield where he had the ability to dictate the pace of games through possession and distribution. Although supposedly a squad player, he made 49 League and Cup appearances and was an important, if rather low profile, member of the Championship winning side.

He scored his first Norwich goal on 26 October 1985 in a 2–0 win at Sunderland, and scored and set up another in a man of the match display against Middlesbrough. Williams scored two doubles that season; two long range efforts in the 6–1 thrashing of Millwall that sent a message to the rest of the League, and a second double on 15 March 1986 in a much closer 2–1 win over Carlisle.

As well as contributing important goals Williams also provided many assists as he became Norwich's set piece expert at free-kicks and corners. He also captained the side in the opening match of the Screen Sport Super Cup, a narrow 0–1 loss at Everton. The Cup was in its maiden year and was established to provide an alternative Cup competition to those English sides banned from European competition. Norwich's opponents in the Cup were three giants of the game: Everton, Manchester United and Liverpool. Williams played in all six games and scored the goal in the 1–1 draw against Manchester United. With one win and three draws, Norwich performed admirably against teams that would all finish in the top four of the First Division that season.

In the 1986–87 season Norwich faced these sides as equals in the First Division. Williams made a well-deserved First Division debut on 23 August 1986 in a 0–0 draw with Chelsea, the

game coming some 11 years after his career had started at Bristol. Williams scored in the first home game of the season – a 4–3 win over Southampton – in a match noted for the opening of the new main stand after fire had destroyed the original one.

During this season Williams represented Wales on five occasions and made a further 10 appearances in the top flight. As 1986–87 ended, Williams moved into a player-coach role and made a further 11 appearances in the 1987–88 season before he was appointed assistant manager to Hall of Famer Dave Stringer.

A shrewd tactician and popular with the players, Williams was part of the management team that led Norwich to record League finishes and two FA Cup semi-finals. He left in 1992 after being touted for the manager's job and has since enjoyed roles at Bournemouth, Everton, Manchester United and the Welsh national team. He did make one further return to Norwich where in 2004 he was Academy Manager and Technical Director.

Dave Williams made 74 appearances for Norwich scoring 12 goals.

Kevin Drinkell

June 1960, Lincolnshire   **Player 1985–88**

A prolific goalscorer, Kevin Drinkell top scored for Norwich City in every season that he spent at the club, including the Championship winning year of 1985–86 and the record fifth place finish in Division One the following year. A scorer of simple tap ins and long range efforts, Drinkell was the complete striker at Norwich.

Drinkell started his career aged just 16 at his local club Grimsby, winning the young Player of the Season award in 1977. He starred in successive promotions in 1978–79 and then as Third Division champions in 1979–80. He won Player of the Season in 1982–83 and led the attack in 1983–84 as Grimsby finished fifth in Division Two.

Throughout his eight seasons at Grimsby, Drinkell never stopped scoring goals. He had scored 89 in 272 games, a statistic which attracted Norwich manager and Hall of Famer Ken Brown as he looked to strengthen the side ready for the promotion challenge in 1985–86. With Drinkell out of contract and in the days before the Bosman ruling, an independent tribunal set the transfer fee at just £105,000, outraging Grimsby, as Norwich landed themselves a bargain.

As with fellow new signings and Hall of Famers Mick Phelan and Dave Williams, Drinkell made his debut on 17 August 1985 in a season opening 1–0 win against Oldham. Including the

Oldham game Drinkell went five games without scoring before breaking his duck with a double in a 4–0 victory against Sheffield United, a win that was to ignite Norwich's season.

After the goals against Sheffield United, Drinkell never looked back, finishing the season with 22 League goals as Norwich romped to the Division Two title. His best spell that season came during Norwich's club record of 10 consecutive wins, running from 23 November 1985 to 25 January 1986. Drinkell scored seven goals including one in the return game versus Oldham, a last minute winner at Fulham, and goals in the top of the table clashes versus Charlton and Portsmouth which Norwich won 3–1 and 2–0 respectively.

On 12 April 1986 Drinkell scored the opener in a 2–0 win at

Bradford's temporary home, The Odsal stadium, to clinch promotion. He also scored in the end of season title party, a comfortable 4–0 win against Leeds. His final total of 22 League goals made him both Norwich's and Division Two's top goalscorer. The accolades continued as Drinkell was voted the Norwich supporters' Player of the Season. He was also selected in the PFA team of the season alongside fellow Hall of Famers, Chris Woods, Steve Bruce and Dave Watson.

Despite the club's championship trophy and Drinkell's personal achievements in 1985–86, the following 1986–87 season was to be even better for both club and player. In Drinkell's first season at Division One level, he made the step up with ease, scoring regularly against the best defenders in the land. His first Division One goal came in the second game of the season in the 4–3 versus Southampton. He then scored twice in a 2–0 win over Newcastle, five weeks later, to keep Norwich second in the League and maintain their unexpected excellent start to the season.

Drinkell was to score against some big teams during the season, as Norwich claimed some significant scalps while consolidating their position among the chasing pack. A goal in the 1–1 draw versus Arsenal was bettered by a late winner in a 1–0 win at Manchester United, representing Norwich's first League win at Old Trafford.

However, the goal Drinkell was best remembered for in the 1986–87 season came on 11 April 1987 when Liverpool came to town. A first half goal from Ian Rush looked ominous as Liverpool had never lost a game in which Rush had scored first. Norwich ended that long standing statistic with an enthralling second half display ending with Drinkell's fine winner late in the game.

Drinkell ended the season as an ever-present with 21 goals in all competitions and collected the top goalscorer and Player of the Season award, both for the second successive season.

After the highs of the previous two seasons, 1987–88 was disappointing with Norwich settling for a 14th place finish after spending much of the season in relegation trouble. Drinkell played his part, finishing the season with 12 goals, six of which came in Norwich victories during a second half resurgence that pulled them away from the relegation pack. Although less than his previous tallies it was still enough to win the Norwich golden boot for the third year in a row.

With Drinkell proving himself capable of scoring in the First Division he became a valuable commodity. After a move to Tottenham fell through, Drinkell joined the English invasion at Glasgow Rangers, signing in June 1988 for £600,000.

Despite 19 goals in his debut season Drinkell was soon back in the First Division at Coventry, before ending his playing days back in Scotland.

Kevin Drinkell made 150 appearances for Norwich scoring 57 goals.

Robert Chase

July 1938, Norfolk   **Chairman 1985–96**

Probably the most controversial member of the Norwich City Hall of Fame, Robert Chase divided opinion among Norwich supporters, local media and the managers that worked under him during his 11 year tenure as chairman.

Norfolk born Chase was a shrewd businessman who made his fortune in property after starting his business from scratch. A Norwich fan since a child, he was keen to become involved with the club and was elected onto the Board in 1983.

For two years Chase worked tirelessly and Norwich managed to make a profit while maintaining a good quality squad. His big break for the top job came in November 1985 after previous chairman and Hall of Famer Sir Arthur South stepped down following a dispute over the building of the new main stand after the previous one had been destroyed by fire.

Chase was appointed chairman of the newly formed Board and with the disputes settled in the Boardroom, Norwich went on to win the 1985–86 Second Division Championship and return to Division One at the first time of asking. Back in the First Division, Norwich were about to enter a golden period for the club, the most successful in their history.

The list of achievements under Chase's stewardship was impressive and included three times breaking the record for the highest ever League position, two FA Cup semi-finals (Norwich had only made one semi-final in the previous 82 years) and the club's first ever European Campaign (Norwich would have enjoyed two other European adventures under Chase had it not been for the Heysel ban).

There were some hard times among the good days but Chase proved equal to the challenge. His first tough decision came after a disappointing run of results at the start of the 1987–88 season. With nine defeats in the first 14 games, Norwich dropped to the bottom of Division One after a 0–2 defeat to lowly Charlton on 7 November 1987. The manager at the time was Hall of Famer Ken Brown, Norwich's longest serving manager who had built up a lot of goodwill with supporters and players alike. Removing him from the job was therefore a big and brave decision by Chase.

Having dismissed the ever popular Brown, Chase held strong despite supporter protest and a no confidence motion by shareholders. He resisted the temptation to turn to a big name manager, instead promoting Hall of Famer Dave Stringer to the post. It proved to be an inspired decision as Stringer not only turned Norwich's season around but went on to become one of the club's most successful managers ever.

Chase's next managerial appointment would not come until the end of the 1991–92 season when Stringer decided to step down. With Norwich about to enter the exciting new era of Premiership football, Chase again made another astute appointment, promoting Hall of Famer Mike Walker from within the backroom staff.

While Norwich were enjoying heady days on the pitch, Chase was also investing in the club's infrastructure which was to become part of his legacy. The new main stand, that had triggered the Board's resignation back in September 1985, was completed and officially opened by the Duchess of Kent in February 1987. This was followed two years later by the opening of the new disabled and family enclosure which was the first of its kind in the country, providing comfortable and modern facilities.

In accordance with the Taylor report after the Hillsborough tragedy, Norwich were at the forefront of stadium redevelopment. The £2.8 million double tier Barclay End and seating of the River End completed the transformation of Carrow Road into a modern sports arena by the 1992–93 season. The training facilities were also revamped in summer of 1994 as Norwich moved from Trowse to a brand new purpose built complex at Colney that became the envy of other clubs and helped attract new signings.

Back to the football, Norwich became a club in free-fall after the departure of Walker. Although blamed for Walker leaving, Chase had fought hard to keep his man, refusing Everton permission to talk and then legally challenging Walker's move to Everton.

As Norwich slipped out of the Premier League at the end of the 1994–95 season Chase presided over a series of high profile transfers out of Carrow Road. Although there were accusations of asset stripping by disillusioned supporters, the sales were necessary as Chase faced the challenge of balancing the books and meeting the bank's demands while losing the revenue stream that the Premiership had provided.

Player sales coupled with high profile fall outs with Norwich managers and disappointing performances on the pitch culminated in anti-Chase protests that sadly Chase would become remembered for, despite Norwich's achievements under him.

Chase's association with Norwich finally ended in May 1996 after he sold his shares to previous chairman and Hall of Famer Geoffrey Watling.

Ian Culverhouse

September 1964, Essex   **Player 1985–94**

Ian Culverhouse's playing career at Norwich directly corresponds with the most successful period in the club's long and eventful history.

A quiet character who was rarely in the media spotlight, Culverhouse would represent all that was good about that Norwich side during an unprecedented period of sustained success at the top level.

An England Youth international, Culverhouse received his footballing education at White Hart Lane, Tottenham. He struggled to break into the first team although he did win a UEFA Cup-winners' medal as an unused substitute in Tottenham's victory over Anderlecht in 1984.

With just two senior appearances to his name, Culverhouse became the first of a new batch of Tottenham trainees that would eventually become legends at Norwich, when he signed in October 1985. At the time he was joining a Norwich side that were struggling to find their feet in Division Two after the previous season's relegation. An indifferent start had left pre-season favourites Norwich ninth when Culverhouse made his League debut on 12 October 1985.

A debut 4–0 win against Carlisle marked the start of an 18 game unbeaten run in which Norwich won 14. It was the best start to a Norwich career of any player and was ended only after a 1–2 defeat to Wimbledon on 8 March 1985.

With a Second Division Championship medal to his name, Culverhouse made his First Division debut in the following seasons opener (1986–87) and was part of a defence that kept a clean sheet in a 0–0 draw against Chelsea. However, despite playing in the opening 25 League games and with Norwich sixth in the League, Culverhouse controversially lost his place to manager and Hall of Famer Ken Brown's son Kenny.

A player of Culverhouse's quality would not be out of the side for long; he returned to the right-back slot playing 40 games in all competitions in the 1987–88 season. In the near double winning season of 1988–89 Culverhouse was an

ever-present in the Norwich defence. He became a model of consistency in a defence that worked as a unit and were all comfortable passing the ball. He rarely gave his opposition winger time or space and excelled at positioning and reading the game.

Over the next three seasons Culverhouse continued to play regularly in a settled Norwich defence. He first captained the side in the final game of the 1989–90 season – a 2–2 draw at home to Arsenal – and was part of a defence that kept four clean sheets in a row during the 1990–91 season. Such was Culverhouse's contribution, he was voted the 1990–91 Player of the Season as Norwich finished 15th, his award coming a year after his fellow full-back and Hall of Famer Mark Bowen's.

The 1991–92 season proved to be a disappointment for Culverhouse after missing a large part of it through injury. Of his 21 League games, he captained the team in seven; the highlight a 3–0 win against Liverpool on 22 February 1992. Culverhouse also captained Norwich to a gritty 0–0 draw away at Southampton in the FA Cup quarter-final, as well as playing in the disappointing semi-final defeat at Hillsborough.

Culverhouse missed just one game in Norwich's historic debut season in the Premiership with only two other outfield players playing more games. He was an integral part of the side that finished in the club record third position.

He went one better in the 1993–94 season, Norwich's second in the Premiership, the only player to appear in every League game that season. He also managed his long awaited first League goal that season. It came on 21 March 1994, a close range effort to open the scoring in a 3–0 win over Everton in a game that was dominated by the eagerly anticipated return of ex-Norwich manager and Hall of Famer Mike Walker.

Just two months after his long awaited goal, Culverhouse played his last game for Norwich before spending the opening half of the 1994–95 season in the reserves. He moved to Swindon in December 1994 and was an ever-present in their 1995–96 Division Two (the old Division Three) Championship winning team. He was also voted into the PFA Second Division Team of the Season.

After retiring from playing, Culverhouse began a coaching career at Brighton before moving onto Orient and Wycombe, where he first worked with Hall of Famer Paul Lambert. Together they worked at Colchester, with Culverhouse in the assistant manager's role, before coming to Norwich in August 2009.

Culverhouse's return to Norwich was popular with the supporters who, during the centenary celebrations of 2002, had voted him Norwich's best ever right-back. In 2008 he was further honoured when he was named in Norwich City's greatest XI. Both were suitable accolades for a man who is 13th in the all-time appearances chart.

Ian Culverhouse made 369 appearances for Norwich scoring two goals.

Ruel Fox

January 1968, Suffolk   **Player 1986–94**

Ruel Fox is the only Hall of Famer born and bred in Ipswich. Snatched from under the noses of Ipswich Town, Fox would go on to haunt his local club for years to come, as he became a Norwich star during the club's early 1990s heyday.

Fox did have a trial at Ipswich but it was his friend and Norwich winger Louie Donowa who persuaded him to come to Carrow Road. Fox joined as a schoolboy in October 1983 before progressing through the ranks to professional in January 1986.

His Norwich debut came during the next season, 1986–87 in a 2–1 victory at Oxford. Despite the Norwich win Fox only made two other appearances that season, both as substitute. One of these was in the 0–1 defeat to Everton which won the Merseysiders the title in front of Norwich's biggest home gate of the season, 23,489.

Like his fellow Hall of Famer Jeremy Goss, Fox's Norwich career got off to a slow start, often in the reserves or on the bench. It was only really in the later days of his time at Norwich that he would become a leading star in the side.

There were early signs of promise as he was voted the club's most improved player in 1987–88; he played 40 games and scored his first goal in a 3–0 win over Chelsea on 28 December 78. However, as an out and out right-winger Fox found his path to the first team blocked by Hall of Famer Dale Gordon, who went on to win the 1988–89 Player of the Season award while Fox made just one first team start.

It was the same story in the 1989–90 season. Fox made just seven appearances, although he did score in three consecutive games against Derby, Aston Villa and Arsenal, the last three games of the season. He actually made it four in a row when he also scored in the opening fixture of the 1990–91 season in a 3–2 win against Sunderland, a game that also saw Gordon on the score sheet.

Two events proved to be the catalyst for Fox's career. Firstly, on 18 February 1991, Fox came off the bench to inspire Norwich to a famous 2–1 FA Cup fifth round victory over Manchester United. Secondly, Gordon's transfer to Rangers in November 1991 allowed Fox to make the right wing his own.

It was in the first ever Premiership season of 1992–93 that Fox and Norwich became the nation's darlings with an exciting brand of attacking football. Fox, with his natural pace and ability to twist and turn, made good viewing for the millions of armchair viewers that Sky TV were to introduce to the top flight, with their new brand of extensive coverage.

Fox played and scored in Norwich's shock 4–2 opening win of the 1992–93 season, away at pre-season favourites Arsenal, a win that really set the tone for the whole season. He then followed this up with a rare header on 22 August 1992 to secure a 1–1 with Everton to maintain Norwich's unbeaten start to the season.

Although Fox missed eight games through injury he returned on 25 October 1992 to play in the rest of the Premiership campaign. He made a total of 34 League appearances; with only two as a substitute compared to 10 in the previous season.

Fox continued his fine form in the 1993–94 season. The big smile and jig of delight were seen twice in the 4–0 win at Leeds on 21 August 1993. It was also his cross that was smashed in by

Goss for his goal of the month. On 4 December 1993 Fox joined a rare group of opposition players who scored a penalty at Old Trafford, in a well-earned 2–2 draw against the champions and runaway leaders Manchester United.

The Manchester United game was broadcast to 23 countries, and Fox's goal in another thriller – this time 3–3 at West Ham – was shown live on Sky TV. Fox's performances in these games, as well as those in Norwich's UEFA Cup run, made him hot property. On 2 February 1994 he became the first high profile transfer since Hall of Famer Mike Walker's departure, when he joined the Kevin Keegan revolution at Newcastle.

The transfer fee of £2,250,000 was a record received by Norwich, and it marked the start of the breakup of the great Walker side. Fox would play just one full season for Newcastle before another big money move of £4.2 million to Tottenham where he would make 106 appearances before injury intervened.

With his professional career over Fox did make a surprise international debut, when he became the only Hall of Famer to have pulled on the Montserrat national shirt in a 4–5 defeat against Antigua in November 2004.

Ruel Fox made 219 appearances for Norwich scoring 25 goals.

Ian Crook

January 1963, Essex   **Player 1986–97**

Ian Crook was the finest passer of the ball in a Norwich side who were nationally renowned for a passing style of football that was pleasing to the eye and applauded by all fans of all clubs.

Crook's superb technical ability was developed at Tottenham as a schoolboy, apprentice and then professional, where he shared the centre midfield with the master of passing, Glenn Hoddle.

While Crook no doubt learned a lot from training and playing with such gifted players as Hoddle, it was because of Hoddle that his first team appearances were limited. After being restricted to just 20 games in four years Crook made the switch to Norwich for just £80,000 in the summer of 1986.

Another clever signing by Hall of Famer Ken Brown, Crook was joining a Norwich side that were back in the First Division after a one year absence. He made his debut in the opening game of the 1986–87 season, a 0–0 draw against Chelsea, and soon became a permanent fixture in the Norwich engine room replacing the injured (and soon to retire) Hall of Famer Peter Mendham.

Crook's first Norwich goal came on 8 November 1986 against his old club Tottenham; a long range effort, it was the type of goal that would become his trademark at Norwich, and it opened the scoring in a 2–1 win. Crook also scored against Spurs' North London rivals Arsenal, on the last day of the season. Again his goal helped Norwich to a 2–1 victory securing a then record fifth place finish.

Crook spent the next two seasons in and out of the side playing 26 games in 1987–88 and 34 in the successful 1988–89 season, before he enjoyed a consistent run of games in 1989–90. By this time he had become an integral part of the team with his ability to pick out passes both short and long with great vision and pass selection. He was revelling in his role as the Norwich playmaker and was credited with many assists.

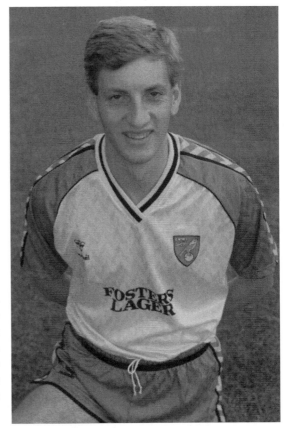

In 1990–91 Crook maintained his high standards in a Norwich side that was struggling to repeat the adventures of the late 1980s. He kept up his fine record against Tottenham, scoring in both the home and away fixtures, with his 25-yard swerving shot the pick of the goals in the 2–1 home win.

After another mixed season in 1991–92, where Crook missed half the League games as well as the FA Cup semi-final at Hillsborough, he became an important member of the 1992–93 Premiership team. He made his first Premiership start on 26 August 1992 in Norwich's first defeat of the season – 1–3 at Manchester City – and scored his first Premiership goal a week later, a stunning drive into the top corner in front of the Sky cameras; a fitting goal for Norwich's first live League game on the revamped Sky TV.

That 3–1 Sky win over Nottingham Forest sent Norwich top of the Premiership. It was against fellow pace-setters Coventry that Crook scored his second Premiership goal, this time as team captain, as Norwich kept top spot after a 1–1 draw.

With Crook playing a starring role in Norwich's record third place finish it was surprising that he did not add to his England B caps with a senior cap, especially when he continued to shine in the 1993–94 season including the UEFA Cup run. Crook missed just one game in Europe and demonstrated his ability to the watching nation in the first leg 3–0 win against Vitesse Arnhem, when he set up the opening goal with a delightful chipped through ball for Hall of Famer Efan Ekoku to finish.

Norwich were relegated at the end of the 1994–95 season, as the team that Hall of Famer Mike Walker built began to break up. Crook stayed loyal to Norwich in the recently rebranded Division One (the old Division Two) and played 32 games in the 1995–96 season. At the end of the season there was time for one last twist in Crook's Norwich career. Released at the end of the season as Norwich looked to trim the squad, Crook signed for Ipswich. However, Walker's return to Norwich led to a change of heart by Crook and a dramatic return to Norwich after exposing a loophole in his Ipswich contract. The whole episode further endeared him to the Norwich support, particularly when he came on as a substitute in the 3–1 victory against Ipswich on 11 October 1996.

Crook captained Norwich for most of the 1996–97 season, making his final appearance on 4 May in a 3–0 defeat by Oldham. It was Crook's 418th Norwich game, leaving him seventh in the all-time appearance listing. He spent 11 years at the club and was rewarded with a testimonial on 10 August 1996 against Sparta Rotterdam.

On leaving Norwich Crook became a globetrotter; playing, coaching and managing in Japan, Samoa and Australia before a brief return to Norwich in 2009.

Ian Crook made 418 appearances for Norwich scoring 24 goals.

Ian Butterworth

January 1964, Cheshire   **Player 1986–94**

Ian Butterworth was Norwich City's captain during two of the most memorable seasons in the club's history, including the record third place Premiership finish and the UEFA Cup campaign.

Butterworth's career began back in 1981 when he signed professional terms at Coventry having joined as a schoolboy in April 1978, while at the same time representing his county at badminton, table tennis and cricket.

Butterworth spent four character building seasons at regular First Division strugglers Coventry, helping them defy the odds as they survived relegation by the closest of margins in 1982–83, 1983–84 and, most famously and to Norwich's cost, in 1984–85 where they won their final three fixtures in controversial circumstances to send Norwich down.

During this period Butterworth played twice against Norwich, with Coventry winning on both occasions. The most important of these games was a nail biting 1–2 Coventry win on 12 May 1984 in the penultimate game of the season, a win that ensured Coventry stayed in the First Division at the expense of Midlands rivals Birmingham.

In the summer of 1985 Butterworth swapped the annual relegation battle for a title challenge when he signed for high-flying Nottingham Forest for £450,000 along with his Coventry teammate and future Forest and England captain Stuart Pearce. After just one season at

Nottingham, Butterworth joined Norwich on loan on 19 September 1986 and made his Norwich debut in a fantastic 4–1 win at Aston Villa.

Butterworth played four games during his loan spell in which Norwich won three and drew one. He formed an instant understanding with Hall of Famer Steve Bruce as Norwich kept three clean sheets in his four loan games, the last of which against Luton sent Norwich top of Division One. It was therefore no surprise when Butterworth's loan spell was made permanent on 29 November 1986.

Coming straight back into the heart of the Norwich defence on 6 December 1986, for the game against eventual champions Everton, Butterworth would miss just one more game that season as Norwich kept pace with the big boys to finish a record fifth place.

The Bruce/Butterworth central-defensive partnership was split during the 1987–88 season after Bruce's transfer to Manchester United. Butterworth represented stability in the Norwich defence playing alongside a number of different partners, as he made 41 appearances in all competitions, including three as captain in the League.

Butterworth's partnership with new signing Andy Linighan blossomed in the hugely successful 1988–89 season. In fact, the entire Norwich defence played together in 35 League games that season forming a consistent base for the eventual fourth place finish. The 1988–89 season also saw Butterworth score his first competitive goal. It came in Norwich's second ever live televised League game, in the hostile surroundings of the Old Den, Millwall. Butterworth's goal, a far post shot from a corner, gave Norwich an early lead in a dramatic game that ended 3–2 in Norwich's favour.

At the start of the 1989–90 season Butterworth was selected as Norwich captain; a role in which he played 31 games until injury and illness ended his season prematurely. He regained fitness and the armband for the 1990–91 season but it seemed his Norwich career may be coming to an end when he put in a transfer request in February 1991.

Butterworth's transfer never materialised and the rest is history. New Norwich manager and Hall of Famer Mike Walker made him his captain for the Premiership season 1992–93. Butterworth was captain for Norwich's first ever Premiership game, that 4–2 win at Highbury, and went on to play 26 Premiership games that season with Norwich losing just eight. He also scored his one and only Premiership goal, a consolation in a 1–4 defeat at Liverpool.

Having captained Norwich to their highest ever League finish, Butterworth would lead his team out to face European giants Bayern Munich and Inter Milan in the 1993–94 European campaign. He would also captain Norwich for 23 games of another exciting Premiership season but was becoming injury prone. Fittingly, his last Norwich game came against his old club Coventry, on 26 March 1994 where his old side beat his current side 1–2, before a knee injury finally ended his career.

After Norwich, Butterworth tried a comeback at King's Lynn before moving to the recently formed Major League Soccer in the USA. He played 17 games with fellow Hall of Famer Chris Woods before returning to the UK to begin a new career in coaching. He made a brief return to Norwich in February 2009 as Hall of Famer Bryan Gunn's assistant and was caretaker manager for two games before the arrival of Hall of Famer Paul Lambert.

Ian Butterworth made 293 appearances for Norwich scoring four goals.

Bryan Gunn

December 1963, Scotland   Player 1986–98
                                                                          Manager 2009

In 2005 BBC1's *Football Focus* ran a poll to identify the cult hero for every professional football club based on fans' votes. The cult hero for Norwich City, with 37 per cent of the vote, was Bryan Gunn.

The results of this poll were not surprising as Bryan Gunn is synonymous with Norwich City Football club. Since signing as a young goalkeeper in 1986 he has represented the club as sales manager, community ambassador, club liaison officer, head of player recruitment, goalkeeping coach and even first-team manager. At Carrow Road you can drink and be entertained in the Gunn suite. He was even made Sheriff of Norwich in 2002. A true legend!

Born on the Northern tip of Scotland and a competitor in Highland Games competitions, Gunn signed for Aberdeen as a schoolboy. Unfortunately for Gunn he joined Aberdeen at a time of unprecedented success and, with an established number one in Jim Leighton, Gunn spent more time babysitting manager Alex Ferguson's young children than he did playing.

In 1986, in recognition of his loyalty, Ferguson secured Gunn a move to Norwich for £100,000. Signed to replace the hugely popular Hall of Famer Chris Woods, who had moved to Rangers for a then British record fee for a goalkeeper of £600,000, Gunn made his debut in a 2–1 win versus Spurs that kept Norwich fourth in the First Division. A clean sheet and Man of the Match award the following week against his old mentor Alex Ferguson's Manchester United established Gunn as Norwich's new number one, in a season that ended with Norwich finishing fifth.

Gunn's success continued during the following two seasons. At the end of the 1987–88 season he won the Player of the Season award as he developed a growing rapport with the Norwich fans.

Gunn took his form into the 1988–89 season as Norwich were establishing themselves as one of the best teams in the country. Wins at Old Trafford and Anfield were particular highlights as Norwich entered April second in the League as well as FA Cup semi-finalists. Gunn was part of the team that lost 0–1 to Everton in what became the 'forgotten' semi-final, as the horrific events at the other semi at Hillsborough unfolded. In the League, Norwich eventually achieved their highest ever position of fourth.

Gunn was rewarded for his consistent performances with his first Scotland cap against Egypt in 1990. Unfortunately a couple of uncharacteristic goalkeeping errors contributed to a 1–3 defeat and Gunn went on to win only another 5 caps for his country.

Norwich began the 1992–93 season that saw the launch of the modern phenomenon that is the Premier League – as pre-season favourites for relegation. After the eye opening 4–2 victory at pre-season favourites Arsenal, the Canaries never looked back and eventually finished in another club record position of third. Gunn, an ever-present in the League that season, put in some outstanding performances epitomizing the spirit in the Norwich camp. He won his second Player of the Season award in a year where he suffered personal tragedy; the death of his 2-year-old daughter Francesca. The Bryan Gunn appeal to this day continues to raise millions for leukaemia and child cancer research.

Norwich's first ever European campaign the following season (1993–94) saw them drawn against the mighty Bayern Munich, four times winners of the European Cup and clear favourites to progress. The first leg in the intimidating Olympic Stadium saw Norwich take a shock 0–2 lead before Munich pulled a goal back. In the second half onslaught on the Norwich goal, Gunn made what he regards as his best ever save when he somehow kept out a bullet header from six yards out with BBC commentator John Motson already calling the goal. Norwich survived and after a 1–1 draw in the second leg, in front of a capacity crowd at Carrow Road and a national TV audience, they progressed to the next round. In the media spotlight Gunn's qualities were witnessed by the nation, though Norwich's European adventure was ended in the next round by another European giant and eventual winners Inter Milan.

The European campaign was the pinnacle of Bryan Gunn's career. During the busy Christmas period of the 1994–95 season, Gunn suffered a broken leg following a routine save. At the time Norwich were seventh and challenging for a European place; four months later they were relegated to Division One.

Despite a decent start to the 1995–96 season there followed a period of mediocrity and a number of mid-table finishes. Gunn was no longer the undisputed number one after 11 goals were conceded in just two games during the 1996–97 season. Finally on 31 January 1998 he played his final match for Norwich in a 0–1 defeat at Crewe.

After a short spell in Scotland, Gunn returned to undertake a number of different roles with Norwich. With the team threatened by relegation in the 2008–09 season Gunn answered the club's SOS to become caretaker manager. At a rejuvenated Carrow Road Norwich stormed to a 4–0 victory over Barnsley in Gunn's first game in charge. However, this was as good as it got and Norwich eventually dropped to Division Three for the first time in 50 years after a 2–4 defeat at already relegated Charlton.

Bryan Gunn was determined to put things right, making 12 new signings including Hall of Famer Grant Holt. However, after Norwich's record breaking 1–7 home loss to Colchester on the opening day of 2009–10, he left the club after a 24 year association.

Bryan Gunn made 477 appearances for Norwich, the fourth highest total in the all-time appearances listing.

Mark Bowen

December 1963, Wales   **Player 1987–96**

Virtually an ever-present during his nine years at Norwich, Mark Bowen has a proud double to his name.

He is Norwich's most capped footballer with 35 international caps won during his time at Norwich, 11 more than second place and fellow Hall of Famer David Phillips. Secondly, he holds the Norwich record for most appearances in the Premiership with 119 games.

Growing up in the 1970s in South Wales Bowen could easily have pursued a career in rugby. He played rugby at district level while representing the Welsh schoolboy side at football.

Having chosen football, he signed as an apprentice for Tottenham where he made a rare first team appearance in the 1984 FA Cup fourth round draw against Norwich. With first team opportunities limited he became part of the famous trilogy of Hall of Famers with Ian Culverhouse and Ian Crooks to swap reserve team football at White Hart Lane for first team football at Norwich, when he signed for £90,000 during the 1987–88 pre-season.

Originally signed as a midfielder, Bowen was in and out of the side until he replaced Tony Spearing as the first choice left-back at the end of the 1987–88 season. It was a position he was to make his own as he missed only three games in the 1988–89 season's fourth place finish.

Bowen was rewarded for his performances on 26 March 1988, winning his third Welsh cap – and the first of his 35 while at Norwich – in an international friendly 1–2 defeat to Yugoslavia, a game that saw Hall of Famer Dave Williams as Wales' caretaker manager. A week after the international and back in a Norwich shirt, Bowen actually appeared in goal for Norwich when he replaced the dismissed Hall of Famer Bryan Gunn in a 1–2 loss at Coventry.

Norwich failed to hit the same heights in the following 1989–90 season with a 10th place finish; however, defensively it was one of the best that the club had had, conceding just 42 League goals (their best ever in the top Division) three better than 1988–89. Bowen played his part as an ever-present

that season in the Norwich defence that managed 18 clean sheets including three against champions Liverpool. Bowen's performances in defence in addition to seven goals scored meant he was a clear winner of the 1989–90 Player of the Season award.

Over the next two seasons Bowen missed just 10 competitive games; he had become the complete full-back. In addition to his defensive qualities he also provided support in attack, making overlapping runs with a quality end product in the form of either a cross or shot. He was made captain during the 1990–91 season and captained Norwich for much of the 1991–92 campaign including the 1992 0–1 FA Cup semi-final defeat to Sunderland.

While fellow defender and Hall of Famer Ian Butterworth was reinstated as captain for the first Premiership season, Bowen was one of only three players to play every Premiership game that season and the only ever-present in all competitive games. He scored his first Premiership goal on 17 October 1992 in a 2–1 win over QPR and followed this up with another five Premiership goals in the following 1993–94 season, including a stunning long range effort at Sheffield Wednesday that sparked a comeback to earn an unlikely point after being 0–3 down.

Bowen's most memorable goal that season came in the epic UEFA Cup game in Munich. Although teammate and Hall of Famer Jeremy Goss rightly gets the headlines for his wonder goal, it was Bowen's far post header that gave Norwich a 2–0 lead and proved to be the winner on a night when Norwich became the first ever British team to win in Munich.

Bowen made a further 36 Premiership appearances in 1994–95 to take his tally to 119, the most for any Norwich player. Sadly his last Premiership appearance for Norwich came the week after relegation had been confirmed as Norwich waved goodbye to the top division in a 1–1 home draw with Aston Villa.

Playing just one season for Norwich in the second tier, Bowen failed to achieve 400 appearances; his last and 399th game coming in a 0–1 defeat to Charlton on 30 March 1996. A few months later, while still under contract with Norwich, he won his 37th Welsh cap (his 35th while a Norwich player) in a comfortable 5–0 World Cup qualifying win versus minnows San Marino.

In the summer of 1996 Bowen moved to West Ham for a season before heading to Japan. Back in English football he made his debut for Charlton in a 0–4 victory at Carrow Road in September 1997 and went on to enjoy success at Wembley with Charlton in the 1998 Division One Play-off Final.

After retiring from playing, Bowen forged a career in coaching. He joined his Welsh teammate Mark Hughes as assistant manager at Blackburn, Manchester City, Fulham and QPR. In 2002 he was voted Norwich's best ever left-back and in 2008 he was selected in the greatest ever Norwich starting XI.

Mark Bowen made 399 appearances for Norwich, ninth in the all-time listing, and scored 27 goals.

Robert Fleck

August 1965, Scotland   **Player 1987–92 and 1995–98**

Robert Fleck was a cult hero at every club he played for, none more so than in his two spells with Norwich, where he was immensely popular with the supporters for his 100 per cent commitment and for the important and spectacular goals that he scored.

Beginning his career at his home town club Glasgow Rangers, Fleck scored 34 goals in 102 games including four hat-tricks in one season. He was already a player of proven quality when he bucked the current trend of players moving from England to Rangers and made the move to Norwich in December 1987.

Fleck was one of new Norwich manager and Hall of Famer Dave Stringer's first signings when he joined for a club record fee of £580,000. He made his debut on 18 December 1987 in 0–1 to Wimbledon that left struggling Norwich second from bottom in Division One. However, it was not long before Fleck would influence matters, scoring in his second game to help Norwich to a 2–1 win at Derby.

The Derby win proved to be a turning point in what had been a dismal season. Fleck went on to score seven League goals, including four in three games as Norwich defeated Manchester United, Tottenham and Oxford. With Fleck in the side Norwich lost just six games in his 18 appearances to ensure a comfortable lower-mid-table finish.

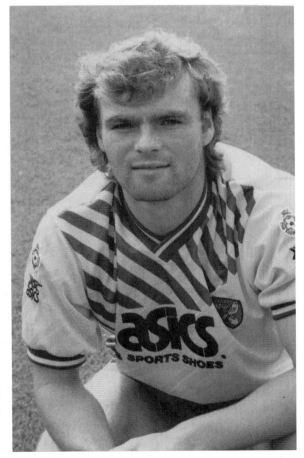

Fleck's first full season leading the Norwich line came in the club's record breaking fourth place finish in 1988–89; a season where he would finish top goalscorer with 15 goals. In a season full of highlights, Fleck got off to a great start scoring four in the first four games as Norwich became the Division's early pace-setters. On 22 January 1989 he scored a quality late winner, a long range half-volley, live on television, as Norwich beat Millwall 3–2.

A week after his heroics at Millwall, Fleck scored a high profile hat-trick in the FA Cup fourth round tie versus non-League Sutton on 28 January 1989. Sutton were the giant killing third round conquerors of First Division Coventry, a win that had captivated the nation's imagination. Sutton's dream ended at Carrow Road with Fleck's hat-trick part of an 8–0 victory, a club record FA Cup win and the biggest fourth round win in 30 years.

Fleck missed the rest of the 1989 FA Cup run, including the semi-final defeat to Everton, but he was back scoring in the 1990 FA Cup when his late equaliser at Fourth Division Exeter spared Norwich's blushes in the third round.

In the 1989–90 League season Fleck was again top scorer with 12 goals, although only seven came in the League as he missed 11 games through injury. Three of his seven goals came against big spending Manchester United who were 'doubled' by Norwich for the first time, with Norwich winning 2–0 in both games.

The home win over Manchester United on 21 January 1990 was shown live on television. A Man of the Match display by Fleck confirmed his status as Norwich's highest profile player with his typical skill and tenacity. The performance made an impression on the watching Scotland manager; Fleck was called up for his first cap in a 1–0 friendly win over World champions Argentina.

Fleck was part of the 1990 Scotland World Cup squad; he played in the second Group game against Sweden and returned to the Norwich camp for the 1990–91 season full of confidence. He again ended the season top scorer although his total of 11 was the lowest since Viv Busby in 1976–77.

Fleck was again top scorer in 1991–92 season, the first player to achieve this in four consecutive seasons since Hall of Famer Terry Allcock in the early 1960s. His total of 19 that season was his best yet at Norwich. He scored two in the FA Cup run to the semi-final, but was lacking match fitness after injury and failed to make an impact in the 0–1 defeat to Sunderland.

In the League Cup he scored six goals as Norwich made it to the fifth round before losing 1–2 at Tottenham. Fleck scored 12 League Cup goals in his Norwich career, the most of any Norwich player, while his total of 11 FA Cup goals was joint second, one behind Allcock.

In the League, Fleck scored in a crucial 1–1 draw against Wimbledon on 25 April 1992. The point was Norwich's first after six consecutive losses and was enough to guarantee them a place as Premiership founder members. Fleck's League and Cup exploits were enough to win him the 1991–92 Player of the Season award with a massive 49 per cent of the fans' votes.

Fleck's goal against Wimbledon was his last in his first spell at Norwich. Inevitably he was attracting interest from clubs keen to make an impression in the Premiership and in August 1992 Norwich accepted a club record £2.1 million bid from Chelsea.

Despite becoming a cult favourite at Chelsea the goals never came, and after just four goals in three years he made a welcome return to Norwich in September 1995. Signed for £650,000 Fleck added another 18 goals to his Norwich total over the next three seasons, adding a touch of quality to a Norwich side now in the First Division. He scored his first derby goal against Ipswich in November 1995 and a classic in the opening game of Hall of Famer Mike Walker's return, a 2–0 win against Swindon.

Fleck ended his playing career at Reading where he scored in their first ever game in their new stadium before returning to Norfolk to become player-manager at Gorleston and Diss.

Robert Fleck made 299 appearances for Norwich scoring 84 goals, the fourth highest in the Norwich all-time listing.

Andy Townsend

July 1963, Kent

Player 1988–90

Andy Townsend typified the strategy adopted by Norwich that would serve them so well during the 1980s.

A player of undoubted potential and hunger to succeed, Townsend was spotted and signed by the Norwich management team under which he would establish himself as a first class top flight footballer, before being sold for a substantial profit.

Townsend had to learn the game the hard way, playing over 100 games for non-League Welling while working as a computer operator. His big break came at Southampton in 1985 where he spent the next couple of seasons in and out of the Saints side before establishing himself as a hard-working midfielder during the 1987–88 season. During that season Townsend twice faced Norwich; both clubs ended the season occupying mid-table positions.

Still a player developing his game, Townsend signed for Norwich in the summer of 1988 for £300,000. He missed the opening game of the 1988–89 season and made his debut on 3 September 1988 in a 3–2 win versus Middlesbrough. He went on to establish himself in the centre of Norwich's midfield for the remainder of the season, finishing with 44 League and Cup appearances.

The 1988–89 season was a watershed moment for Norwich as it represented the first time in the club's history that a Norwich side would be serious contenders for the First Division title. Nine of the first choice XI are Hall of Famers from a Norwich side that captivated and entertained the watching public.

Playing in the spine of the team, Townsend was central to Norwich's attractive brand of passing football. He was full of energy and was a real box to box midfielder with a hard tackle and the vision to pick out the right pass. He chipped in with seven goals that season and became one of the few opposition players to score at both Old Trafford and Anfield in the same season.

His goal at Old Trafford on 26 October 1988 proved to be a late winner in a 2–1 victory against Manchester United. It was Norwich's first win that season against one of the 'big four' at the time (Manchester United, Liverpool, Everton and Arsenal) and it maintained Norwich's excellent start to the season, keeping them top of the League.

Manchester United were going through a turbulent time; however, in contrast, Liverpool were continuing to dominate English football. The holding champions were again among the leaders when a Townsend strike gave Norwich a 1–0 victory at Anfield on 17 December 1988, a win that would finally confirm Norwich as a force to be reckoned with that season.

The week after the shock win at Liverpool, Townsend was on the score sheet again in Norwich's first ever televised League game on 27 December 1988. In front of the BBC cameras, Townsend capped a Man of the Match display with Norwich's second goal in the 2–1 win over West Ham.

Norwich also made an impression in the FA Cup that season, reaching their first semi-final since 1959. Townsend played every game in the Cup run with his best performance coming in the third round at Port Vale. After taking the lead, Third Division Port Vale were looking to pull off a Cup shock before Townsend intervened with two goals, both high quality finishes, to see Norwich through to the fourth round with a 3–1 win.

In February 1989, Townsend made his international debut for the Republic of Ireland having qualified for selection through his Irish grandmother. The friendly versus France would be the first of 17 caps that Townsend would win while a Norwich player.

Eventually Norwich fell just short in both the League and Cup, but on a personal note Townsend was named in the PFA First Division team of the season, the first and, to date, only Norwich player to have achieved this honour.

After having one of the best ever debut seasons of any Norwich player, the following 1989–90 season failed, not surprisingly, to live up to such heights. Townsend was again a regular, missing just three League games, and captaining the team on 15 occasions. His first game as captain was a 0–0 draw against QPR on 26 August 1989, and his two goals scored while wearing the armband came in games against Millwall and Luton.

The highlight for Townsend that season came on the international front where he was to play in every game of Ireland's 1990 World Cup campaign, which included an opening 1–1 draw with England, a dramatic win on penalties versus Romania (Townsend was one of the penalty scorers) and a 0–1 quarter-final defeat to hosts Italy.

Soon after returning from Italy Townsend was sold to Chelsea for £1.2 million, much to the dismay of the Norwich supporters. Unlike his fellow Hall of Famer Robert Fleck, Townsend enjoyed a successful time at Stamford Bridge making 100 appearances and scoring 12 goals, including one against Norwich in the opening Premiership season.

He would become a regular Premiership footballer with Aston Villa – where he won a League Cup medal – and Middlesbrough, while he captained the Republic of Ireland in the 1994 World Cup. He has now swapped his boots for a microphone and pen as a pundit and co-commentator on television, as well as writing articles in the national papers.

Andy Townsend made 88 appearances for Norwich scoring 10 goals.

Gordon Bennett

June 1946, Bristol　　　　　　　　　　　　　　　　　**Executive 1988–99**

During his decade at Norwich City, Gordon Bennett filled the positions of Youth Development and Chief Executive – two of the most important functions at any club.

He undertook both these roles at a crucial and challenging time in the club's history and is one of the few characters that the club can thank for its very existence.

Born in Bristol, and an avid Bristol Rovers supporter, Bennett's playing career never got beyond the backwaters of the local Bristol League. He did achieve the next best thing to playing for Rovers when he was offered a job at the club which involved developing the Youth structure.

An intelligent and ambitious man, Bennett would soon progress through the ranks to become the Chief Executive where his biggest challenge would be ensuring the club's survival during a

10 year exile outside the city after the sale of their Eastville ground in 1986.

Bristol Rovers survived and a new ground was found back in Bristol. Meanwhile, Bennett moved up the M5 to WBA where he demonstrated his legal knowledge, serving the club as company secretary. After three years in the role, Bennett decided to return to the job that he had enjoyed at Bristol when he became Norwich's Youth Development Officer in 1988.

Youth Development had always been integral to Norwich with many Hall of Famers over the decades having emerged from the schoolboy/youth set-up to become first team legends. Norwich had regularly relied on income generated from the sale of players developed at the club either as schoolboys or signed as promising youngsters from other clubs.

When Norwich were relegated from the Premiership at the end of the 1994–95

season the need for the emergence of youth into the first team became paramount to the club's future. Fortunately, by the time of the relegation Bennett had already laid the foundations by establishing a centre of excellence, growing the youth coaching team and ensuring that a comprehensive scouting system was in place both locally and nationally.

Seven Hall of Famers would emerge from the Norwich youth academy under his guidance, as well as numerous other players who would represent the first team. Players such as Darren Eadie and Chris Sutton would play in Europe and eventually move for big money; Sutton went on to move for a British transfer record.

Later, after Eadie's and Sutton's departures, new talent would emerge. The Under-14s had enjoyed success in the Milk Cup tournament in Northern Ireland, the same tournament that featured the famous Manchester United youth teams of Beckham, Butt, Neville and Scholes. Many of the Under-14s squad would play in the Norwich youth team that won the 1996–97 South East Counties title, the first since 1982–83. Of that squad, 13 members were offered professional contracts; nine went on to play for the first team and three became Hall of Famers, playing at the top level of English Football.

By the time the Youth squad lifted the trophy, Bennett had been engaged to manage Norwich's affairs through a difficult period in the club's history. Increasing financial pressure coupled with mounting pressure from supporters saw the sale of shares and a switch of ownership between Hall of Famers Robert Chase and Geoffrey Watling.

After overseeing the Watling deal, Bennett was promoted to Chief Executive where he was ultimately responsible for cutting costs via player sales, staff redundancies, and offloading out of contract squad members, some of whom were Hall of Famers and stars of the club's time in the Premiership. Bennett had the added challenge of the Bosman ruling – where players could leave for nothing once their contract expired – it was therefore becoming increasingly difficult to guarantee a transfer income stream.

Bennett's ability to make tough decisions and his negotiation skills with the banks – he managed to restructure £8.5 million of debt – helped ensure Norwich's survival as a football club as they came within 48 hours of liquidation.

With Norwich City in a much better place, Bennett left in September 1999 to become the first Chief Executive at Scottish Premiership side Aberdeen, where he would encounter new challenges faced by Scottish clubs regarding television revenues and the influence of the old firm Glasgow clubs.

Bennett returned to England and now works as Head of Youth at Plymouth. He still keeps touch with happenings at Norwich via the Friends of Norwich City Youth (FONCY), a group that he helped set up during his time at Norwich.

David Phillips

July 1963, Germany   **Player 1989–93**

David Phillips' Norwich career started with a bang when he scored just two minutes into his debut to equal a club record held since 1927.

Phillips' quick goal on 19 August 1989, that helped Norwich to an opening day 2–0 win at Sheffield Wednesday, was just the start of a special period for both Phillips and Norwich that was to continue throughout his four seasons at the club.

Born on the German/Dutch border to a Welsh father serving in the RAF, Phillips received the very best schooling within one of the famous Dutch academies.

On his family's return to the UK, Phillips played rugby and competed in athletics but ended up choosing football, joining Plymouth in August 1981. Phillips helped Plymouth, a Third Division club, to an unlikely FA Cup semi-final appearance in 1984, scoring the winning goal direct from a corner in the quarter-final versus Derby.

After 73 appearances on the South coast, Phillips moved to Manchester City and then on to Coventry, where he scored a double against Norwich in November 1986. He was part of the Coventry team that won the club's first FA Cup in the thrilling 1987 Final and was a regular first teamer for all the clubs that he played for.

Norwich manager and Hall of Famer Dave Stringer was therefore getting an experienced professional when he signed Phillips for £525,000 to replace departing captain and Hall of Famer Mike Phelan in the Norwich midfield, in preparation for the 1989–90 season.

Phillips was an ever-present in his debut season of 1989–90 as he made the left midfield position his own. After his quick-fire debut goal he would play nine games in a Norwich shirt before experiencing a defeat, which came on 21 October 1989 1–4 at Luton. Prior to this first loss he scored his first home goal in a 2–2 draw at home to Tottenham a game that saw England internationals Gary Lineker and Paul Gascoigne on the score sheet.

It was during this period of the season that Phillips won his first Welsh cap as a Norwich player, representing his country in a 0–1 World Cup qualifying loss to Finland. He would play 24 times for Wales while he was at Norwich, leaving him second behind fellow Welshman and Hall of Famer Mark Bowen as Norwich's most capped player while at the club.

Phillips was Norwich's only ever-present during the 1990–91 season. Offering balance to the team he would interlink with Bowen on the left side, with both players comfortable either attacking or defending. Phillips scored four goals that season, all coming in wins for Norwich. It was a distinctly average season that saw Norwich finish 15th, one place above Phillips' old club Coventry.

After 104 consecutive appearances since his debut Phillips missed his first Norwich game, a 2–1 win over West Ham on 14 September 1991. He would miss a further 10 games through injury including the FA Cup semi-final defeat to Sunderland; he scored just two goals all season.

Following the disappointment of 1991–92, Phillips and Norwich got the 1992–93 season off to a sensational start. Phillips scored the equaliser in the 4–2 opening day win at Arsenal that meant Norwich were the first ever team to top the Premiership. He then followed this up with Norwich's first ever home Premiership goal in the 2–1 versus Chelsea.

More was to follow on 29 August 1992 with Phillips scoring an acrobatic scissor kick to earn a 2–1 win at Crystal Palace. The next week Phillips scored with another fierce drive that was becoming his trademark. This time it came in front of the Sky cameras, in Norwich's first Monday night League fixture, where a 3–1 win against Nottingham Forest took Norwich back to the top of the Premiership.

Phillips scored five in the first eight Premiership games. He would add a further four goals that season all coming in wins, including a winner in the penultimate game of the season against Liverpool that kept Norwich on course for their record third place finish. He was one of three ever-presents in Norwich's best ever season and finished as second top goalscorer.

With the joys of the 1992–93 season still fresh in the mind and a UEFA Cup campaign to look forward to, it was a big surprise when Phillips moved to Nottingham Forest in August 1993. The move was even more surprising when you consider that Forest had just been relegated from the Premiership.

In 1993–94 his first season at Nottingham Forest, Phillips helped the club to an instant return to the Premiership before seeing out his playing days at Huddersfield and Lincoln.

David Phillips made 186 appearances for Norwich scoring 20 goals.

Daryl Sutch

September 1971, Suffolk   **Player 1990–2003**

With 61 appearances from the Norwich bench, Daryl Sutch holds the uninspiring record of being Norwich's most used substitute. However, while this statistic suggests a bit part role in Norwich's history, 291 games in the starting XI tells a different story; Sutch would become part of the club's fabric over his 12 years at Carrow Road.

Born just south of the border in Lowestoft, Sutch was one of the first products from the Canaries School of Excellence where he would make 55 youth team appearances, outscoring Hall of Famer Chris Sutton. Having also represented the County and England Youth, Sutch was offered a professional contract in July 1990.

Sutch made his debut and the first of his record 61 substitute appearances on 9 October 1990 in the 3–0 League Cup victory over Watford. His first two games as a starter in the League would prove to be a real baptism of fire as Norwich lost 0–3 and 0–5 to Liverpool and Nottingham Forest respectively.

The highlight of the 1991–92 season for Sutch came at International level when he was called up to make his debut for the England Under-21s in a 2–2 draw with Hungary. Also playing for England that day were future Norwich players Matt Jackson and Mike Sheron, while fellow Norwich youth player and Hall of Famer Chris Sutton played alongside Sutch in the 0–0 European Qualifier with Turkey in what was Sutch's fourth and last Under-21s cap.

Back at club level it was not until the 17 October 1992, in that first Premiership season, that Sutch would experience his first Norwich victory as a starter in a 2–1 victory against QPR, his 10th game in the starting XI.

Sutch's first Norwich goal soon followed the QPR game, a late equaliser in a 1–1 draw with Middlesbrough. On 28 November 1992, an assist and a goal came in what was one of Norwich's best results of the season, 3–2 against fellow title challengers Aston Villa.

Altogether Sutch made a commendable 22 appearances (eight as substitute) in 1992–93 in what was Norwich's best ever season. His game time was again limited the following season (1993–94), but he did start in one of the biggest games in Norwich's history; the 0–1 UEFA Cup home defeat to Italian giants Inter Milan as well as coming off the bench in both games against Bayern Munich.

It was not until the 1996–97 season, a long way from the heady days of Europe, that Sutch finally had a consistent run in the first team. By now Norwich were struggling in mid-table of the Nationwide League Division One (or the old Second Division). Now a senior member of the squad, Sutch's experience and versatility were necessary to prevent Norwich from getting sucked into a relegation battle. Normally playing at full-back, Sutch would often sacrifice himself for the greater good of the team, covering every position and doing the less glamorous jobs such as man marking a key opponent or protecting the back four.

It was during these tough days that he became particularly popular with the Norwich supporters who recognised his loyalty, modesty and commitment to any job that he was asked to do by the manager. He was also a symbol of the good old days as the last remaining member of the Premiership and European successes.

Between seasons 1996–97 and 2000–01 Sutch would make 227 appearances with only six as a substitute. One of these appearances came as a replacement goalkeeper in the match against Huddersfield on 24 March 1999. For 80 minutes Sutch performed heroics in goal, conceding just one in a 1–1 draw with Huddersfield.

1999 also marked the year of Sutch's testimonial when Norwich played Dutch side AZ Alkmaar on 30 July 1999, fittingly for a defender the game finished 0–0.

By the 2001–02 season Sutch found himself out of favour and back on the bench; he made 19 appearances, only six of which were starts. His last Norwich game would be one of the club's biggest in years, the Play-off Final versus Birmingham at the Millennium Stadium in Cardiff. Although he had little involvement in the game himself, it was Sutch's miss in the penalty shoot-out that finally condemned Norwich to another season in Division One.

Although his final career moment was a sorry one, Sutch can look back on many highs. His 352 appearances placed him 16th in the all-time listing while his 12 seasons at the club are comparable with the likes of Hall of Famers Duncan Forbes and Bryan Gunn.

Daryl Sutch made 352 appearances for Norwich scoring nine goals.

John Polston

June 1968, London   **Player 1990–98**

Having taken the well-trodden pathway between White Hart Lane and Carrow Road, John Polston would emerge from the fringes of the Tottenham side to captain and score for Norwich in their first ever European game.

Off the three Hall of Famers (Ian Culverhouse, Ian Crook and Mark Bowen) that had made the same move before him in the 1980s, Polston was probably the most established at Tottenham having made 28 first team appearances as well as winning England youth and U19's caps.

Polston's career had been derailed in 1986 by a serious back injury but by summer 1988 he had returned to fitness and was looking to fulfil the potential that his youth had promised. Tottenham obviously rated Polston as they requested a fee of £750,000 from Norwich; however, the Football League tribunal sided with Norwich and the final transfer fee was set at £300,000 in July 1990.

Polston's arrival at Norwich on 20 July 1990 was overshadowed by the signing of

Paul Blades from Derby County. Blades, also a central-defender, had played 166 games for Derby and he became Norwich's record signing when he joined for £700,000 on 3 July 1990. Both men were under pressure to replace the ever popular Andy Linighan who had been sold to Arsenal for £1,250,000.

It was therefore all change in the Norwich central defensive department as the 1990–91 season got under way, with Blades the favourite to partner captain and Hall of Famer Ian Butterworth. Both Polston and Blades made their debuts on 25 August 1990 in a 3–2 victory over Sunderland before, as expected, manager and Hall of Famer Dave Stringer went for the Blades/Butterworth pairing.

On 8 December 1990 Polston was recalled to the team for the 3–1 win against Southampton. After an impressive performance he kept his place in the team for the rest of the season making 36 competitive appearances in total. He also scored four goals including a winner in the 1–0 home win against Everton.

Having seemingly cemented his place in the Norwich defence, Polston experienced an indifferent season in 1991–92 and Stringer turned to record signing Blades. However, Polston did play in all six FA Cup ties that season including the disappointing semi-final loss against Sunderland. His selection in Norwich's biggest game of the season was a vote of confidence and, with Blades' departure in the summer of 1992, Polston would finally make the number-five jersey his own.

Polston played in that first Premiership game at Highbury, before missing a few games through injury. He made a welcome return to the defence the week after Norwich had conceded seven at Blackburn, when the ship was steadied with a 2–1 win over QPR.

Polston became an important member of that Norwich team that took the Premiership by storm. He took over the captaincy in Butterworth's absence and led Norwich to a 0–0 against challengers Blackburn in his first game with the armband. This was the first of four clean sheets in five games as Norwich returned to the summit on 17 March 1993 and set things up perfectly for the the title deciders against second and third place Aston Villa and Manchester United.

Polston put in a true captain's performance in the first of these games on 24 March 1993. The Norwich defence withheld sustained pressure before Polston himself netted a late close range winner to send Carrow Road wild, as title rivals Aston Villa were defeated 1–0. Unfortunately Norwich could not repeat the trick a week later; Manchester United's 1–3 victory would be the beginning of the end of the Premiership dream.

The following 1993–94 season marked another landmark occasion for Polston as he led the team out for Norwich's much anticipated debut in European football against Dutch side Vitesse Arnhem. As with the Villa game, Polston marked the historic event with another close range effort, the icing on the cake in a 3–0 first leg win on 15 September 1993.

After the highs of the last two years, Polston played 46 games (his best total) in the 1994–95 relegation season and, like many at the club, stayed to help Norwich's promotion attempt despite, no doubt, having options elsewhere. By this time he was no longer a regular but he did make 36 appearances in 1995–96 and another 34 appearances in Hall of Famer Mike Walker's returning season, 1996–97, which included a headed goal in the televised 3–1 derby victory over Ipswich on 11 October 1996.

After just 14 games in the 1997–98 season, including five as substitute, Polston made a cameo appearance in the last home game – a 5–0 thrashing of Swindon. His last Norwich game came on 3 May 1998 away at Reading, the club he was to join on a free transfer that summer.

Polston's time at Reading was injury plagued and he made few appearances before retiring in 2001 to take up sports therapy and personal training.

John Polston made 263 appearances for Norwich scoring 12 goals.

Chris Sutton

March 1973, Nottinghamshire   **Player 1991–94**

At his peak with Norwich former academy player Chris Sutton was Britain's most desired footballer, with every major club in the land keen to secure his services.

Big spending Blackburn Rovers eventually won the race as Norwich accepted a £5 million offer, at that time it was by far and away the biggest transfer fee ever seen in English football.

£5 million was a particularly good return for a local lad who had come through the youth system. Sutton's father Mike had made 54 appearances for Norwich between 1963 and 1966 and together they would become the fourth father and son to both play for Norwich.

Sutton emerged from the youth team to sign professionally in June 1991, two months after he had made two appearances as substitute at the end of the 1990–91 season. Sutton started as a centre-back when he replaced injured captain and Hall of Famer Ian Butterworth for his first start on 7 December 1991 in a 3–3 draw with Crystal Palace.

After eight games in defence, Sutton was switched to centre-forward in the impressive 1–1 draw away to Arsenal; from then on he made the forward's position his own. In terms of goals, it was in the 1991–92 FA Cup run that Sutton would make his mark. He scored a double in the fifth round 3–0 win against Notts County and then an extra-time winner – a looping header – in the quarter-final replay against Southampton to seal a 2–1 win in what was to be the last big game played in front of the Barclay End terrace.

Sutton started the first Premiership game in the 1992–93 season as Norwich's number nine, but after a two goal debut by summer acquisition Mark Robins, Sutton reverted back to the centre-back position where he admirably covered injured Hall of Famer John Polston in a run of just two defeats in 10.

It was during this run that Sutton made his England Under-21 debut in a 1–0 win against their Spanish counterparts. This was the first of 13 Under-21 caps that Sutton would win while at Norwich, the most for any Norwich player while at the club, but he would have to wait until his time at Blackburn before winning his one and only full England cap in November 1997.

Meanwhile in the Premiership, after a spell on the bench, Sutton returned to spearhead the Norwich attack for the Boxing Day 0–0 against Spurs. Three goals in three games soon followed before he was back in defence, this time replacing the injured Butterworth. Sutton did finish the season with a bang, scoring a fine hat-trick in a 4–2 win over Leeds on 14 April 1993, a win that kept Norwich in third position and on course for European football.

The 1993–94 season was the year everything came together for Sutton as he enjoyed an unbroken spell up front. He scored two in a 3–2 victory over Blackburn, eroding the memories of last season's 1–7 thrashing. This was Sutton's first of seven doubles that season including two at Tottenham, two in consecutive weeks against West Ham and Liverpool and one in the FA Cup third round tie against Wycombe, the first game after Hall of Famer Mike Walker's departure.

The goals flowed throughout the season, with the pick of the bunch a long range half-volley in the 2–2 draw at champions Manchester United in a match beamed to a global audience. Sutton scored a total of 28 League and Cup goals that season to finish top goalscorer by some margin. His total was the highest since Hall of Famer Ted MacDougall's in 1975–76, while his 25 League goals were the most scored by a Norwich player in a single season in the top division. Not surprisingly, the Player of the Season award followed as did the bidding war for his signature.

Sutton's £5 million move to Blackburn was vindicated when, alongside Alan Shearer, he helped fire Blackburn to their first Championship in 80 years, with 20 League and Cup goals including one in his return to Carrow Road on 1 October 1994. He ended the season on a personal high when he was voted in the 1994–95 PFA team of the season.

Injury meant that Sutton missed out on much of the 1995–96 season. By the time he returned, his old striking partner Shearer had left for Newcastle in a move totalling £15 million – a fee that dwarfed Sutton's £5 million record. Sutton himself was soon on the move for £10 million to Chelsea, which netted Norwich £500,000 thanks to a clause inserted in the original contract with Blackburn.

Sutton had one more big money move, this time to Celtic for £6 million taking his career tally to £21 million. At Celtic he enjoyed a successful time under former Norwich manager and Hall of Famer Martin O'Neill before he eventually saw out his playing days back in England with Birmingham and Aston Villa.

Chris Sutton made 127 appearances for Norwich scoring 43 goals.

Rob Newman

December 1963, Somerset   Player 1991–98

A total of 483 competitive appearances for Bristol City – the seventh highest in the all-time listing – many as club captain, and a testimonial versus Aston Villa; Rob Newman had all this to his name before he had even begun his career with Norwich, where he would add Premiership and European football to that already distinguished list.

As with fellow Hall of Famer Dave Williams, Rob Newman was a one club man this time from the red half of Bristol. He had progressed through the ranks at Bristol City to become a professional in October 1981 at a time when Bristol City were fighting for their very existence.

The club survived and Newman went on to make his 483 appearances, the vast majority in the Third Division until Bristol City's promotion to the Second Division in 1989–90. At the time it appeared that Newman would see out his career at his local club, but in July 1991, aged 28, he was offered a shot at the big time with a £600,000 move to Norwich.

Signed by manager and Hall of Famer Dave Stringer, Newman would offer Norwich some experience, versatility and a high work ethic after their disappointing 15th finish in 1990–91. Newman made his debut on 17 August 1991 in an opening day 2–2 draw versus Sheffield United. He soon found his shooting boots with two goals in the next two games, earning Norwich a point at Oldham and three at QPR.

The whole of Newman's debut 1991–92 season was spent wearing the number-nine shirt. Despite not being a natural striker he contributed nine goals, just two fewer than Norwich's record signing and out and out forward Darren Beckford. Newman scored some important goals in his first season, including goals in two exhilarating 4–3 wins against Crystal Palace and Everton – wins that would ultimately keep Norwich in the First Division.

Newman also played all six FA Cup games, scoring a fine equaliser to calm the nerves in the semi-final replay against Southampton which Norwich went on to win 2–1 in extra-time. In total Newman made 53 appearances for Norwich in his first season, more than any other player that season.

He started the first 11 opening fixtures in the brand new

Premiership, in a run that included seven Norwich victories. Newman scored his first Premiership goal in a 1–0 win against Sheffield Wednesday on 19 September 1992, which was Norwich's fifth successive win, a club record in the top flight.

Although goals were generally hard to come by, and after a spell on the side-lines, Newman returned to the side in the centre-back position where he helped the side to two successive clean sheets against Tottenham and Leeds, doubling the number of clean sheets achieved so far that season. Unfortunately for Newman a broken ankle in the Leeds game meant that he would miss the next 18 games. He returned in the penultimate match of the season, another clean sheet in a 1–0 win over Liverpool.

In the 1993–94 season Newman would demonstrate his versatility, playing for Norwich in defence, attack and midfield. He turned 30 during the season and enjoyed the greatest moment of his career when he captained the side in the world famous San Siro stadium. Here he played against and was equal to the likes of Dutch wizard Denis Bergkamp, as Norwich eventually succumbed to an undeserved 0–1 defeat, 0–2 on aggregate.

After Europe came relegation in 1994–95, a campaign that saw Newman make 41 appearances including 10 as substitute. It was a season short of highlights, but Newman's opener at Portman Road on 19 September 1994 helped Norwich to a 2–1 victory, their first in their rivals' backyard since 1982.

Newman was used as a squad player during Norwich's first season back in the second tier since 1985–86. He became a bit of a scapegoat for frustrated fans but never hid out on the pitch. His late equaliser on 2 April 1996 in a 2–2 draw at Barnsley ensured that Norwich would avoid a second successive relegation.

A resurgent Newman missed just two League games in the 1996–97 campaign as returning manager and Hall of Famer Mike Walker recognised his qualities. He played 14 games as captain including a 3–1 home win against Ipswich that kept Norwich top, before a run of 10 games without a win consigned Norwich to another mid-table finish.

The 1997–98 season would be the last in a Norwich shirt for Newman. His last game saw him again come off the bench to help earn Norwich a 1–1 draw against QPR on 3 December 1997. At the end of the season, Newman moved to Southend on a free transfer where he would eventually have a spell as caretaker manager. His last job was the glamorous sounding role of Manchester City's scout based in Spain.

Rob Newman made 249 appearances for Norwich scoring 17 goals.

Mike Walker

November 1945, Wales   **Manager 1992–94 and 1996–98**

In the first of his two short but hugely contrasting periods at Norwich, Mike Walker oversaw the most monumental 18 months in Norwich's 110 year history.

During the Premiership title challenge and a UEFA Cup campaign, Norwich consistently got the better of the bigger and more glamorous clubs, playing an exciting and attractive brand of football that was beamed across the country and the world in the growing media spotlight; an 18 months of which the likes may never be seen again for a club of Norwich's size.

When Norwich decided to promote from within, following Hall of Famer Dave Stringer's resignation in May 1992, few had heard of Walker or knew much about his credentials. As a player he spent most of his career at Colchester where he played in goal 656 times including 310 consecutive games between 1977 and 1983. His managerial career also took place at Colchester until he left to become Norwich reserve team coach in November 1987 with Colchester sitting top of Division Four.

With Walker's lack of experience and Norwich's lowly finish in 1991–92 they were the bookies' pre-season favourites for relegation, making Walker's achievements in the 1992–93 season all the more remarkable.

Walker made a couple of astute pre-season signings, bringing in some experience in Hall of Famer Gary Megson for £800,000 and a goalscorer from Manchester United reserves, Mark Robins, who would top score for Norwich that season with 15 Premiership goals. Largely though, Walker managed to get the best out of the existing squad that had only just avoided relegation the previous season, highlighting his man-management skills as well as his tactical nous; he played a system that got the maximum out of the players at his disposal.

Under Walker, players that had been at Norwich for many years, often on the fringes, suddenly

came to the forefront. Players such as Hall of Famers Ruel Fox and Jeremy Goss would emerge to become household names and key components in the team's success.

In Walker's first game in charge on 15 August 1992 he faced his first test, a half-time team-talk with Norwich 0–2 down to title favourites Arsenal. A stirring second half comeback and a 4–2 win shocked the nation and set the standard from which Norwich rarely dropped. By 31 August Norwich were top and Walker had won the Premiership's first ever Manager of the Month trophy. By the time he won his second Manager of the Month award, for November, Norwich were eight points clear at the top.

Despite injury set-backs and the odd thrashing, Norwich showed character to regain top spot in March and were still top with just six games to go; the closest ever to that first title.

Norwich under Walker proved they were no one season wonders as they started the 1993–94 season with some wonderful results. Blackburn, Leeds, Tottenham and Everton were all ruthlessly put to the sword away from home, with Norwich scoring 15 goals in the process. The glory continued in the UEFA Cup; they beat Bayern Munich and pushed Inter Milan, the eventual winners, all the way in the third round, with the fans singing Walker's name for an hour after the full-time whistle at the San Siro.

Norwich had an air of invincibility about them, but as Walker wanted to push the team on to the next level he came to loggerheads with the chairman. With the relationship soured, Walker left for Everton in January 1994. He left Norwich with a 45 per cent win ratio, the best of any Norwich manager in the top division.

One of the best known managers in the English game at the time, Walker experienced a tough time at Goodison, with Everton almost getting relegated for the first time in over 60 years. Things were no better the following season (1995–96); Everton went 12 games without a win and Walker was sacked just two days after a 0–0 draw at Norwich.

Walker's second coming at Norwich came with much expectation in the summer of 1996. With Norwich now in the old Second Division, Walker instantly worked his magic with a 2–0 opening day win over Swindon as the style and swagger returned to Norwich's football. With just one defeat in the first 10 games, Norwich topped the League after a 4–1 win at Grimsby. A win over Ipswich followed before the tide turned dramatically with a run of just one win in 12, and the season ended in a disappointing mid-table finish.

The 1997–98 season was no better, with a 0–5 loss to Ipswich and the first home gate below 10,000. Only a couple of late wins saved Norwich from relegation as Walker left the club at the end of the season. The second spell brought a win percentage of just 32.7 per cent.

Mike Walker managed Norwich for 179 games, and led Norwich to a record League finish and their first European campaign.

Gary Megson

May 1959, Lancashire   Player 1992–94
                                                          Manager 1995 and 1995–96

Fifteen years after his professional debut and with over 400 senior appearances at some of England's biggest and most historic clubs, Gary Megson became Hall of Famer Mike Walker's first Norwich signing when he joined on a free transfer in July 1992.

Under Walker, Megson would enjoy a fitting swansong to a successful playing career before a spell as Norwich manager which would be spent in the most difficult and trying of circumstances.

Megson's professional career began at Plymouth in 1977 before taking him to Everton, Newcastle, Nottingham Forest and Manchester City.

However, it was at the club his father captained, Sheffield Wednesday, that Megson would enjoy his best days. Having joined in August 1981, Megson would miss just three games in three seasons. He faced Norwich in the tense final fixture of the 1981–82 season where Norwich gained promotion despite a 1–2 defeat. Two seasons later Megson enjoyed his own promotion as an ever-present in the 1983–84 Sheffield Wednesday team that won promotion to the First Division.

It was while at Manchester City that Megson made his move to Norwich, having been deemed surplus to requirements at the age of 33. He arrived at Carrow Road with a wealth of experience coupled with the energy and enthusiasm of a player half his age. He needed all these attributes in his Norwich debut away at Arsenal on 15 August 1992 as he helped the team to a famous 4–2 win in the opening fixture of the new Premiership season.

Megson started the first nine games in the Premiership, of which Norwich won seven. He scored his one and only Norwich goal in a 1–3 loss at his old club Manchester City and he captained Norwich to a 3–2 win at Chelsea. After a 1–0 win on 19 September 1992 against another old club, Sheffield Wednesday, injury intervened and disrupted his season. Megson made a total of 25 appearances for Norwich, of which 23 were in the Premiership; a telling contribution towards a record third place finish.

A similar number of games were played in the following 1993–94 season, the highlight of which came on 8 December 1993 in the intimidating surroundings of the San Siro stadium, Milan. Megson had missed the two games against Munich and the first leg defeat to Inter Milan but returned to a Norwich side weakened by injury and suspension in the second leg. In a Man of the Match display Megson rolled back the years, organising the Norwich team, harassing his illustrious opponents and commanding the midfield. Only a late Denis Bergkamp goal would kill off a tie where Norwich had run the eventual UEFA Cup winners close over both legs.

In the 1994–95 season Megson began to make the transition from player to coach during Hall of Famer John Deehan's tenure. A post-Christmas loss of form for Norwich coupled with an injury crisis saw Megson briefly back on the pitch in a 0–1 defeat to Leicester on 5 April 1995. Three days later after another defeat, this time at Newcastle, Deehan resigned leaving Megson as caretaker manager for the last five games.

With no opportunity to freshen the squad and faced with a tough fixture list Megson, was left with a tough battle to keep Norwich in the Premiership. He relished the challenge, and while Norwich were eventually relegated, four defeats in the last five games were all by the odd goal.

Bad luck also accompanied the team, particularly at Tottenham where Norwich hit the woodwork, and at Leeds where they conceded a disputed penalty.

With relegation confirmed Megson spent a brief period away from Norwich as assistant manager at Bradford. He returned to the firing line in December 1995 to take over after the controversial departure of Hall of Famer Martin O'Neill.

It was a thankless task with supporters unhappy and an ugly atmosphere within the stands. Megson stuck gallantly to the task despite being severely handicapped by the sale of two senior players, Hall of Famer Jon Newsome and striker Ashley Ward for a combined price of £2.6 million. Megson shared the fans' frustrations and to his credit managed to ensure that Norwich avoided a second successive relegation.

Unfortunately for Megson, a change of ownership resulted in another managerial change, with his old manager Walker returning to replace him in the summer of 1996. Megson meanwhile went on to enjoy success at Stockport and then WBA, where he took Albion back into the top flight in 2001–02 after a 15 year absence, winning Manager of the Season in the process.

Gary Megson made 54 appearances for Norwich scoring one goal. He was manager of Norwich for 32 games.

Darren Eadie

June 1975, Wiltshire   Player 1993–99

Flying winger Darren Eadie would make his first-team debut in Norwich's first ever European game, the UEFA Cup first round tie at home to Vitesse Arnhem.

Later, as Norwich struggled back in the second tier of English football, Eadie would become a symbol of optimism to the supporters during the dark days. He was a player guaranteed to lift you off your seat and a match winner on his day.

Eadie's arrival at Norwich was a glowing testament for Norwich's scouting and youth policy at the time. A member of the Southampton school of excellence and Wiltshire County Under-13s and 15s, he chose to join Norwich over a number of interested clubs based on the strength of Norwich's youth system.

Having joined Norwich as a schoolboy he progressed to trainee in 1991 and then to professional in February 1993. Seven months later, aged 18, he made his famous debut in Norwich's historic UEFA Cup opener coming on for Hall of Famer Gary Megson with the tie safe at 3–0. He then went one better, starting in the electrifying home draw with Bayern Munich, the 1–1 result enough to see Norwich progress over the two legs.

Eadie made his Premiership debut on 18 September 1993, scoring a goal in a 2–2 draw against QPR. In total in the 1993–94 season he made nine Premiership starts, six appearances as a substitute and scored three goals. At the end of the season Eadie made his England Under-21 debut in the Toulon Tournament in a 0–3 defeat to hosts France. It was the first of seven Under-21 caps that Eadie would win while at Norwich.

The 1994–95 season marked the beginning of the decline for Norwich. Eadie's career, however, was just getting started. He played 36 games in all competitions including six games in the League Cup where Norwich progressed to the quarter-finals before losing 0–1 to Bolton. He scored two Premiership goals, the second of which came in a 3–0 derby win over Ipswich on a Monday night in front of the Sky cameras. The win was Norwich's first in 12 games and a rare highlight in a disappointing season that ended in relegation.

Eadie's class would show in the second tier as he became a regular for Hall of Famer and new manager Martin O'Neill. His first goal actually came in O'Neill's last game in charge, a 2–2 draw with Grimsby in December 1995. A week later he scored again, this time against Leicester, where a shell-shocked Norwich eventually lost 2–3.

After the disruption of 1995–96, the 1996–97 season would start with hope under the returning manager and Hall of Famer Mike Walker. Playing for the man who had shown such faith in him during those European nights, Eadie was to have his best season in a Norwich shirt.

Eadie played 46 games that season on the Norwich wing, where his pace and directness scared defenders. He was a classic winger who could finish; he ended the season with 17 goals, the most scored by a winger since Hall of Famer Ken Foggo back in 1970–71. He scored four doubles including one in the first 10 minutes in a 4–1 win at Grimsby that put Norwich top on 1 October 1996.

Despite Norwich slipping down the League in the second half of the season, Eadie scored 11 goals from late January onwards. It was a run of form that would see him selected for the

full England squad, some feat for a player outside of the Premiership, and was enough to win him the Player of the Season award to add to the golden boot.

After that season Eadie had offers to play in the Premiership but stayed loyal to Norwich. His form was disrupted by injuries which now began to plague his career, causing him to miss large chunks of the next three seasons. When he did make a comeback it would often inspire the team, such as his first game in the 1999–2000 season where his goal versus Crewe on 11 September 1999 helped Norwich to their first win in the opening six games.

Eadie's last Norwich game came on 4 December 1999 in a win over WBA before a £3 million transfer fee was accepted from Leicester. It was Norwich's third largest fee received and while at the time it upset many fans, it would turn out to be a good bit of business. Eadie went on to play just 40 times for Leicester before injury forced an early retirement in 2003 aged just 28.

Darren Eadie made 204 appearances for Norwich scoring 38 goals.

Efan Ekoku

June 1967, Lancashire   **Player 1993–94**

Although he was only at Norwich for one full season, Efan Ekoku achieved two claims to fame that would guarantee him a place forever in Norwich folklore.

Both events came within 10 days of each other in September 1993. The first was scoring Norwich's first ever goal in European competition when he scored the opener versus Vitesse Arnhem. The second was a four-goal haul away at Everton, which was a joint club record for most goals scored by a Norwich player in one game in the top division and the most scored in a single game away from Carrow Road. At the time it was also a Premiership record and today is still an equal best scoring performance on an away ground.

These were two great achievements for a player who was a relative late comer to professional football. At school his focus was on rugby, where Ekoku stood out for his pace and jumping ability; two attributes which would make him such an effective centre-forward.

His footballing break-through came at Bournemouth when he was signed by then manager Harry Redknapp in the summer of 1990. He made his professional debut at the grand old age of 23.

After enjoying relative success at Third Division Bournemouth, Ekoku – nicknamed 'The Chief' – signed for Norwich for £500,000 on 25 March 1993 just hours before the transfer window deadline. His signing reignited the old link between the two clubs that was so prominent during the 1970s as he joined a Norwich squad top of the Premiership and looking to make a final assault on the title.

His first game on 5 April 1993 came in the top of the table clash at home to Manchester United which ended in a 1–3 loss. The next week he scored his first goal but in another defeat, this time 1–5 at Tottenham. These two defeats effectively ended Norwich's title hopes.

With the title challenge over, Ekoku still managed to leave his mark on the season when he scored two in his first start, the 3–3 final day draw at Middlesbrough. The point was enough to secure Norwich third place, a record Norwich League finish and enough for a shot at Europe.

The 1993–94 season started off indifferently for Ekoku with the strikers rotated in the first month of the season. Luckily for Ekoku it was his turn to lead the attack in the opening UEFA Cup game against Vitesse Arnhem on 15 September 1993. Arnhem were not the most glamorous of opponents but provided a good test for Norwich with their distinctively continental style of football. The breakthrough, and Ekoku's historic goal, came in the 51st minute – a stunning controlled volley that swerved into the bottom corner of the net, a fitting goal for such an occasion.

Ten days later, on 25 September 1993, came Ekoku's quadruple at Everton to set that Norwich and Premiership record. His goals included a run and finish from a through ball, a far post header, an open goal from a rebound and, his fourth and best, a flick over the defender to round the 'keeper and score. The goals were scored past former Footballer legend Neville Southall, and the 5–1 win put Norwich fifth in the Premiership.

Ekoku ended the season with 14 goals, second top scorer behind Hall of Famer Chris Sutton. He could have had more but missed six games in March and April 1994 while away representing Nigeria (who he qualified to play for through his father) in the Africa Cup of Nations. He also went to the 1994 World Cup with Nigeria but failed to make an appearance.

After Sutton's record transfer to Blackburn in the summer 1994, Ekoku started the 1994–95 season as Norwich's main striker. However, after just seven games he himself was off to pastures new, joining Wimbledon for £900,000 on 14 October 1994. The transfer was another disappointment for the Norwich fans who felt there was much more to come from Ekoku and were surprised at selling to a club perceived as being 'smaller' than Norwich. The disappointment was further compounded when he scored winners for Wimbledon in both games against Norwich that season as Wimbledon finished ninth and Norwich were relegated.

At Wimbledon, Ekoku enjoyed a successful few years with further top 10 finishes and appearances in two semi-finals. He was their main target man for 123 Premiership games before he moved overseas to Swiss side Grasshoppers.

After ending his career at Brentford, Ekoku moved into the media as a match analyst and co-commentator while at the same time obtaining his FA and UEFA coaching badges.

Efan Ekoku made 45 appearances for Norwich scoring 17 goals.

Andy Marshall

April 1975, Suffolk   **Player 1993–2001**

After being thrown in at the deep end aged just 18, Andy Marshall emerged to become one of the best and most popular of Norwich goalkeepers, as he helped keep relegation at bay almost single-handedly at times during a turbulent period in the club's history.

Such was the respect he gained with the club and its supporters during those difficult seasons that Marshall's inclusion in the Hall of Fame was never in any doubt, despite one of the most controversial transfers in the club's history when he crossed the Norfolk/Suffolk divide to join Ipswich Town in the summer of 2001.

Born in Suffolk, Marshall was another product of Norwich's excellent scouting and youth system. Having just turned professional he was still learning his trade when he was suddenly thrown into the Premiership fray after a serious injury to long serving number one and Hall of Famer Bryan Gunn. Gunn's injury, a broken leg, happened in the first half of the away game at

Nottingham Forest on the 27 December 1994. It proved to be a shaky start for Marshall with Forest's winner in a 0–1 coming direct from a corner.

Marshall did not have much time to reflect on the error with his home debut coming just four days later on New Year's Eve 1994, in front of a packed 21,172 at Carrow Road. The visitors were Kevin Keegan's high-flying and free scoring Newcastle but a Man of the Match display from Marshall restricted them to just the one goal in a 2–1 victory for Norwich. Marshall pulled off a number of stunning saves during the game earning praise from both managers. The performance also convinced Norwich manager and Hall of Famer John Deehan that he could rely on the young Marshall for the remainder of the Premiership season.

Marshall played 21 Premiership games that season and was in no way to blame for a terrible run that ended in relegation. He kept a clean sheet on 25 February 1995 away at champions elect Blackburn, the first time Rovers had failed to score at home all season. Another clean sheet was obtained in the 3–0 win over Ipswich that was shown live on Sky.

Marshall ended the 1994–95 season on a personal high when he made his England Under-21 debut, in a team that included David Beckham, keeping a clean sheet in a 2–0 win against Malaysia.

With Gunn back to fitness for the 1995–96 season Marshall went from Premiership football to loan spells at Bournemouth and Gillingham in the Second and Third Divisions as he looked to maintain his game time and increase his experience.

It was not until the 1997–98 season that Marshall would establish himself as the Norwich number one; he played 42 out of the 46 Division One games in what was to be a difficult season. In the first game that he missed, Norwich conceded five at Wolverhampton. Marshall returned to the team to keep a clean sheet against Manchester City in a 0–0 on 7 February 1998, while three clean sheets in the last four games were enough to earn Norwich three wins and a 15th place finish.

Marshall played 91 games over the next two seasons although on both occasions Norwich fell some way short of the Play-offs. In the 1998 League Cup Marshall became the centre of attention as the third round tie against Bolton went to penalties, with Norwich losing despite Marshall saving Bolton's first. In the League two clean sheets against promotion contenders Ipswich proved to be the highlights in 1999–2000.

The 2000–01 season was Marshall's best in a Norwich shirt and also his last. A number of fine displays and 14 clean sheets helped ensure Division One football for another year. His season was summed up in his last game for Norwich where he made a number of crucial saves to earn Norwich a point at Wimbledon on 6 May 2001. His efforts that season were recognised by the Norwich support who voted him their Player of the Season.

At the top of his game and ambitious to play in the Premiership to further his international prospects, no Norwich fan would begrudge the out of contract Marshall his dream move. Unfortunately for them the move to the Premiership took him to rivals Ipswich who had finished 5th in the Premiership, qualifying for the UEFA Cup.

Marshall's move to Ipswich was the first time a player at his peak had moved between the two rivals and it soured relations on both sides. Marshall struggled to settle, with a clean sheet in a hostile return to Carrow Road on 2 March 2003 a rare highlight for him.

On leaving Ipswich, Marshall played for Millwall where he appeared in the 2004 FA Cup Final 0–3 defeat to Manchester United. A move to Coventry followed where he won Player of the Season in 2006–07. Now at Aston Villa, Marshall splits his time in the reserves with work at a goalkeeping academy.

Andy Marshall made 219 appearances for Norwich.

Neil Adams

November 1965, Staffordshire   **Player 1994–99**

A familiar voice to Norwich fans through his match day media work with radio Norfolk, Neil Adams was Norwich's dead-ball expert and a player Norwich could always rely on for a pinpoint cross or a cool finish during his five years at the club.

Adams' qualities, including his set-piece skills, were first seen at his local club Stoke, where he made such an impression that the Division One runners-up Everton came calling in the summer of 1986.

Although never a regular he made enough appearances to receive a Division One winners' medal at the end of the 1986–87 season, Everton's last as champions of England.

Just 20 games in three seasons for Everton meant that Adams had to move to progress his career. In January 1989 he joined former Norwich striker Joe Royle's revolution at Second Division Oldham. Adams was joining Oldham at the start of a glorious period in the club's history. As well as a Wembley appearance in the 1990 League Cup Final, which ended in a 0–1 defeat to Nottingham Forest, Adams was also involved in an epic 1990 FA Cup semi-final that finished 3–3 against Manchester United. He was also a member of the Oldham team who won the Second Division title and with it promotion to the top flight.

Oldham were a founder member of the Premier League, with Adams playing a part in both Premiership games versus Norwich as Oldham pulled off an unlikely escape from relegation. During the second Premiership season, 1993–94, Adams was bought by new manager and Hall of Famer John Deehan. He signed in February 1994 for £250,000 as a replacement for departing Hall of Famer Ruel Fox. However, Adams was a very different player to Fox, being more defensively minded and more focused on delivering the final ball rather than beating a man with pace and a trick.

Adams made his Norwich debut on 19 February 1994 in a 3–3 draw at Swindon and went on to play in all except one of the remaining 14 Premiership games, including the 1–1 final day draw that would send his old team Oldham down.

The relegation year of 1994–95 saw Adams make the left-midfield slot his own, playing in 33 League games (10 as a substitute) in that ill-fated season. For Norwich the season had started well as Adams' last minute winner against Leeds in October 1994 put Norwich eighth, while another goal, this time in the first minute in a 2–1 win against Newcastle on New Year's Eve 1994 saw Norwich rise to seventh before a run of one win in 20 games confirmed their relegation.

Adams was a regular in Norwich's first season back in the second tier of English football in nine years, as he created many opportunities with his quality crosses both in open play and from corners or free-kicks. He was the mainstay of a Norwich side that had to ride out a rough period in the season before ending clear of the relegation zone.

In the 1996–97 season Adams added goals to his repertoire, with 16 in all competitions, 10 more than he had scored in the previous three seasons together. Nine of his goals came from the penalty spot, a Norwich record for most penalties scored in a season and a 100 per cent success rate for Adams. In total he would score 13 out of 14 penalties during his Norwich career, the club's most successful penalty taker.

As well as his highest goals tally, Adams played more games than any other player that season, missing just one game. He also captained the side for the first time when he was given the armband for the last game of the season in a 0–3 defeat at his old stomping ground, Boundary Park, Oldham.

In contrast to 1996–97 Adams missed a large part of the 1997–98 season through injury and his goals tally was down to five. Two of his goals came from the penalty spot, and one from open play on 20 September 1997 gave Norwich a 2–1 win at Manchester City, a win which helped Norwich break one of football's longest records by winning their first match at Maine Road in 33 years.

After missing large parts of the 1998–99 season, again through injury, Adams' last game for Norwich was on 6 February 1999, a disappointing 0–2 home defeat to a Stockport side managed by ex-Norwich manager and Hall of Famer Gary Megson. After being released at the end of the season Adams split his time between coaching and media work. He became one of the voices of local football in his role as co-commentator on Radio Norfolk, as well as hosting Canary Call, the regular football phone-in that followed each of City's games.

Neil Adams made 206 appearances for Norwich scoring 30 goals.

Jon Newsome

September 1970, Yorkshire   **Player 1994–96**

By the summer of 1994 nine Norwich City players, eight of whom are Hall of Famers, had left the club for fees exceeding the magical £1 million mark.

Jon Newsome finally bucked the trend when he became Norwich's first £1 million signing when he joined from Leeds United in July 1994. He was to remain Norwich's record signing for another 11 years until Hall of Famer Dean Ashton joined for three times the amount in January 2005.

Newsome had begun his career at Sheffield Wednesday before making his name at Leeds. He joined the Leeds title winning side of 1991–92, the last team to win the old First Division, and he was a scorer in the 3–2 victory over Sheffield United that was to clinch the title.

In contrast to Norwich, Leeds struggled in the new look Premiership. Newsome was a used substitute in the games versus Norwich which included a draw and two wins for Norwich (including the 4–0 thrashing at Elland Road).

Newsome struggled to become a first team regular at Leeds but had still made 76 League appearances when the Norwich Board decided to reinvest some of Hall of Famer Chris Sutton's transfer income. The final fee of £1 million represented a calculated gamble and seemed a fair price in the current transfer market.

Immediately made team captain for his debut on 20 August 1994, a 0–2 opening day defeat away at Chelsea, Newsome would captain Norwich in every game he played for the club except for one substitute appearance towards the end of his career there.

After the Chelsea defeat Newsome settled in quickly as part of a defence that kept four clean sheets in a row. His first goal came on 1 October 1994 when high-flying Blackburn, with new signing Sutton, came to town. Not only did Newsome manage to restrict the lethal Blackburn forward line of Shearer and Sutton to just one goal, but his mazy run and shot proved to be the winner in a 2–1 victory.

Newsome also scored in another 2–1 victory, this time with a powerful header to beat Leicester, a win which put Norwich ninth going into December and had the team looking up towards Europe rather than down to the relegation zone in which they would eventually finish.

As Norwich's confidence began to fall apart in the second half of the season with just one win in 20, Newsome never gave up, with his battling displays earning respect from the Norwich fans during a time when club/supporter relations were at a low point. He hit the bar with a 30 yard effort in a narrow 0–1 defeat to Tottenham on 17 April 1995 and he kept on driving the team until relegation was confirmed after a 1–2 defeat at his old club Leeds.

Despite Norwich's relegation Newsome was actually part of a defence that conceded just 54 goals, the lowest tally since the 1989–90 season when there were four fewer games. Even in the third place finish of 1992–93 Norwich conceded 65 goals, 11 more than 1994–95. Newsome was part of a defence that had kept nine clean sheets and had only let in three or more goals on three occasions. In recognition of these statistics and his efforts over a tough season Newsome won the 1994–95 Player of the Season award, the first debutant to win it since Hall of Famer Kevin Drinkell in 1985–86.

Newsome could have stayed in the Premiership but remained loyal to Norwich and was determined to help them bounce straight back up. He remained club captain in spite of a change in manager and started the 1995–96 season off with intent, scoring two in the opening 3–1 win at Luton.

He scored a headed goal in the 2–1 win over Ipswich on 19 November 1995 to keep Norwich in the Play-off places after a promising start to the season. An injury then forced Newsome to sit out eight games after which Norwich had fallen to 13th.

Newsome was to play just one more game, a 1–1 draw at home to Portsmouth on 9 March 1996, before his sudden and shock transfer to Sheffield Wednesday. Apparently against manager and Hall of Famer Gary Megson's wishes, Newsome's sale came out of the blue as a financially strapped Board took £1.6 million off Sheffield to the dismay of Norwich fans.

Newsome made more appearances for Wednesday than in his first spell there but could not prevent their relegation from the Premiership during the 1999–2000 season. By this time injury had taken its toll on Newsome and he retired from the game aged just 29.

Jon Newsome made 76 appearances for Norwich scoring eight goals.

Delia Smith

June 1941, Woking

Michael Wynn-Jones

June 1941, Wales   Majority Shareholders 1996–current

Delia Smith was born in Woking and left school with no qualifications. After a short stint as a hairdresser she began working as a kitchen hand in a small restaurant in Paddington – perhaps the most unusual background of all the Norwich Hall of Famers.

Michael Wynn-Jones meanwhile had carved out a successful career in media to build his own publishing company.

Wynn-Jones' family had relocated to South Norfolk in 1953 where he would become a regular at Carrow Road at a time when the 1959 Cup team were capturing the city's and county's imaginations.

It was thanks to Wynn-Jones that Smith became a Norwich supporter when he took his fiancée to her first game in 1969. By now she had worked herself up through the culinary ranks to become a best-selling cookery author with a regular slot on television, the nation's first celebrity chef. It was a busy lifestyle but she still found time to attend matches regularly with season ticket holder Wynn-Jones.

As her media career continued to grow during the 1980s, so did her love for football. She became a Norwich season ticket holder, on the River End terrace, alongside her now husband Wynn-Jones.

As fans first and foremost, they both enjoyed the club's successes of the early 1990s before relegation, falling attendances and a fire sale of players illustrated the dire financial situation the club had found itself in. The situation was so bad that in 1996 the club was rumoured to have come within 24 hours of going out of business.

Initially the club was saved by Hall of Famer Geoffrey Watling in April 1996. The feel good factor had returned to the Carrow Road; however, the club was still in dire financial straits and with Watling now well past retirement age, Smith and Wynn-Jones were approached. For a £500,000 investment, they both took a seat on the new look Board in November 1996.

Their initial investment was to be the first of many, with an estimated £12 million invested in total to date, at a time when football finances are continually tested. The investment earned them a majority shareholding of 61 per cent with the first instalment in the summer of 1996 effectively saving the club from extinction as the debt was brought down to manageable levels. It is to their credit that, throughout the remainder of the 1990s and early 2000s, they continued to put their own money into the club as Norwich struggled on the pitch and despite the criticism from some sections of the fans.

They proved to be a great double act with Smith becoming the vocal point through her national fame. Both continued to attend games, sometimes in the stands with the fans, wearing their Norwich scarves and Wynn-Jones his distinctive yellow tie.

Together they displayed energy and business acumen as they set about revolutionising the catering facilities, not only to improve the match day experience but also to generate a revenue stream for the club outside of match days. Such was their success in this field that Arsenal adopted the Norwich model when building their new Emirates stadium.

Their support for the club and the passion shown was often evident. The most famous incident was Smith's rousing speech to the Norwich faithful at half-time during the home match against Manchester City on 28 February 2005. With Norwich deep in a relegation battle, and having let slip a 2–0 lead, the speech on the pitch in front of the Sky cameras was to become legendary.

Wynn-Jones also displayed his passion on many an occasion. In 1998 he even gave the first team squad a pep talk after the departure of Walker and with relegation a possibility. On a happier note there was also the dancing on the Portman Road pitch to celebrate Norwich's 2–0 victory that took them top of Division One on 21 December 2003.

As supporters of the club they owned, Smith and Wynn-Jones would become the envy of many other clubs who had lost their souls, and in some cases their financial security, through the trend of foreign ownerships. While they were open to investment, both Smith and Wynn-Jones were adamant that it would only be to the right people and only if the club's best interests were at heart.

Smith was to gain a CBE, OBE and an honorary degree from the University of East Anglia during her long and successful career. However, given her passion for the club, I imagine that she got just as much joy from watching Norwich achieve back to back promotions in 2009–10 and 2010–11, ending up with her and her husband again enjoying the boardroom hospitality of the country's top clubs.

Delia Smith and Michael Wynn-Jones continue to this date to hold the majority shareholding in Norwich City Football Club.

Michael Foulger

March 1954, Norfolk   **Director 1996–Current**

After the upheaval experienced at Norwich City Football Club at the end of the turbulent 1995–96 season, and the formation of a new board in November 1996, the attention and media focus was for obvious reasons all on the incoming Hall of Famers Delia Smith and her husband Michael Wynn-Jones.

Smith in particular was to grab the column inches as a national treasure and now 'celebrity' football fan and owner. A female in a traditional man's world only heightened the attention. However, on 28 November 1996, Michael Foulger also joined the board, where he would serve the club with distinction and purpose away from the limelight.

Foulger was born and bred in Norfolk in a Norwich supporting family. He claimed on his induction to the Hall of Fame that he had had a trial with Norwich in his younger days, but it was the family meat business that he entered at a young age, ensuring that the company continued to

thrive and grow. With money to spend, a good and experienced head for business and as a passionate supporter, Foulger became an ideal candidate to join the newly formed Board, and in doing so he contributed to a £2 million capital investment.

At the time of the Board's formation the feel good factor had returned to Carrow Road, with Hall of Famer Mike Walker and supporters who had been boycotting, both returning to the club. On the pitch Norwich were riding high in third place in Division One, but a sudden downturn in form meant that Foulger had to wait until the seventh game before witnessing his first win as a director, a 2–0 victory over Bradford on 28 December 1996, a month after he joined the Board.

Norwich's poor run of form had included a couple of heavy defeats but, in a refreshing change from the previous regime, money was made available to spend on the team. Matt Jackson arrived for £450,000 from Everton to shore up the defence and helped Norwich to finish the season in 13th place.

As the club continued to struggle throughout the rest of the 1990s Foulger, proud to serve his club, worked tirelessly behind the scenes. He focused his resources on the academy continuing the good work put in place by Hall of Famer Gordon Bennett.

Another aspect of the club that the board, and particularly Foulger, improved was the relationship and communication between the club and the supporters. A number of supporter initiatives and forums were set up with links established to the Board to ensure that supporter feedback was received. Foulger would attend many supporter events in an effort to engage with the fans and answer their concerns. One such concern was the club's finances and the continual sales of star players or assets.

The Board made an effort to ensure a decent proportion of cash received went straight into the manager's transfer kitty. This was evident when midfielder Andy Johnson's sale to Nottingham Forest for £2.2 million was followed by the purchase of Hall of Famers Iwan Roberts and Craig Fleming for a combined cost of £1.5 million. Against a backdrop of annual losses and increasing debts it was the directors' use of their own money that ensured that the club remained liquid.

Out of all Foulger's hard work behind the scenes, two particular gestures were especially appreciated by the club and fans alike.

His first gesture came at a point in time when the club needed it most at the end of the 2008–09 season. Having just been relegated to the third tier for the first time since 1959–60, Norwich had reached a new low in their recent history. As a result of the relegation, fans who had purchased season tickets for the following 2009–10 season were entitled to a 20 per cent rebate as compensation for the fact they would now be watching League One (Third Division) football. With the financial ramifications of relegation evident, Foulger agreed to match every supporter pound for pound that waived their rebate. His actions bought in a personal donation of £718,608 cash which was used to bring Hall of Famer Grant Holt to the club, while Foulger remained on the Board to help see the club through this difficult period.

His second gesture came during the happier times of February 2011. With Norwich not only back in the Championship (Division One) but gunning for promotion to the Premiership, Foulger made a £2 million investment on the condition that the money was to be used purely for transfers. The investment increased his shareholding to 15 per cent and was made at a time when the country was in recession.

Michael Foulger continues to sit on the Norwich City Board as well as being a Trustee of the club's Community Sports Foundation.

Craig Bellamy

July 1979, Wales   **Player 1997–2000**

At £5.2 million Craig Bellamy's transfer fee was the highest ever received by Norwich. Twelve years on, having graced the top levels of the game with some of the biggest clubs in the country, his total accumulated transfers come to an incredible £45 million.

As Bellamy has become one of the icons of the Premiership over the years – loved by fans at all the clubs he has played at for his skill, pace and commitment – there remains an element of pride from Norwich staff and fans alike for the achievements of their one time youth product.

Bellamy first arrived at Carrow Road in 1993 aged just 14 where he was the star player in the 1996–97 youth team that won the South East Counties League title. In the same season he emerged in the first team with three substitute appearances.

In 1997–98, his first full season, he finished Norwich's top goalscorer with 13 goals and became a beacon of light for the long suffering supporters after a couple of seasons of underachievement. He was a player who excited the fans with skill and desire, a clever player whose confidence gave him the edge that would take him eventually to the top of the game.

His first Norwich goal came on 1 November 1997 in a 2–2 draw at Bury in just his fifth full game. He would go on to play in most of the remaining games that season although injury forced him to miss the embarrassing 0–5 defeat at Ipswich. Bellamy returned to score a double in the 3–3 draw at home to Birmingham on 4 March 1997, a game watched by just 9,819. It was Norwich's lowest home gate for 26 years and reflected the fans' feelings towards the relegation battle that the club found itself in.

A fine individual goal in the 1–1 versus WBA lifted spirits, and a goal and a Man of the Match display in the last home match versus Swindon helped Norwich to a 5–0 victory that ensured Norwich would survive the drop that season.

Bellamy's fine debut season also included his first Welsh cap,

in a 0–0 against Jamaica, and the winner against Reading on 3 May 1998 which was the last goal ever scored at Elm Park, Reading's home for the last 102 years.

The 1998–99 season was very much a tale of what could have been as Bellamy's partnership with Hall of Famer Iwan Roberts flourished, with both men complementing each other's games. Bellamy got the season off to a great start with five goals in three games as Norwich started the season with three straight wins. His goals included a hat-trick in a 4–2 win over QPR on 22 August 1998 with two coming from the penalty spot.

Bellamy continued his scoring run with a headed winner at Portman Road, the first goal conceded by Ipswich in four games. This was then followed by classic doubles by both Bellamy and Roberts in a game that summed up their partnership; the Huddersfield defence was given a torrid time during a 4–1 Norwich win.

Bellamy's and Norwich's season was defined on 12 December 1998 when he was injured in a crude tackle in the 2–2 draw at Wolverhampton. At the time Norwich were sixth and Bellamy had scored 13 goals in a 23 goal partnership with Roberts. Although Bellamy would miss just five games, when he returned the momentum had gone and he scored just four more goals as Norwich finished ninth.

While the injury at Wolves got the attention from fans and media alike it was an injury in the 1999–2000 pre-season friendly at Southend that would be much more critical. The cruciate knee ligament rupture meant Bellamy would miss virtually the entire 1999–2000 season, returning in the 0–0 against Port Vale with just four games remaining.

Bellamy did end the season on a high when he took his club partnership with Roberts onto the international stage in the prestigious friendly against World champions Brazil, a 0–3 defeat in front of 72,500 in the Millennium stadium. It was Bellamy's ninth and last Welsh cap while playing for Norwich.

Bellamy played just one game, the opener, in the 2000–01 season before the record breaking move to Premiership Coventry. After Coventry's relegation he then went on to earn big money moves to Newcastle, Blackburn, Liverpool, West Ham and Manchester City, starring for each club, playing in the Champions League and winning the 2002 PFA Young Player of the Season award.

He made a loan spell to his boyhood club Cardiff in 2010–11 as Cardiff challenged and lost out to Norwich in the promotion race for the Premiership. He has now signed for Cardiff on a permanent basis. Outside of Football Bellamy has invested £1.2 million into his academy work in Sierra Leone.

Craig Bellamy made 91 appearances for Norwich scoring 34 goals.

Darren Kenton

September 1978, London   **Player 1997–2003**

'You'll never beat the Kenton' was a chant often heard from the Barclay End in recognition of Darren Kenton's presence in the Norwich defence.

In many ways there was a lot of truth in the chant as Kenton would progress from the academy to become one of the best defenders in Division One.

Joining Norwich as a trainee, Kenton was a member of the 1996–97 Championship winning youth team, many of whom would progress to senior level. Kenton signed his first professional contract in the summer of 1997 to become part of manager and Hall of Famer Mike Walker's first team squad for the 1997–98 season.

Kenton made his debut on 4 October 1997 in the 0–2 defeat at Tranmere; not the easiest of debuts with Norwich down to nine men following two red cards. It was not until February 1998 that he played his next game and his first as a starter in a 0–0 versus Manchester City. The

Manchester City game started a run of ten games for Kenton, but they were ten games without a win as Norwich struggled with injuries and poor form. It was certainly a tough environment for the young defender to come into.

The 1998–99 season got off to a much better start for both Kenton and Norwich. He scored in the opening game of the season, 2–1 over Crewe, and played in four wins in the first five games. Under new manager Bruce Rioch, Kenton's defensive qualities were further developed and he ended the season with 27 appearances as Norwich finished in an improved ninth position.

The 1999–2000 season was a bit unsettling for Kenton after a period on the transfer list and his future uncertain. The Norwich back four was also evolving with a number of different players selected in defence over the course of the season. Kenton made 28 appearances, the highlight being seven clean sheets in 10 games including defensive shut-outs versus title challenging Manchester City and Ipswich.

With a new contract signed and his future settled, Kenton had an impressive 2000–01 season playing 33 games and scoring two goals. He was proving to be a versatile defender comfortable at either full or centre-back. He had pace combined with good decision making that made him very hard to beat.

As Kenton's performances continued to impress so too did Norwich's, with the club reaching the 2001–02 end of season Play-offs for the first time since their conception in 1987. Kenton was a key part of the defence that included fellow Hall of Famers Adam Drury, Craig Fleming and Malky Mackay and would concede just 16 goals at Carrow Road.

Kenton also contributed with four goals including a quick-fire double on 3 February 2002 to earn Norwich a 2–1 win against Sheffield United. Just as important was his winner in the 2–1 victory at home to Gillingham on 19 March 2002. This win, coming on the back of a 0–1 defeat at home to Birmingham, was the starting point of a seven match unbeaten run, including five wins that saw Norwich rise from 10th to squeeze into the Play-offs in sixth position on the last day of the season.

The 2001–02 season also saw Kenton test himself against the best as Norwich were drawn against big spending Chelsea in the third round of the FA Cup. Traditionally a good Cup side Norwich had been starved of success since the 1992 semi-final. Although they were eventually knocked out in a replay, the 0–0 in the first game illustrated Kenton's potential as star strikers Jimmy Floyd Hasselbaink and Gianfranco Zola were both kept quiet.

After the disappointment of losing to Birmingham on penalties in the Play-off Final, Norwich were to suffer a post-Play-off hangover in the 2002–03 season, although for Kenton this was probably his best season in a Norwich shirt. Defensively Norwich got off to a sound start and had conceded just seven goals by the start of October.

With Norwich unable to build on this good start it soon became clear that another season in Division One was beckoning. Kenton was ambitious and had the ability to play at the higher level. Therefore, to progress his career, he decided against signing a new contract and became a free agent at the end of the 2002–03 season.

Kenton signed 'on a Bosman' for Premiership Southampton where he put in some Man of the Match performances as he quickly adjusted to life in the Premiership. However, as is common in football, a change in management meant he spent more time on the sidelines than on the pitch. After just 29 League appearances in three seasons Kenton transferred to Leicester, where back in the Championship (Division One) he was to score after just 40 seconds against Norwich in a 2–1 Norwich win on 14 April 2007.

After leaving Leicester, Kenton had spells at Leeds, Cheltenham and in the US before retiring in 2009 to pursue interests outside of football.

Darren Kenton made 175 appearances for Norwich scoring nine goals.

Craig Fleming

October 1971, Yorkshire   **Player 1997–2007**

Craig Fleming was the rock at the back in the Norwich defence, a reliable figure and fans' favourite during a decade of highs and lows for the club.

By the time Fleming signed for Norwich in June 1997 he had already enjoyed a successful career which had included two seasons in the Premiership with Oldham Athletic.

Before Oldham, Fleming had broken into his home town team Halifax aged just 16. He soon established himself as a first team regular with a series of eye-catching performances that earned him his move to Oldham, who had just been promoted to the First Division.

Alongside fellow Hall of Famer Neil Adams and ex-Norwich midfielder Mike Milligan, Fleming enjoyed three seasons in the top division with Oldham. They were founder members of the Premier League in 1992–93 and preserved their status after surviving a traumatic relegation battle on goal difference. In the following 1993–94 season Oldham were not so fortunate, with Fleming part of the team that were relegated at Carrow Road after a 1–1 draw on 7 May 1994.

Fleming would face Norwich again, after their own relegation from the Premiership meant they joined Oldham in Division One for the 1995–96 season. However, it was after another relegation – this time Oldham's drop to Division Two at the end of the 1996–97 season – that Fleming made his £600,000 switch to Norwich.

Signed to add some authority to a Norwich defence that had struggled in the previous season, Fleming made his debut as captain in the opening fixture of the 1997–98 season, a disappointing 0–2 defeat to Wolverhampton. It set the tone for a poor season in which Fleming experienced just five wins in his 22 League appearances as Norwich struggled. He did score a crucial goal, the important opener in a 5–0 victory over Huddersfield that ended a barren run of 14 games without a win and helped keep relegation at bay for another season.

Over the next three seasons Fleming would establish himself in the Norwich defence, eventually switching from full-back to centre-back. He captained the side again on 20 October 1998, this time to a 1–0 win away at Ipswich just eight months after Norwich had suffered a 0–5 humiliation on the same ground. He scored six goals over this three year period including Norwich's first goal of the new millennium when Portsmouth were beaten 2–1 on 3 January 2000.

By the time of the 2001–02 season Fleming had established a formidable central defensive partnership with Hall of Famer Malky Mackay, a partnership that would provide the bedrock not only for that season's Play-off Final appearance but also for the Championship winning team of the 2003–04 season.

Fleming was an ever-present in the 2001–02 season, a long season that ended in Play-off defeat to Birmingham on 12 May 2002. He was also an ever-present in the 2003–04 title winning team, playing in all 46 League games as Norwich won the title with 94 points. Fleming was part of the defence that conceded just 39 goals – only three more than the record breaking 36 in 1971–72 but with four more games played. At the end of Norwich's most successful season since the early 1990s Fleming was awarded the Player of the Season award, a fitting tribute in a season where there were many candidates.

In Norwich's first campaign back in the Premiership after a nine season absence, Fleming was an ever-present; an impressive achievement in the era of squad football and team rotation, and the only outfield player in the whole of the Premiership to play every game.

He scored his one and only premiership goal that season in the 3–2 win over relegation rivals WBA on 5 February 2005. He also cemented his reputation as one of the best man markers in the game as he starred in the 2–0 shock win over Manchester United on 9 April 2005, a win that would kick start an unlikely and ultimately unsuccessful push for survival.

After relegation Fleming decided to stay with Norwich and attempt to lift the club back to the Premiership at the first attempt; however, the 2005–06 season proved to be disappointing as pre-season favourites Norwich finished outside the Play-off places in ninth. The season did end positively for Fleming as he was granted his testimonial on 26 July 2006 against Newcastle.

After his testimonial Fleming played just 10 games during the 2006–07 season, his last and his 382nd Norwich game coming on 16 December 2006 in a 1–2 defeat at Southampton. In January 2007 he moved to Rotherham on a free transfer and was missed by Norwich as results continued to go against them in a poor season.

Fleming had a short spell at Rotherham before returning to Norfolk where he splits his time between charity work, his duties as Ambassador of Sport in Norfolk and his coaching-management role at Lowestoft Town.

Craig Fleming made 382 appearances for Norwich, 11th in the all-time list, and scored 13 goals.

Iwan Roberts

June 1968, Wales   **Player 1997–2004**

Iwan Roberts is one of the most popular players to have ever worn the famous yellow jersey, a cult hero with the fans and Norwich's third highest goalscorer in the club's history.

His goalscoring records were even more impressive when it is considered that he did not join Norwich until he was nearly 30.

Roberts started his career, some 11 years before his arrival at Norwich, with Watford in 1986. From Watford he moved to Third Division Huddersfield where 50 goals in 142 games got him his first break in the Premiership with Leicester, at £300,000 he was their record signing at that time.

Roberts finished top goalscorer in each of his three seasons at Leicester which included two promotions both via the Play-offs, and a relegation from the Premiership in the same season as Norwich in 1994–95.

A popular player at Leicester, Roberts moved to Wolverhampton for £1.3 million in summer 1996 where he would spend just one season. He endeared himself to the Wolves supporters with a hat-trick against Black Country rivals WBA before his £900,000 transfer to Norwich in July 1997.

Roberts endured a difficult first season at Norwich. Expectations were high with attacking talent such as Hall of Famers Darren Eadie, Craig Bellamy and Robert Fleck all starting alongside Roberts in his debut against his old club Wolverhampton on 9 August 1997. A 0–2 defeat to Wolves set the tone for a disappointing campaign as injury, the weight of expectation and a loss of form, all weighed on the team.

With Norwich struggling at the wrong half of the table the big money striker Roberts bore the brunt of the supporters' dissatisfaction, with little sign of the hero worshipping he would later enjoy. Roberts ended the season with only seven goals in 33 games, although a double against Huddersfield and one against Swindon helped dispel any fears of relegation.

Roberts put the disappointment of his debut season behind him returning fitter and stronger for the 1998–99 campaign. It was the season that his

partnership with Bellamy clicked as he became the target man but with a good touch and eye for a pass. Together they scored 23 goals until an untimely injury to Bellamy disrupted the partnership. Roberts, now playing with confidence, scored 23 goals to finish Norwich's top scorer. More importantly, after the first season doubts, he was voted as the fans' Player of the Season.

Despite losing his playing partner Bellamy for much of the 1999–2000 through injury, and then Bellamy's record transfer at start of the 2000–01 season, Roberts still managed to score regularly even though Norwich struggled in both seasons and he played with a number of different striking partners.

In both seasons Roberts finished top scorer with 19 and 18 goals respectively, with his goals often being the difference between a mid-table finish and a relegation battle. In a difficult time for the club he scored a memorable double to earn an unlikely 2–0 victory at Portman Road and on 20 February 2001 he scored his first Norwich hat-trick in a 4–0 win against Stockport. The 1999–2000 season ended with Roberts winning the Player of the Season award, becoming only the fourth player at the time to have won it in consecutive seasons.

Roberts would miss a number of games in the Play-off season of 2001–02 although he would still finish the season as top scorer with 14. It was the fourth consecutive season he had finished top scorer putting him in a distinguished group with Hall of Famers Terry Allcock and Robert Fleck.

His most famous Norwich goal, and one of the most memorable in his career, came in the last game of the 2001–02 season: the Play-off Final against Birmingham. Having been a used substitute in the two semi-final games, Roberts came off the bench in the Final to score a trademark extra-time header to give Norwich a 1–0 lead. The goal was all the sweeter coming in the Millennium stadium where Roberts had worn the red shirt of Wales with pride. Unfortunately it did not prove to be a winner; Norwich lost 2–4 on penalties despite Roberts converting his.

After the despair at the Millennium, Norwich and Roberts both had a disappointing season in 2002–03; Roberts failed to hit double figures for the first time since his debut season.

The arrival of big name players Peter Crouch and Hall of Famer Darren Huckerby followed by strikers Leon McKenzie and Mathais Svensson in 2003–04 meant that Roberts would have to settle for a bit part role in Norwich's Championship winning season. Roberts still contributed eight goals but with promotion won it was announced that his contract would not be renewed.

Although the decision no doubt disappointed Roberts, it allowed him to take centre stage in an emotional farewell in the last home game of the season, a 3–2 win over Preston. He was made captain for his last game against Crewe on 9 May 2004 and scored twice in a 3–1 win.

Roberts moved to Gillingham but after just one season he retired and returned to Norfolk where he is often seen/heard/read in his work in the media.

Iwan Roberts made 306 appearances for Norwich scoring 96 goals, the third highest in the club's history.

Robert Green

January 1980, Surrey   Player 1999–2006

After making his debut aged just 19 and keeping a clean sheet against Norwich's biggest rivals Ipswich, Robert Green was destined to become a Norwich great.

Behind the maturity and ability shown in that exceptional debut performance were the efforts of the Norwich coaching staff who had worked with Green throughout his time in the schoolboy, academy and youth teams.

A graduate of the academy, he was the third member of the 1996–97 Championship winning youth team to go on to a successful career and a place in the Hall of Fame.

Green had also featured for England Under-16, Under-18 and B sides. Therefore, although he was a relative unknown to Norwich fans when he made his debut on 11 April 1999, he had the confidence of manager Bruce Rioch to handle the pressure in what was Norwich's biggest game of the season.

Despite his fantastic debut, Green was still young for a 'keeper and when Hall of Famer Andy Marshall returned from injury Green continued his education with a period in Italy at Parma, who had formed a partnership with Norwich sharing resources and experiences.

Green's break back at Norwich came in the summer of 2001 when Marshall left for Premiership Ipswich. Again the Norwich management had faith in their young goalkeeper, deciding not to replace Marshall during the 2001–02 pre-season, the foresight of which was to be ratified by Green's performances as Norwich would go all the way to the Play-off Final in his first full season.

Green quickly set the standard for the 2001–02 season with four consecutive clean sheets in the first five games. The season ended with another four blanks in the final six games as Norwich embarked on a late push for a Play-off place. In total, Green played 47 games in his first full season keeping an impressive 17 clean sheets (16 in the League) – a record comparative to the Championship winning years of 1971–72 and 1985–86.

Unfortunately the 2001–02 season would end in tears with a Play-off Final defeat to Birmingham on penalties. Green, however, would add to his growing reputation with a competent performance including a world class save from a Geoff Horsfield effort late in extra-time, all in front of 71,597 in the Millennium Stadium and the watching millions at home.

The Play-off experience would prove to be valuable for Green as he went on to have a superb 2002–03 season where his consistently high class performances spread confidence throughout the team. He was the only ever-present that season and went one better with a club record 18 clean sheets, although incredibly for such a statistic Norwich would finish eighth.

Green took his good form into the Championship winning season of 2003–04 where another 18 clean sheets by the ever-present 'keeper were this time enough to seal the Division One title. One particularly breathtaking save against Stoke on 27 March 2004 helped Norwich to a 1–0 win and typified the reflexes that would see Green end the season selected in the PFA team of the season and receive a call up to the England senior squad.

In the 2004–05 season, Green would see plenty of action against some of the world's top strikers who now graced the Premiership. Six clean sheets and a Man of the Match display away at Tottenham on 12 September 2004 would further enhance his reputation on a national scale.

As one of only two ever-presents in Norwich's first season back in the Premiership, Green was one of Norwich's better performers and was again rewarded with selection for England in the tour of the USA in May 2005. On the 31 May 2005 Green won his first England cap coming on as a second half substitute in the 3–2 win over Colombia. In doing so he became the first Norwich player to win an England cap since fellow 'keeper and Hall of Famer Chris Woods back in 1986.

As an England International Green was subject to much transfer speculation following Norwich's relegation at the end of the 2004–05 season, but he decided to stay and help the pre-season favourites in their attempt at an instant return. However, Norwich fell some way short of expectations and after a disappointing ninth place finish Green was sold to West Ham for £2 million in August 2006.

Green returned to the England side after his return to the Premiership and would represent his country in a World Cup. At West Ham he was a popular player, helping the Hammers survive relegation with a 1–0 win at Old Trafford. In the 2007–08 season he was voted West Ham Player of the Year. In summer 2012 after helping West Ham back into the Premiership, Green moved across London to begin the next stage of his career at QPR.

Robert Green made 241 appearances for Norwich.

Malky Mackay

February 1972, Scotland   **Player 1998–2004**

In the 1970s it was Dave Stringer and Duncan Forbes, in the 1980s Steve Bruce and Dave Watson and in the 2000s it was Craig Fleming and Malky Mackay; great defensive partnerships in Norwich title winning sides.

Each one a Hall of Famer, these defenders all shared common attributes and characteristics that would make them a success at Carrow Road.

Mackay, the last of the six to join Norwich, was no exception. He had begun his career at Scotland's oldest side Queen's Park, where he followed in his father's footsteps.

Queen's Park were an amateur side; therefore Mackay combined League football with a career at the bank, before a dream move to Celtic in 1993 meant he could leave the desk job behind for good. At Celtic Mackay would struggle to hold down a regular place in the starting XI and after five seasons decided to make the move south, joining Norwich in September 1998.

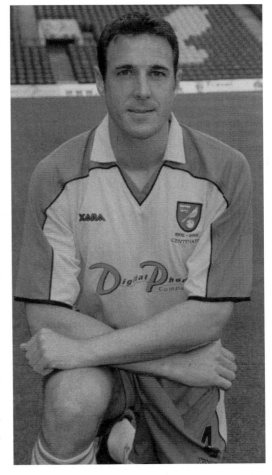

Mackay was signed initially on a three month loan but after an impressive debut in a 1–2 defeat to Sheffield United on 19 September 1998 his move was made permanent for £350,000. His first Norwich goal followed 10 days later in a 2–2 draw with eventual champions Sunderland and he went on to make 31 appearances in the 1998–99 season.

A similar number of games were played in the 1999–2000 season before Mackay cemented his place at centre-back with 40 appearances during the 2000–01 season.

The Fleming/Mackay partnership was finally established early in the 2001–02 season after the departure of central-defender and Norwich captain Matt Jackson allowed Fleming to switch to central defence alongside Mackay. Together they played 45 League games at the heart of the Norwich defence with Mackay missing just one game, a 0–4 defeat at Preston on 26 September 2001; it was a game in which Norwich were 0–4 down by half-time as they badly missed Mackay's organisation and physical presence.

Norwich's success in making the Play-offs that season was based on the defence, particularly at home where just 16 goals were conceded and only two defeats suffered – the second best home record in the division.

Mackay also scored three important goals, all coming at the business end of the season as Norwich pushed on for a Play-off place. After a late run of six unbeaten, Norwich went into the final fixture at home to Stockport on 21 April 2002 having to better Burnley's result. With both sides winning 1–0 and the tension mounting, Mackay's towering header in the 75th minute proved to be enough to see Norwich snatch the final Play-off place by just one goal.

Mackay would score another key goal in the Play-off semi-final versus Wolverhampton where his last minute header would win the first leg 3–1 and give Norwich a crucial two goal cushion for the second leg at Molineux. In the second leg it was Mackay's defensive qualities that shone through as Norwich held their advantage despite relentless Wolves attacks in front of a passionate home support.

The 2002–03 season was another good one for Mackay in the Norwich defence. Despite Norwich finishing eighth the defence stood strong with just 49 goals conceded. It could have been even better but Mackay missed nine games including the 0–2 home defeat to Ipswich. The corresponding fixture earlier in the season on 15 September 2002 had seen Mackay score in a 1–1 draw. He would go on to score six goals in total – his highest return for Norwich.

The 2003–04 season was Mackay's finest and also his last in the Norwich defence. Again the team's success, this time in the form of the Division One title, was built on a strong defence that let in just 39 goals; the average of 0.84 goals conceded per game that was just marginally lower than 0.85 in 1971–72 and 0.88 in 1985–86 and therefore a club record.

Mackay missed just one game of the Championship winning season, while two of his four goals that year came in the home derby versus Ipswich. In front of a season's best crowd of 23,942 Mackay's two headers helped settle the nerves to see Norwich to a 3–1 win and keep top spot after two consecutive draws.

After contributing so much to the club's promotion it was a shame that Mackay's contract was not renewed at the end of the season. Mackay joined Hall of Famer Roberts in the last game for them both, the season's finale at Crewe.

In the summer of 2004 Mackay stayed in Division One with West Ham and was part of their promotion squad via a 1–0 Play-off Final win against Preston. Mackay missed out on Premiership football again though, as he was released to Watford. At Watford, for the third time, he was part of a squad that gained promotion to the Premiership, and this time he would get his well-deserved opportunity in the top flight.

Mackay retired in 2008 and became a highly respected coach and manager, first with Watford and currently with Cardiff.

Malky Mackay made 232 appearances for Norwich scoring 17 goals.

Paul McVeigh

December 1977, Northern Ireland   **Player 2000–07 and 2009–10**

Whether playing out on the wing, behind the main striker or as an out and out striker himself, Paul McVeigh was one of those players that galvanised the team and supporters alike.

He was a quick, agile player with a trick and an eye for the spectacular goal; a player that earned his own terrace chant during his seven years at Carrow Road.

McVeigh had been part of the youth set-up at Tottenham but found first team opportunities limited and was released towards the end of the 1999–2000 season.

Meanwhile Norwich's new manager Bryan Hamilton was trying to make his mark on the squad. He brought in six new faces, one of whom was McVeigh who made his debut in the final game of the season in a 0–1 defeat at Bolton.

Of the six newcomers only McVeigh would go on to make the grade at Norwich; his fellow new starters gradually drifted away from the club making very few appearances between them. For McVeigh it would take another season before he would establish himself in the first team after just six starts in the 2000–01 season which included his first Norwich goal, the winner in a 1–0 win over Wolverhampton on 24 February 2001.

Under new manager and Hall of Famer Nigel Worthington, McVeigh became a key player in the 2001–02 Play-off season. After forcing his way

into the team in the third game of the season, he went on to make 48 appearances in all competitions in what was to be a long season for the Norwich squad.

McVeigh scored 10 goals in the 2001–02 season, finishing second highest goalscorer behind Hall of Famer Iwan Roberts. He opened his account with the second goal in the first home game, a 2–0 win over eventual champions Manchester City in a game made famous for Marc Libbra's debut goal 20 seconds after coming off the bench.

In the same month as the Manchester victory McVeigh was selected for the Northern Ireland side to face Denmark and Iceland in the World Cup Qualifying double header. He would win a total of 19 caps while at Norwich and 20 in total.

The interplay and inventiveness that McVeigh brought to the team was particularly evident on 3 November 2001 when an assist and a goal saw Norwich beat leaders Wolverhampton 2–0 and really set the tone for the season.

McVeigh played a vital part in Norwich's late charge for a Play-off place; he scored three goals (two of which were winners) as Norwich won four out of the last five games to finish sixth. McVeigh carried this form into the Play-off semi-final where a superb glancing header into the top corner put Norwich into the lead in a tight first leg encounter with Wolves.

It did not take McVeigh long to get over the disappointment of defeat in the 2002 Play-off Final; he scored two in a 4–0 win over Grimsby in the opening fixture of the 2002–03 season. Working in tandem with Roberts, McVeigh finished the season as Norwich's top goalscorer with 15 goals, many of which were long range efforts.

McVeigh played an important role in the 2003–04 title winning side; in McVeigh and Hall of Famer Darren Huckerby Norwich had pace and skill in abundance on both wings. As well as providing the ammunition for the Norwich forward line, McVeigh scored five goals as Norwich stormed to the Division One title.

In the 2004–05 season McVeigh got to display his skills at the 'Theatre of Dreams' with Norwich's first away game coming at Manchester United on 21 August 2004. In front of 67,812 at Old Trafford Norwich gave a good account of themselves with McVeigh's late goal, a shot after cutting in from the right, a consolation in a narrow 1–2 defeat.

McVeigh's goal at Old Trafford would be his first and last Premiership goal as he found himself utilised mostly as an impact player from the bench with 14 of his 17 Premiership games starting as a substitute.

Following Norwich's relegation from the Premiership, McVeigh remained an important part of the squad looking for an instant return to the Premiership. Back as a regular starter he played 40 games in all competitions in the 2005–06 season scoring eight goals, including a double in a 2–1 win at Crewe.

With a change in management, McVeigh found himself back on the bench for much of the 2006–07 season before spending the last three months on loan at Burnley. In the summer 2007 he joined Luton on a free transfer but his move coincided with a difficult time for the club, with two consecutive relegations following a severe 30 points deduction for financial irregularities.

Without a club McVeigh made a surprise return to Norwich for the 2009–10 season, where he added another 11 appearances, his last coming off the bench in the 3–0 win at Bristol Rovers on 1 May 2010 with the League One title already in the bag.

After retiring from football McVeigh has followed a career in media with work on Radio Norfolk and Radio 5 Live as well as embracing the Twitter revolution.

Paul McVeigh made 246 appearances for Norwich scoring 40 goals.

Nigel Worthington

November 1961, Northern Ireland   **Manager 2000–06**

After five managers had tried and failed, Nigel Worthington was the man who finally took Norwich back to the promised land of the Premiership and with it the financial and footballing riches that come to members of what is branded 'the best league in the world'.

Since Norwich's relegation from the Premiership at the end of the 1994–95 season, the club had endured a series of mid-table finishes with relegation often looking more likely than promotion. It was a malaise that would take a man of Worthington's qualities and experience to turn around, culminating in the promotion and the title winning team of 2003–04.

Worthington had built up a wealth of experience as a dependable left-back at Sheffield Wednesday. In ten years at Hillsborough he played under some of the game's top managers such as Howard Wilkinson and Ron Atkinson. He won a League Cup and promotion to the First Division where Sheffield Wednesday would become a regular top 10 side. On 10 January 1993 he scored the winner in a 0–1 versus Norwich – a loss that knocked Norwich off the top of the Premiership – and he ended that season a runner-up in both the League and FA Cups.

Worthington also had years of experience of international football with 66 caps for Northern Ireland including two at the 1986 World Cup Finals. He was made captain of his country by manager Bryan Hamilton and it was under Hamilton that Worthington would begin his career at Norwich, joining as his assistant manager in the summer 2000.

Before joining Norwich Worthington had managerial experience at Second Division Blackpool and was therefore a suitable candidate to replace Hamilton as caretaker manager when he resigned on 6 December 2000, after a run of five consecutive defeats. Worthington's impact on the struggling side was instant; just one defeat in the next six games resulted in him being offered the permanent post in January 2001.

For the rest of the 2000–01 season, Worthington focused on trimming down the squad, getting rid of the deadwood while making a couple of astute signings in Hall of Famers Gary Holt and Adam Drury. A comfortable 15th place finish was achieved, although Norwich were only mathematically safe after a 1–0 win over Sheffield Wednesday in the penultimate game of the season.

In his first full season (2001–02) Worthington transformed Norwich from relegation strugglers to a Play-off team within a penalty-kick of the Premiership. He had established a settled team with a strong spine and excellent team spirit that was evident in Norwich's late push to grab the final Play-off place.

Much of the squad remained in place and continued to evolve as a team during the 2002–03 season during which Worthington would give a debut to Ryan Jarvis who, at 16 years and 282 days, would become Norwich's youngest ever player.

The 2003–04 season would go down in history as one of Norwich's finest but it would take an inspired bit of management to make this happen. After an indifferent start to the season and a first round League Cup exit, Worthington, with the backing of the board, persuaded three players – Peter Crouch, Kevin Harper and Hall of Famer Darren Huckerby – to swap life in the Premiership for a loan spell at Norwich. All three made a great impact which, combined with the signings of Leon McKenzie and Mathais Svensson, transformed Norwich from a mid-table side to eventual run away leaders. They finished with 94 points, a club record at that level.

At the end of the title winning season Worthington showed that he could make tough decisions when he released Hall of Famers Malky Mackay and Iwan Roberts, but also showed a human touch in allowing Roberts a suitable farewell in the final games against Preston and Crewe.

Now a Premiership manager, Worthington added a couple of players with big reputations in Europe namely Thomas Helveg and Mattias Jonson but it would not be enough for Norwich to ensure Premiership football for a second season. He kept together the core of the team and kept calm when Norwich played 13 games before getting their first win.

Worthington was proactive in trying to keep Norwich up; he signed Hall of Famer and club record signing Dean Ashton while changing team tactics and players. It was almost enough as Norwich put together a late run, but relegation was confirmed in difficult surroundings after a 0–6 loss at Fulham.

Norwich took time to get over the thrashing at Fulham as Worthington looked to rebuild the squad, but they never recovered from a poor start to the 2005–06 season, which included a 2–4 defeat to Luton after being 0–4 down at half-time. A manager of the Month award in December, to add to three won in 2003–04, would not be enough to turn Norwich's season around and it ended in a ninth place finish.

The 2006–07 season did not get any better. After a dismal 1–3 loss at Plymouth and a high profile 1–4 home defeat to Burnley in front of the Sky cameras, Worthington left the club on 1 October 2006 after nearly six years in charge.

A short spell at Leicester was followed by four years managing his country.

Nigel Worthington managed Norwich for 280 games with a 40.7 per cent win ratio.

Gary Holt

March 1973, Scotland   **Player 2001–05**

As an ex-soldier in the British Army, Gary Holt knew all about hard work and team work, two qualities which he would become associated with during his time at Norwich.

A member of the Army football team, Holt got his break in professional football at his local side Kilmarnock for whom he signed in 1995.

Holt's time at Kilmarnock coincided with a golden period in the club's history. He played in the 1997 Scottish Cup Final win which took Kilmarnock into the UEFA Cup as well as being a member of the team that achieved consecutive fourth place finishes in the Scottish Premier League.

With domestic success came international honours; Holt made his Scotland debut in September 2000 in a 1–0 win over Latvia. Norwich were therefore getting themselves an international player for just £135,000 when manager and Hall of Famer Nigel Worthington signed Holt in March 2001.

After just four appearances in the 2000–01 season, Holt made one of the central-midfield positions his own during the 2001–02 season. He was an ever-present that season and added some much needed steel to the Norwich midfield. Holt became popular with the Norwich supporters for his work rate, covering every inch of the pitch, closing down the opposition and winning possession back for the team.

Holt's role that season was to protect the back four but he did manage a couple of goals, both spectacular long distance strikes. The pick of the two was a 30 yard piledriver at Sheffield Wednesday on 29 December 2001, which was the icing on the cake in a 5–0 victory – Norwich's biggest away win in the League since 1951.

Holt's season was summed up in the season's last and biggest game, the Play-off Final versus Birmingham. Over 120 minutes, Holt ran himself into the ground with a Man of the Match display as Norwich kept Birmingham at bay, only to be eventually beaten by the lottery of the penalty shoot-out. In recognition of his efforts in that game and over the course of the season Holt was voted Norwich Player of the Season for 2001–02.

Holt continued to protect the back four throughout 2002–03 and played his part in a good season from a defensive perspective with just 49 goals conceded. He played 49 games in all competitions including a fifth round FA Cup 0–2 loss at Premiership Southampton, the first time Norwich had reached the fifth round since 1994–95. The only League game he missed was a 0–1 defeat to Gillingham in February 2003.

Holt was again an ever-present in the engine room of Norwich's Championship winning side of 2003–04. Nicknamed 'three lungs' by the Norwich support, his efforts in a more defensive role allowed his fellow central-midfielder Damien Francis to play a more attacking role which saw him score seven vital goals.

Holt's one goal of the season came on Valentine's Day 2004 when he scored the opener from close range in a 2–0 win at Coventry, Norwich's third win in a row cementing their place at the Division One summit.

It was also during 2004 that Holt's international career would take off after a two year spell in the wilderness. During 2004 Holt won seven Scottish caps and scored his one and only international goal in a 4–1 friendly win over Trinidad and Tobago on 30 May 2004. His total of eight Scotland caps is the most of any player while at Norwich.

Holt started Norwich's first game back in the Premiership and played the next 12 games as Norwich searched for their first win after eight draws and five losses. He finished the season with 27 Premiership appearances as he became hampered by injuries and a loss of form which had singled him out for criticism by sections of the Norwich supporters.

Holt's last game as a starter came on 2 April 2005, a 1–4 defeat to a Thierry Henry inspired Arsenal. After Norwich's relegation was confirmed on 15 May 2005 he transferred to League One side Nottingham Forest.

Holt spent two years at Forest but after defeat in the 2007 League One Play-offs to Yeovil he transferred to Wycombe. At Wycombe Holt played under Hall of Famer Paul Lambert, and followed him first to Colchester and then back to Norwich where he currently works in the academy.

Gary Holt made 182 appearances for Norwich scoring three goals.

Adam Drury

August 1978, Cambridgeshire   **Player 2001–12**

When Adam Drury signed for Norwich in March 2001, he was described by his former boss at Peterborough as 'the best full-back outside of the top flight'.

Over his 11 years Drury has more than lived up to this statement, proving to be not only one of Norwich's finest ever full-backs but also one of the best in the land.

Drury's professional career began at Peterborough, despite a very brief spell at Norwich as a kid. He would soon make the first team where he would play 175 games in all competitions including one at the old Wembley stadium in the Third Division Play-off Final. On a personal front he was voted Player of the Season and was highly regarded within the game when joining Norwich for what proved to be a bargain £500,000.

One of manager and Hall of Famer Nigel Worthington's first signings, Drury would go on to play under five Norwich managers in a career that would take him to 361 appearances, leaving him 13th in the all-time listing.

The first of Drury's 361 games was on 31 March 2001 in a 2–1 win over Grimsby while his second was a 3–4 defeat to Gillingham after Norwich had been 0–4 down.

Over the next two seasons (2001–02 and 2002–03) Drury became part of a settled Norwich defence with Hall of Famers Robert Green, Malky Mackay and Craig Fleming. It would prove to be one of the best in the League, particularly in 2002–03 where just 49 goals were conceded, including only 17 at Carrow Road. Of that watertight defence it would be Drury who won the fans' 2002–03 Player of the Season award.

Drury was promoted to captain for the 2003–04 season, where he commanded respect for his ability, consistency and professionalism in a team that included some star names as well as some natural leaders. As captain, Drury played 44 games in a season that marked many club bests at that level including most away wins

(10), most home wins from the start of the season (eight) and the most points clear of third place team (15). The season would culminate with Drury lifting the famous old Division One trophy on the balcony of City Hall in front of thousands of fans.

Drury looked at home in the Premiership in the 2004–05 season where he made 33 appearances and even managed a rare goal on 22 January 2005, a late equaliser in the thrilling 4–4 draw against Middlesbrough in which Norwich had been trailing 1–4 after 80 minutes.

After Norwich's relegation from the Premiership Drury would remain the cornerstone of the Norwich defence where his pace, ability to read the game and attacking support would prove invaluable. He was sorely missed during his seven games out injured in the 2005–06 season of which Norwich lost six. It was much the same story in 2006–07 where Norwich lost five of the seven games that Drury missed.

After missing much of the 2007–08 and 2008–09 seasons through injury, Drury started in the horror show that was the 1–7 home defeat to Colchester in Norwich's first game in the old Division Three since 30 April 1960. However, under new manager and Hall of Famer Paul Lambert, Norwich would recover and prosper with Drury playing 35 League games as he became the first Norwich player to win two Championships.

Back in the Championship Drury played 20 games in the 2010–11 season as Norwich completed remarkable back to back promotions and Drury became the first Norwich player to have achieved three promotions with the club.

In his 11th year at Norwich and by far the club's longest serving player, he was still an important member of the squad, with a further 12 Premiership appearances to add to those played back in 2004–05. His experience proved crucial in ensuring that Norwich would avoid the fate of 2004–05 and enjoy at least another season in the top flight.

On a personal note, Drury's long anticipated induction into the Hall of Fame came in March 2012, while at the end of the season he was rewarded with his testimonial against Celtic before his transfer to Leeds United.

Adam Drury made 361 appearances for Norwich scoring four goals.

Roger Munby

January 1946, Yorkshire   Chairman 2001–09

At the time of his resignation in May 2009, Roger Munby was Norwich's longest serving member of the executive group.

During his time in office he contributed to and oversaw a revolution off the pitch, as the club made great progress both commercially and with the supporters, even during times of hardship on the pitch and against the backdrop of a global recession.

Munby was already a successful businessman when he first became associated with Norwich in January 1986. After the fallout over the building of the new stand, Munby was a member of the newly appointed Board under the chairmanship of Hall of Famer Robert Chase.

His time on the Board would be brief, lasting only until September 1987 before a period spent away from football to concentrate on his business. However, Munby maintained his association with the club and returned to a new look Board in 1996 after the successful takeover by Hall of Famers Delia Smith and Michael Wynn-Jones.

After five years serving the club in his capacity as a director, Munby was promoted to chairman in 2001 shortly after the appointment of manager and Hall of Famer Nigel Worthington.

Under Munby's reign as chairman, Norwich City would make a number of significant developments that would help shape the club's future. First and foremost was the continued focus on building the occasionally fragile relationship between the football club and its supporters. Communication improved through the medium of supporters' groups and the hosting of various focus groups, and the club began to understand supporter concerns as well as developing a product that would attract fans to games.

One of the great achievements under Munby's chairmanship were the increases in Norwich's home gates and season ticket sales. When he joined the board, in the 1996–97 season, the average gate at Carrow

Road was 14,719. In 2000–01 season when appointed chairman it was 16,525. At the end of Munby's last season with Norwich, 2008–09, it was 24,543, which was impressive considering Norwich were relegated at the end of the season. Even at the heights of the 1992–93 Premiership season the average home gate was just 16,154.

The levels and growth of Norwich's support became the envy of many clubs. Carrow Road, bucking the national trend, was often full to capacity, as Norwich became far more sales focused. Norwich also rediscovered their links with the local community through various initiatives such as the community sport facilities behind Carrow Road and events such as the 'ability counts' soccer weeks for disabled children.

One of the factors in the increased gates was the further improvements made to the stadium, namely the building of the new 8,500 capacity Jarrold Stand which was opened in February 2003. This included corporate boxes and later an infill between the Jarrold and River End stands. Meanwhile at the Barclay End a hotel complex was added, and apartments were built alongside the river outside of the ground.

The match day experience also became a focal point under Munby, with supporters able to buy into various 'experiences' such as training with ex-players or singing *On the ball city* out on the pitch before kick-off. The catering facilities also grew to the extent that, in 2008, they generated profits of £700,000.

Norwich's success off the pitch helped attract international sponsorship, contributing to an increase in turnover which tripled during Munby's time at Norwich. However, in the increasingly expensive world of football finance, and heightened by Norwich's relegation from the Premiership in 2004–05, financial investment was always a priority. Munby would become involved in the process of attracting and seeking new investment that could take the club forward.

While Norwich continued to thrive off the pitch the team, in contrast, would experience a difficult period after relegation from the top flight. Four managers worked under Munby, each of them backed with funds to spend on players or loan deals in order to rebuild the squad.

Munby was reactive to supporter feelings and prepared to give a young manager an opportunity as he did with Peter Grant, while his appointment of Glen Roeder in November 2007 ultimately spared Norwich from relegation that season.

Norwich were eventually relegated to League One (the old Division Three) at the end of the 2008–09 season, just four seasons after they were a Premiership club. Munby recognised that a change was needed as the club looked to a fresh start, and he stepped aside in May 2009.

Roger Munby served the club in an executive capacity for 13 years and was chairman for eight years.

Darren Huckerby

April 1976, Nottinghamshire   **Player 2003–08**

The ambitious signing of Darren Huckerby in 2003, a player of proven Premiership quality, was the catalyst for Norwich's long awaited return to the top division.

Huckerby was one of Norwich's biggest ever signings in terms of his experience and stature, a player who had been known at a national level ever since he signed for Kevin Keegan's Newcastle for £400,000 in November 1995.

The teenage prodigy joined Newcastle at the height of Keegan's free flowing attacking revolution, but with appearances limited and after impressing on loan at Millwall, Huckerby signed for Coventry for £1 million.

At Coventry the potential was fulfilled. Partnering Hall of Famer Dion Dublin, Huckerby scored 14 Premiership goals in the 1997–98 season including a contender for goal of the season, a solo effort versus Manchester United. England Under-21 and B caps followed as did a nomination for PFA Young Player of the Season.

Now very much on the footballing map there was a big money move to Leeds before another large transfer to Manchester City, where Huckerby's 26 goals helped City to the Division One title in 2001–02.

As Manchester City spent big back in the Premiership, Huckerby had a loan spell at his home town club Nottingham Forest where he was a scorer in a 0–4 win over Norwich on 22 March

2003. A move to Forest never materialised after their defeat in that season's Play-offs and the following season, 2003–04, he arrived at Norwich in a move that would lift the Norwich support.

Huckerby's debut came in the 2–0 win over Burnley on 13th September 2003 before goals in three consecutive games won him the Player of the Month award. In total his 18 games on loan saw Norwich lose just twice as they rose from 10th to second in Division One.

Huckerby saved his best performance for his last loan game where he put on a classic display of wing play with pace, trickery, skill and finishing. Two goals and an assist gave Norwich a 4–1 victory over Cardiff leaving Norwich fans wishing for more.

Their wish came true 13 days later. Hard work by the Board and Hall of Fame manager Nigel Worthington coupled with Huckerby's desire to play for Norwich resulted in his £750,000 transfer.

The cash outlay represented a gamble by the club that would pay huge dividends following Norwich's promotion to the Premiership at the end of the 2003–04 season. As Norwich raced to the title, Huckerby was the focal point of a free flowing attacking side that won 13 of the 19 games that he played in after his permanent move. His many dazzling displays produced nine goals (taking his season total to 14) and numerous assists, with winners against Ipswich and a fine individual effort against Wigan proving to be the highlights. Huckerby's season ended with a Championship medal, the PFA Division One Player of the Season award and the golden boot as Norwich's leading goalscorer.

Huckerby's quality was at home in the Premiership during the 2004–05 season, scoring Norwich's first goal back in the top flight in the opening day 1–1 against fellow new boys Crystal Palace. He would be a constant threat to opposition defences despite Norwich struggling to settle.

With seven goals that season, Huckerby shared the golden boot with three other players. However, he was far ahead of anybody in terms of assists including four in one game, the 4–4 draw at home to Middlesbrough. His efforts over the course of a difficult season won him the supporters' Player of the Season award for 2004–05.

Having again proved himself at Premiership level, Huckerby had offers to stay in the top flight including rumoured interest from Liverpool. Staying at Norwich he was again a highlight in a disappointing 2005–06 season where he would score the winner at Portman Road (1–0) on 18 September 2005, Norwich's first away win in 18 months.

Huckerby was again voted Player of the Season for 2006–07 where he scored 13 goals in 44 games. This time his presence would be critical in ensuring that Norwich avoided relegation; winners against Leeds, Birmingham and Stoke would earn Norwich crucial points just as the nerves were setting in. His goal in the game against Birmingham on 13 March 2007 was another candidate for goal of the season, a run from his own half leaving a number of defenders trailing in his wake.

His last season at Norwich would end in disappointment when he was released after scoring in a 1–4 defeat at Sheffield Wednesday on the last game of the 2007–08 season. By now a Norwich fan himself he decided against playing for another English club instead moving to the MLS with San Jose Earthquakes.

Huckerby was a success in the US winning the September Player of the Month, 2008 best newcomer of the year and top goalscorer. However, injury intervened and after one season Huckerby returned to settle in Norfolk. He now performs various functions for Norwich Football Club as well as supporting local charities and community projects through his Trust.

Darren Huckerby made 203 appearances for Norwich scoring 48 goals.

Dean Ashton

November 1983, Wiltshire   Player 2005–06

While Dean Ashton's career at Norwich was short, just 46 games in one year, his impact on a team struggling for confidence and form was instant; as he helped inspire Norwich to an unlikely battle against Premiership relegation in which they would fall just short.

Throughout his earlier career at Crewe, Ashton was always singled out for attention as the next big star to emerge from Crewe's famous football academy.

After excelling at all levels he made his football League debut on 28 October 2000 aged just 16.

Over the next four years Ashton would complete his soccer education under long serving boss Dario Gradi. He would score 74 goals in total including two versus Norwich, one of which was in Hall of Famers Iwan Roberts and Malky Mackay's final game in May 2004. That season he top scored for Crewe with 20 goals, the most scored by a Crewe player at that level.

Having also represented England at Under-17 and Under-21 level, and with 20 goals in the first 27 games of the 2004–05 season, Ashton was one of the hottest young properties in English football. It was therefore a significant coup for Norwich when manager and Hall of Famer Nigel Worthington made Ashton the club's record signing, paying £3 million in January 2005; an amount that tripled the previous record set by Hall of Famer Jon Newsome back in 1994.

Ashton made his Premiership debut on 15 January 2005 in a disappointing 0–3 loss at Aston Villa. His first Premiership goal came in the next game, his first at Carrow Road, in the enthralling 4–4 draw with Middlesbrough.

Soon settling into a struggling Norwich side, Ashton would become the answer to Norwich's goalscoring shortage. He was a natural finisher with the combined qualities of technique and strength. He linked play well and brought the best out of his fellow attackers. His ability was shown to the watching nation with a superb lobbed finish in the televised 2–3 defeat at home to Manchester City, a loss that left Norwich second from bottom.

By the time Norwich lost to Arsenal on 2 April 2006 they were bottom and with Manchester United next at Carrow Road, Norwich were almost resigned to their fate. On 9 April, and again in front of the Sky cameras, a typical powerful header by Ashton set the platform for a shock 2–0 win over United and with it renewed hope.

Over the next nerve-racking five games, Ashton would score four goals as Norwich put together a run of three wins and a draw to take them to the brink of survival. Ashton's goals included a double at relegation rivals Crystal Palace, an injury time winner versus Newcastle and a coolly converted penalty in a tight 1–0 win over Birmingham in the last home game of the season.

Unfortunately Norwich fell just short, falling through the trapdoor after a last day thrashing at Fulham. Despite the hurt experienced at Fulham, Ashton, with seven goals (Norwich's joint top goalscorer) had proved himself a Premiership footballer.

Staying at Norwich despite plenty of interest from other clubs, Ashton started the 2005–06 season strongly with two in the first three games, all ending in 1–1 draws. Norwich never really recovered from this stalled start and became quickly marooned in mid-table. An Ashton hat-trick in a 3–1 win against Southampton on 17 December 2005 was a rare highlight and with an instant return to the Premiership out of the question, Ashton was sold to West Ham as the transfer window opened in January 2006.

Despite leaving in January, Ashton was still Norwich's top goalscorer for the 2005–06 season with 11 goals, while his transfer fee of £7,250,000 was a club record fee received for a Norwich player.

Ashton got off to a great start at West Ham with five in his first seven games; Norwich, meanwhile, continued to struggle. Ashton ended the season playing and scoring in the FA Cup Final which West Ham lost on penalties to Liverpool after a thrilling 3–3 draw.

Success at West Ham meant Ashton would break into the England senior squad, but while on international duty he suffered the ankle injury that would eventually end his career aged just 26.

After some time away from football, Ashton has settled in Norfolk with his young family and begun to explore work in the local and national media.

Dean Ashton made 46 appearances for Norwich scoring 18 goals.

Dion Dublin

April 1969, Leicestershire   **Player 2006–08**

On 20 September 2006 the prodigal son returned to Norwich, 18 years after he had originally been shown the door as a teenager back in 1988.

Norwich Football Club, as the Hall of Fame demonstrates, has always had a fine reputation for producing top class footballers through the youth, apprenticeship and academy set-ups who would go on to represent the club. Dion Dublin, however, was very much the 'one that got away'. He played just six Norwich reserve games, before going on to enjoy a glittering career in the Premiership as well as representing England on four occasions.

Dublin's first club after his Norwich rejection was Cambridge United who were a Fourth Division club at the time. However, Cambridge under John Beck were a club on the up and with Dublin scoring the goals they reached the 1991–92 Division Two Play-off semi-finals, just two wins from becoming founder members of the Premier League.

The impressive League form was matched in the FA Cup with a run to the 1991 quarter-finals where Dublin scored in the 1–2 defeat at favourites Arsenal. The goal certainly helped put Dublin on the footballing map and in August 1992 he joined Manchester United for £1 million.

A badly broken leg disrupted Dublin's time at United and he left for Coventry in 1994. At Coventry he would finish top scorer over the next four seasons, helping Coventry survive relegation after some epic last day battles. His tally of 18 League goals in 1997–98 were the joint highest in the Premier League that season.

A big money move to Aston Villa followed in November 1998, as did his England debut. Dublin also played in the last FA Cup Final at the old Wembley in May 2000, in which Villa lost 0–1 to Chelsea.

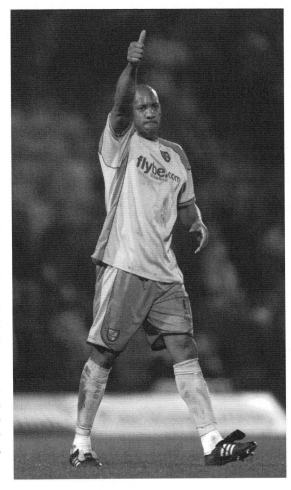

Dublin would spend six years at Villa followed by moves to Leicester and Celtic before he eventually went full circle with his return to Norwich, as one of manager and Hall of Famer Nigel Worthington's last signings.

Dublin's debut for Norwich was on 23 September 2006, in an abject 1–3 defeat at Plymouth that showed how far Norwich had fallen in the last year. It was followed by a defeat and a draw that left Norwich sixth from bottom in the Championship by mid-October.

With Norwich going through a difficult time they would come to need Dublin's experience, composure and versatility throughout the 2006–07 season. An inspiration to the team, Dublin scored seven goals that season, including an important winner against QPR on 30 December 2006 and the opener in a 2–1 win against bottom club Leeds after three defeats on the trot had sucked Norwich back into the relegation battle.

Dublin also scored a double in the FA Cup third round as Norwich travelled to non-League Tamworth, with a watching public tuned into the BBC for a Cup shock that did not emerge; Dublin scored the opener just before half-time to settle Norwich in what ended up a comfortable 4–1 win.

The 2007–08 season was Dublin's 20th as a professional footballer and would be his last. Again he proved to be a leader when the chips were down as Norwich slipped to the bottom of the Championship after a run of 11 games without a win. The sequence was broken on 24 November 2007 with a 2–0 win against Coventry, and in the next match away at Blackpool Dublin scored twice as Norwich recorded their first away win of the season.

Dublin was involved either as a starter or used as a substitute in a run of 13 games undefeated that ultimately saw Norwich pull clear of the relegation zone. Dublin ended what was to be his last season before retirement with 41 appearances in all competitions and nine goals.

His last Norwich goal came on 5 April 2008 in a 2–0 win versus Burnley, and his last game as a professional was on 4 May 2008 in a 1–4 loss to Sheffield Wednesday. At the end of the game he received a standing ovation from all four stands at Hillsborough in recognition for his services to football over the years, which showed the popularity of Dublin both as a player and a person. Norwich supporters backed up this sentiment voting him Player of the Season, the oldest winner of the award at 38 years old.

After retirement Dublin focused on a career within the media and he can often be seen on BBC Sport or heard on Radio 5 Live as a pundit or co-commentator.

Dion Dublin made 79 appearances for Norwich scoring 16 goals.

Wes Hoolahan

May 1982, Ireland   **Player 2008–present**

After a difficult first season, Wes Hoolahan would emerge to be a central figure in Norwich's meteoric rise from the bottom of League One to the Premiership – a journey that would take just two joy filled seasons.

Hoolahan's quality had always been evident from an early age, playing his football with Shelbourne in the Republic of Ireland.

Hoolahan won three League of Ireland Championships with Shelbourne and, as a result, experienced champions League football in the qualifying rounds. Playing against the likes of Hajduk Split and Deportivo La Coruna helped polish Hoolahan's technical abilities, but career opportunities were limited in the Irish League and Hoolahan moved to Livingston in Scotland for the 2006–07 season.

A brief spell at Livingston was followed by a switch to Blackpool where Hoolahan became an instant hit with the fans. Operating either on the wing or in a free role, Hoolahan scored 10 goals as Blackpool won promotion to the Championship after a 2–0 Play-off Final win versus Yeovil. He ended a terrific first season named in the League One PFA team of the season.

It was during the 2006–07 season that Hoolahan first came onto the radar of the Norwich management team with two clashes in the FA Cup fourth round. Hoolahan impressed in both games as Blackpool took Norwich to a replay. Then, following Blackpool's promotion to the Championship for the 2007–08 season, he again impressed in Blackpool's 1–2 League win at Carrow Road.

In June 2008, just a month after Hoolahan won his first Republic of Ireland cap, he was signed by Norwich manager Glenn Roeder for £250,000 and was one of six debutants in the opening game of the 2008–09 season, a 0–2 defeat at Coventry.

The optimism for the 2008–09 season would soon disappear as it became clear that Norwich would face a long struggle at the bottom. There

was a brief moment of hope when Hall of Famer Bryan Gunn took control and Norwich won the first game of his tenure 4–0 against Barnsley, with Hoolahan scoring his first Norwich goal.

Often Norwich's inspiration with his ability to create space and pick out a pass, Hoolahan's injury in the 1–0 win against Plymouth on 14 March 2009 would prove critical; he sat out the last seven games of the season. Norwich managed just one victory in these seven games and were relegated.

Hoolahan stayed at Norwich as they looked to rebuild in League One (old Third Division) and after a difficult start he became one of the best players in the League. Playing at the tip of the diamond formation favoured by manager and Hall of Famer Paul Lambert, Hoolahan was the creative force behind a free scoring Norwich front line.

In addition to his assists Hoolahan scored 14 goals in 42 games, as Norwich romped to the League One title with a club record 95 points. Hoolahan capped an excellent campaign with his inclusion in the PFA League One Team of the Season.

Back in the Championship, Hoolahan continued to prosper at the top of the diamond. He made 41 League appearances (with 36 as a starter) and scored 10 goals. He scored one double in a Man of the Match performance against Leicester on 28 September 2010, with his second goal – a long range shot into the top corner – sealing a 4–3 victory.

Half of Hoolahan's 10 goals came from the penalty spot. These included two second half penalties in the 4–2 victory over Sheffield United, where his coolness from 12 yards brought Norwich back into the game after being 1–2 down at half-time. A late breakaway goal secured Hoolahan's first Norwich hat-trick, all the more remarkable as he had only played 45 minutes after coming on as a substitute at half-time.

Hoolahan scored a rare headed goal on 8 March 2011 to set Norwich on course for a 3–2 win at in-form Leicester, a win that gave the club belief that a second successive promotion could be achieved.

With promotion confirmed after the 1–0 win at Portsmouth, Hoolahan was named in the PFA Championship Team of the Season, the third time he had made a PFA team of the season, twice as a Norwich player.

On 13 August 2011, and on the stroke of half-time, Hoolahan scored Norwich's first Premiership goal after a six year absence in an opening day 1–1 draw at Wigan. The goal was followed up with the captain's armband in a 2–1 win at Bolton on 17 September 2011, Norwich's first win of the season and their first away win in the top division since 17 December 1994.

Hoolahan's 33 appearances and four goals in 2011–12 helped ensure another season of Premiership football next year.

To date, Wes Hoolahan has made 121 appearances for Norwich and scored 30 goals.

Grant Holt

April 1981, Cumbria   **Player 2009–present**

The talisman of the team, club captain, goalscorer supreme and fans' favourite, Grant Holt epitomises the qualities and attitude shown by Norwich City over the last few dramatic seasons.

A player that fans can relate to, when Holt started his first Premiership game on 13 August 2011 he joined a unique group of players that had played in all four Divisions of the English Football League. He had therefore lived the dreams of many watching on the terraces.

His career actually started in non-League football with his local clubs Workington and Barrow where he combined football with work as a tyre fitter. His first break in the professional game came at Sheffield Wednesday but it was at his next club, Rochdale, that he would start to find the net on a regular basis, with 34 goals in 75 games.

Holt's performances at Rochdale earned him a move to fallen giants Nottingham Forest in League One. He finished top scorer in his first full season, winning the supporters' Player of the Season award. However, a difficult second season, much of it spent out of position on the wing, resulted in a move to Shrewsbury for a club record fee of £170,000.

In Holt's one season (2008–09) at Shrewsbury he finished joint League Two top goalscorer (joint with now Norwich teammate Simeon Jackson) and Player of the Season, and was selected in the PFA League Two Team of the Season. However, despite Holt's personal accolades, Shrewsbury missed out on promotion, losing in the League Two Play-off Final.

Holt on the other hand would start the 2009–10 season in League One, after Hall of Famer Bryan Gunn made him his big summer signing. Gunn spent £400,000 on the striker as Norwich faced their first season back in the third tier since 1959–60.

He had scored on his debut for four of his previous clubs, but Holt's Norwich debut on 8 August 2009 will go down as being arguably the

darkest day in the club's history. Seven goals conceded at home (five by half-time) to local rivals Colchester was Norwich's heaviest home defeat ever and sent shock waves around the football world. It left Norwich rock bottom after the slow decline over the last few seasons.

Such were the repercussions of the Colchester defeat that Holt's hat-trick in a 4–0 versus Yeovil three days later went pretty much unnoticed. However, by the time he had scored a double in Norwich's next home match, in a 5–2 victory over Wycombe, Norwich's season was up and running.

When Holt scored the winner in a 2–1 victory over Stockport on 5 April 2010, Norwich were top and marching on to the title. The goal was also Holt's 30th of the season in all competitions, the first Norwich player to hit 30 since Hall of Famer Ron Davies in 1963–64 and one of only five Norwich players to achieve this feat. The tally included six doubles and earned Holt the Player of the Season award and another place in the PFA team of the year.

Taking his sparkling form into the 2010–11 Championship season, Holt continued to score regularly at a higher level. His last minute winner in the season's second game at Scunthorpe set the standard from which Norwich rarely dropped.

Holt's legendary status with the Norwich fans was confirmed on 28 November 2010 when he became the first Norwich player to score a League hat-trick against rivals Ipswich in an exceptional 4–1 win. It was the first of two hat-tricks that Holt would score that season, the second coming in the 6–0 thrashing of Scunthorpe.

In total Holt scored 23 goals in 48 games – three of which were late winners and three were penalties – to win him the Norwich golden boot for the second successive season. His goals, overall performances and sheer hard work throughout that amazing promotion season won him another supporters' Player of the Season award, another selection in the PFA team of the year and the runner-up position in the PFA Championship Player of the Year.

Holt completed his incredible journey when he made his Premiership debut in that first game versus Wigan. As the season progressed, Holt proved that he could cut it at the very top level despite the pre-season doubters. During Norwich's successful first season back Holt would score against Liverpool (in front of the Kop), Arsenal, Chelsea and Manchester United. He scored a last minute penalty to earn a 3–3 draw against Blackburn, and three doubles to help Norwich to important wins versus Newcastle, Swansea and Wolves.

In his first Premiership season Holt scored 17 goals, 15 of which were in the League. His goals demonstrated his range of strengths: powerful headers, composed finishes, and moments of skill as per the equaliser at Everton. He completed a unique hat-trick which saw him finish, for the third successive season, as both Norwich's top scorer and also the fans' Player of the Season – the first player to have won the award three years in a row.

To date, Grant Holt has made 129 appearances for Norwich and scored 70 goals, leaving him joint seventh in the all-time goalscorers' listing.

Paul Lambert

August 1969, Scotland   **Manager 2009–12**

Paul Lambert's achievements at Norwich over the last three seasons are unprecedented, not only at Norwich but in English football in general, as Lambert has become one of the most highly regarded managers in country.

His success as a manager reflects that which he enjoyed as a player; Lambert spent most of his career winning trophies. His first, aged just 17, was a Scottish Cup with St Mirren, and he went on to win the biggest trophy of the lot, the Champions League, with Borussia Dortmund in 1997.

Championships followed at Celtic as did 40 Scotland caps, including 15 as captain and appearances in the 1998 World Cup Finals. However, Lambert's first step into management did not come easy; he failed to last the season after a difficult spell at Livingston.

In June 2006 Lambert moved south of the border to Wycombe where he would learn his trade in English football's bottom division. After serving his time at Wycombe, Lambert moved up a League to Colchester where he would inflict Norwich's heaviest ever home defeat, leading his side to a 1–7 victory in the opening game of the 2009–10 season.

The magnitude of the win triggered a remarkable chain of events that would end with Lambert in the Norwich hot seat just 10 days later; he was no doubt impressed by the potential offered at Norwich with 25,217 watching the Colchester horror show. For his services Norwich would later pay Colchester £425,000 in compensation.

Lambert's first game in charge was a 5–2 win over Wycombe on 22 August 2009 and from that point onwards Lambert's stock rose, as Norwich began their rapid ascent towards the Premiership.

Norwich's success in League One in 2010–11 was very much down to Lambert getting the best out of the squad he inherited, while players that he brought in would all contribute to the team's success. A change of formation to the diamond made Norwich the League's most potent attacking force with 89 goals – the most scored by Norwich since the 1958–59 season.

As Norwich marched to the title with a record 95 points and a record 11 successive home wins, they gained their revenge on Colchester with an emphatic 5–0 victory on a rain soaked 18 January 2010. The scoreline meant that in the two fixtures between the sides, Lambert's teams had come out 12–1 on top.

During the 2009–10 season Lambert was inducted into the Scottish Football Hall of Fame, while inevitably he ended the season with the League One Manager of the Year award to go with his three Manager of the Month awards.

With Norwich expected to consolidate in their first season back in the Championship, the 2010–11 season was nothing more than a minor miracle as rare back to back promotions were achieved for the first time since Manchester City in 2000.

As in League One, promotion was achieved on the back of high fitness levels, unbreakable team spirit and a winning mentality. These attributes were highlighted by 12 games, nine of which were victories, where goals were scored in injury time. Late winners – in particular in games versus Millwall, Reading, Bristol City and Derby – would prove to be decisive in the battle to finish second, as Norwich gained a reputation for playing until the very end.

Of the many highlights in the 2010–11 season, the double over Ipswich stands out. The 5–1 win at Portman Road was the club's best ever, as was the aggregate win of 9–2 in the two derbies.

With promotion came another Manager of the Year award for a manager who had never lost back to back games while at Norwich.

In 2011–12 Lambert was the seventh Scottish manager in the Premiership as he more than achieved his pre-season brief of keeping Norwich in the top flight. Norwich's final position of 12th was the club's joint highest finish since 1993–94. The 12th place finish was achieved with a relatively small budget by Premiership standards, as Lambert again added to his squad well, bringing in players from the lower Leagues with the ability, hunger and desire to succeed.

Lambert would also demonstrate his tactical awareness at the very highest level as well as optimizing squad rotation. During the season Norwich would play a variety of formations, often changing within a game, which would see them take points off four of the top six clubs, as the team played a brand of exciting, positive football.

His tactical knowledge in hand with man-management skills and ability to spot a bargain in the transfer market have made him one of the top and most sought after managers in the game earning him a move to Aston Villa in the summer of 2012.

Paul Lambert managed Norwich for 142 games with a win ratio while at Norwich of just under 50 per cent, by far the best of any Norwich manager.

Hall of Fame – Facts and Figures

- There are 128 members in the Norwich Hall of Fame including 106 players (eight of whom also managed the club); nine managers; eight executives including members of the board and chairman; three founders of Norwich City Football club; and finally a physio and a groundsman who between them have given over 60 years service to the club.
- Of the 106 players in the Hall of Fame, 36 played in Midfield; 32 were forwards; 31 defenders and seven goalkeepers. These numbers are based on their main positions with the club, although many would serve Norwich in more than one position.
- In today's global game – where over 50 per cent of Premier League footballers are from overseas, and an incredible 92 different nations have been represented in the Premiership – it is surprising that only seven Norwich Hall of Famers were born outside of the UK, and of those, three were born to British parents based in the military. Of those born in the UK, five were born in Northern Ireland; 11 in Wales; 18 in Scotland and the remaining 87 in England. 17 Hall of Famers were Norfolk born.
- The club has been in existence for 110 years covering 11 decades, since its foundation in 1902. The Hall of Fame covers the entire history of Norwich City Football Club. Based on when players joined or turned professional, the post-war/1950s period is best represented with 27 Hall of Famers, and the 1980s is the second best with 26 Hall of Famers joining Norwich. Both of these decades represented successful periods in Norwich's history. The rest of the Hall of Fame is split along the following timelines; Foundation to World War Two (16), 1960s (12), 1970s (16), 1990s (20) and the new millennium (11).
- It is to the club's credit that 26 of the 106 players in the Hall of Fame were products of the Norwich youth system or were signed at youth level and developed by the club. The remaining 80 players were signed from clubs throughout the UK and Ireland.
- There are particular links with two clubs, Bournemouth and Tottenham, that stand out. A total of six players joined from Bournemouth, predominantly in the 1970s (in addition to two managers in the Hall of Fame), while Tottenham Hotspur have provided Norwich with seven players who have gone on to become part of the Hall of Fame.
- One club where no Hall of Famers were signed from is East Anglian rivals Ipswich Town, although Ruel Fox did play for Ipswich Juniors before making the switch to City.
- Generally speaking, players in the Hall of Fame either ended their careers at Norwich or obtained their 'dream' move to one of the biggest clubs in the country. The current Premier League's 'big five' (Arsenal, Manchester United, Liverpool, Chelsea and Manchester City) have signed nine players and two managers from Norwich, while three players in the 1980s joined the Graeme Souness revolution at Glasgow Rangers. Two players (Andy Marshall and John Deehan) left Norwich directly for Ipswich and five players left for clubs based overseas.
- Norwich has always had a reputation as a selling club, often to the frustration of supporters who saw potentially great teams dismantled for a profit. In total the Hall of Famers have cost £14.4 million to bring to Norwich, the highest fee being the £3 million spent in 2005 for Dean Ashton. In contrast, total fees of £40.6 million have been received for players sold by Norwich which has generated a net profit of £26.2 million. The largest fee received also involved Dean Ashton when he was sold in 2006 for a reported £7.3 million. Thirteen Hall of Famers were

sold for fees exceeding £1 million including Chris Sutton's £5 million transfer to Blackburn in 1994 which at the time was a British record.

- The 115 players and managers have represented Norwich on 25,373 occasions between them (League and Cup) and scored 2,938 goals. The most appearances were the 673 made by goalkeeper Kevin Keelan in a career spanning 17 years. In contrast to Keelan, Alf Kirchen made the least appearances of all the Hall of Famers (18) reflecting the affection and pride held for the Norfolk born man as he went on to win trophies with Arsenal and later to represent England.
- Norwich's top 13 all-time goalscorers (led by Jonny Gavin's total of 132) are all members of the Hall of Fame. Gavin may be the club's all-time top goalscorer but Percy Vargo has the best goals/appearances ratio of 0.72 (nearly a goal per game).
- The 17 Hall of Famers that have managed Norwich oversaw a grand total of 3,078 games, with Ken Brown's 367 games between 1980 and 1987 the highest for one manager. Brown won a respectable 41 per cent of his games in charge, although Norman Low and Paul Lambert boast the best records with win percentages of around 50 per cent.
- There is one World Cup winner in the Hall of Fame (Martin Peters).
- Of the 106 players in the Hall of Fame, five are still playing: two at Norwich (Wes Hoolahan and Grant Holt), and three (Craig Bellamy, Robert Green and Adam Drury) at other clubs.
- Two Hall of Famers are currently managers (Paul Lambert and Malky Mackay).
- And finally, one Hall of Famer is the assistant manager to arguably the most successful manager of all time (Mick Phelan to Alex Ferguson).